The Combined Family

A Guide to Creating Successful Step-Relationships

The Combined Family

A Guide to Creating Successful Step-Relationships

Taube S. Kaufman, M.S.W.

With the editorial assistance of
Glenn D. Slovenko

Foreword by
Helen W. Coale, L.C.S.W., L.M.F.T.

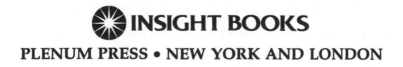 **INSIGHT BOOKS**

PLENUM PRESS • NEW YORK AND LONDON

Library of Congress Cataloging-in-Publication Data

Kaufman, Taube S.
   The combined family : a guide to creating successful step
-relationships / Taube S. Kaufman ; with the editorial assistance of
Glenn D. Slovenko ; foreword by Helen W. Coale.
      p.   cm.
   "Insight books."
   Includes bibliographical references and index.
   ISBN 0-306-44500-X
   1. Stepfamilies.   2. Stepfamilies--Psychological aspects.
3. Children of divorced parents--Family relationships.
4. Stepchildren--Family relationships.   I. Title.
HQ759.92.K38   1993
306.874--dc20   93-27748
                                                          CIP

10 9 8 7 6 5 4 3

Permission is acknowledged from Warner/Chappell Music, Inc. to reprint in the United States and Canada the lyrics to "I'm My Own Grandpaw" by Dwight Latham and Moe Jaffe © 1947 COLGEMS–EMI Music Inc. Copyright renewed 1975 COLGEMS–EMI Music Inc. All Rights Reserved. Used by Permission.

Permission is acknowledged from EMI Music Publishing to reprint internationally the lyrics to "I'm My Own Grandpaw" by Dwight Latham and Moe Jaffe © 1947 renewed 1975 COLGEMS–EMI Music Inc. All Rights Reserved. International Copyright Secured. Used by Permission.

Permission is acknowledged to print a vignette based on the film *The Last Emperor* courtesy of Hemdale Film Corporation.

ISBN 0-306-44500-X

© 1993 Plenum Press, New York
A Division of Plenum Publishing Corporation
233 Spring Street, New York, N.Y. 10013

An Insight Book

All rights reserved

Printed in the United States of America

Dedicated to the memory of my dearest friend,
my partner and helpmate
My Beloved Husband,
Harold A. Simon

Foreword

The structure of the "typical" American family has been in continuous flux for several decades. The traditional nuclear family of the 1950s, comprising two adults in a first marriage and their biological children, is no longer the normative family structure. Single-parent–headed households and stepfamilies, as well as other groups of people who recognize themselves emotionally (even though they may not be recognized legally) as "families," have leaped onto the stage of American family life.

As more people live in family forms which differ significantly from the "traditional" family, new ways of understanding family life are required and new standards for evaluating "success" must be developed. Attitudes and beliefs about families, however, are slow to change. Even as more people are living in varying family structures, they often still judge themselves—and are judged by those around them—based on the values about family living from times past. Since these values no longer "fit" the family structure in which they are living, using them as a yardstick for measuring success does not work. Instead, new values and ways of doing things must be developed—values and ways which are congruent with the demands of a different kind of family structure.

Because of the high divorce and remarriage rates in the United States, stepfamilies have become the most prevalent "nontraditional" family form needing new guidelines for negotiating successful family living. They must navigate complicated relationships with both "insiders" and "outsiders" in a family system that extends across two, and often more, household lines. Remarried couples must develop a strong marital bond in a family system in which parent and child have an emotional attachment and history that predate the marriage. Stepparents must function in a role that is ambiguous, ill-defined, and laced with negative meanings. Children must deal with a residue of losses accompanying each change in the structure of their family and learn to adjust to at least two sets of rules and ways of doing things as they go back and forth across household lines.

Things that were taken for granted in the original family must be carefully discussed and negotiated in the stepfamily. Holidays and family celebrations, daily routines, allocations of space and time—these and many other aspects of family life are "up for grabs" and often loaded with conflicted emotional meaning for family members. Even the language with which negotiations must occur is fraught with problems. The vocabulary of the English language is insufficient to positively define the many different kinds of relationships created when a stepfamily forms.

Taube Kaufman addresses the many issues inherent in stepfamily living with clarity, compassion, and creativity. She explains the dilemmas facing stepfamilies as "normal" dilemmas that can be solved with a clear understanding of the intricacies of all the "in" and "out" and "old" and "new" relationships in the family and with a willingness to do the hard work required to facilitate family integration. Her discussion of the issues is thorough and filled with interesting practical examples gleaned from a lifetime of obviously rich professional and personal experience. Every issue, however problematic, is addressed from an optimistic, hopeful—but not Pollyannaish—perspective. Even the problem of language she approaches head-on—with a new vocabulary she invented for describing step-relationships!

I think that *The Combined Family* is an excellent resource for any couple considering remarriage as well as for those already living in a marriage and feeling "stuck." One of the primary dilemmas faced by stepfamilies, especially in the early stages, is the complex task of trying to function as a family before there has been time to work out *how* that will occur. Families often feel as though they are floating in a boat on the open sea with no map, no destination, no paddles or engine, no navigational instruments, and only very limited resources on board to sustain life. In order to minimize the helplessness and the sense of loss of control that family members feel in this kind of situation, they may try to propel the boat in *any* direction that they can just to get *somewhere*.

Ms. Kaufman's book offers clear ideas about why stepfamilies might feel chaotic and out of control, suggests hopeful destinations for them to navigate toward, and provides them with the tools to facilitate their journey. She also addresses the perils of the trip in a refreshingly matter-of-fact manner that allows for many possible solutions, thus avoiding the danger of establishing idealistic expectations that may work for some—but not all—stepfamilies.

Helen W. Coale

Helen W. Coale, LCSW, LMFT, is Founder and Director of the Atlanta Area Child Guidance Clinic, Atlanta, Georgia.

Preface

In this book, we are dealing with a new frontier—where the explanations offered may sometimes leave you feeling, "I need to know more." The author wishes she could give you more, but such information may not yet exist; this field is in its infancy.

Wherever possible, I have attempted to give you perspective on how and what various individuals in a combined family might be thinking or feeling at a particular time or in a particular situation. In specific instances, a variety of possible solutions is offered to assist you in resolving some of the issues that you confront on a daily basis.

This book, however, is intended for two audiences. It has been written for those of you who are, or are about to become, members of combined families and are desperately hoping that this book will provide you with answers to problems you have not been able to resolve on your own—and that no one else seems to understand. At the same time, this book has been written for students of this burgeoning societal issue. It is offered as yet another piece of the groundwork that is so urgently needed to help all of us gain a clearer understanding of the difficulties all combined families face.

As the reader starts out on this journey with the author into the mysterious realm of step-relationships and the combined family, neither can help but recognize that the words that are available for describing such families come from the past. As the scarlet letter *A* used to brand a woman as an adultress, the word *step* in front of mother, father, or child seems to conjure up all the negative stereotypes that have become associated with step-relationships over the centuries.

To this day, there is a stigma associated with *step* that seems destined to leave persons in step-relationships feeling "less than equal." For example: How do we feel inside when we think that someone is treating us unfairly? For many, the answer is "like a stepchild." Whom do children seem to fear most in fairy tales? Stepmothers! To the author, these images of past step-relationships still serve to block members of these families from being allowed to integrate comfortably into our present-day society.

In order to circumvent what I see as one of the greatest obstacles to the integration of the combined family into our society, I have coined a language that does away with the word *step* entirely. The language is defined in Chapter 21. It has not been used throughout the book for the simple reason that the language is the future, and I wanted to write this book in a language that everyone would understand today—the language of yesterday!

Taube Kaufman

Northbrook, Illinois

Acknowledgments

I wish to express my profound thanks to the hundreds of people whose firsthand experiences helped me to come to a greater understanding of the underlying dynamics of combined family life. Many have granted me permission to use disguised versions of their true life stories. One courageous combined family has been gracious enough to allow all of us to enter their lives to get a feeling for what it was like for them to establish their identity as a combined family. I hope I speak for all of us when I say to all of you: Thank you for sharing your lives with us.

The following portion of this acknowledgment is bound to be as nontraditional as the family forms discussed within this book. Because I have both an eye disease and a syndrome which keeps my eyes dry, I have been limited for most of my adult life, both in what, and how much, I can read. Thus it is that I wish to express my thanks to the Blind Service Association for all their efforts in my behalf.

Without the Blind Service Association's providing me with volunteer readers over the years, I would not have established two very important relationships in my life. Zinette Yacker, first my reader and then my friend, read to me weekly between 1983 and 1988. I can never adequately thank her for her loyalty and devotion. For years, the Northbrook Public Library was our friend, our confidant, and our greatest resource for materials related to combined family life. Anything we needed, the reference department obtained for us. I truly appreciate and applaud the library's staff for their efforts.

When I moved closer to their offices, the Blind Service Association continued to provide me with a variety of readers. One in particular, Susan Marks, became a surrogate for all of you; it was she whom I had to make understand my message. It was also Susan who persuaded me that I needed someone to read, write, and edit with me. My friend, Nora Herbst, found the perfect person to fill the bill: her sister, Margaret. Without the loyal and dedicated assistance of Peg Herbst, this book would have been far less than it has become.

I would also like to thank Leslie Williams and the staff of readers at the branch of the Blind Service Association at the Skokie Public Library who assisted me through their reading of manuscript pages, and subsequently page proofs, of this book.

There is another element in this acknowledgment that is not only hard to explain, but painful to discuss. In May 1985, I had a face-lift to remove lines on my face that came about following my husband's diagnosis of colon cancer, and his death, just three months later.

An undetected abscessed tooth complicated my facial surgery, and an errant earring punctured my newly healing scar tissue. Together, these two events combined to produce a bewildering array of symptoms. Much to my dismay, the doctors I consulted seemed more willing to write me off as a kook than they were to figure out what was causing me to have such terrible problems with my hearing, my memory, and my ability to think straight. All this was going on while I was first contemplating, and subsequently undertaking, the writing of this book.

By 1986, I had developed the language that appears in Chapter 21. My son, Glenn Slovenko, later insisted that I have the new vocabulary copyrighted. Once this was done, and I started writing, I began to see just how much difficulty I was having with my thought processes. I could not put four words together, add a fifth, and remember the first four words.

It was my friend and neighbor, Herb Edisis, who first tried to make sense of what I was writing, but his efforts bore little fruit. My thoughts came and went in a wasteland. Without the invaluable assistance of my dear friend, John Roberts, D.O., I might never have gotten out of the quagmire I was in. It was Dr. Roberts who first helped me get a handle on the bacterial infection in my head, and it was he who led me to establish contact with Richard Novak, M.D., whose "milk of human kindness" has helped to restore a good deal of my memory—as well as my faith in the medical profession.

My thanks also go to Gale Grubman—for refreshing my memory on the subject of the English language and for directing me to Larry McEnerney, from the University of Chicago's Little Red Schoolhouse. His class in "Effective Writing for Business and the Professions" proved inspirational. Never have I learned so much, so fast, so dynamically.

On a more personal level, I would like to take this opportunity to thank my stepson-by-choice, Jonathan Simon, who introduced me to a new way of outlining. The unique diagram he drew became the outline for Chapter 20, and the model for five others.

My thanks also go to my daughter, Karen, who for a time typed my dictation while I babysat my most marvelous grandchildren, Bryce and Jillian. I truly appreciate my children's and grandchildren's consideration of my time, and their forgiveness for the time I could not spend with them. I also wish to thank my mother, my family, and my friends for their love and support, and the memory of my father—for strength and determination.

As for the final stages of this book, it has been my son, Glenn, who has given up more than a half-year of his time and effort to edit six and one-half chapters, while his lovely wife, Jay, sat silently by. Obviously, there is no way to thank the two of them for "being there" for me. I hope Glenn's efforts were a labor of love; I am certain he derived little personal pleasure from the monumental task set before him.

I also would like to thank Linda Sorkin Eisenberg, Robert Eisenberg, and all the members of their combined family for sharing their story—with me, as well as with you (Chapter 19). They have shared their family at the risk of not receiving societal support, but with the hope that they will be giving hope to all of you who live in combined families and are, at this particular moment, finding it difficult.

And, finally, I want to thank Norma Fox, and subsequently

Frank Darmstadt, of Plenum Press for understanding the kind of book I was writing, for calling me immediately to let me know Insight Books wanted to publish it, and for supporting me throughout this period of having to pass up one deadline after another in order to produce a book I could look back upon with pride, and forward to with hope.

Contents

The Combined Family

A Guide to Creating Successful
Step-Relationships

ONE

"... and lived happily ever after."

Once upon a time a dashing young Prince rescued a maiden in distress, whereupon the couple fell madly in love, married, and lived happily ever after.

From our earliest memories, fairy tales have programmed us to believe that when we find our true loves we shall live "happily ever after." But what does "happily ever after" mean? Does it mean that when Snow White marries Prince Charming and Cinderella marries her charming prince nothing will ever go wrong in their married lives? Does it mean that no domestic problems will ever arise in their households, and that Snow White will never leave her husband and children in order to run off with the woodsman? Does it mean that each adult will live exactly the same length of time as the other, so no one will be left widowed or wanting?

As with all good fairy tale characters, it seems reasonable to presume that the parents of Snow White and Cinderella started their marriages expecting to live "happily ever after." But both couples learned that over the course of a lifetime reality and expectation often part company: spouses die, couples divorce, children are hurt—yet life goes on. Fairy tales do not shield us from life's harsh realities; they keep us ever mindful of them.

1

Stories such as "Snow White," "Hansel and Gretel," and "Cinderella" focus on the fate of children whose parents failed to choose their remarriage partners well. Their story lines point out the differences between poor choices and second chances, and between blood ties and marriage ties. However, the real value of these stories may lie in their focusing our attention on the problems single parents face in trying to balance their own needs against the best interests of their children.

Parents who are left alone with their offspring, either by choice or by chance, may find little to comfort them in previously written works concerning remarriage and combined families. Fairy tales do not tell single parents how to build new family structures on parent–child foundations. They offer no help when it comes to telling heads of one-parent households how to add new marriage partners to their preexisting families. Fairy tales simply warn of terrible consequences to children if single parents fail to choose their remarriage partners well.

Society, too, sends its own stark message to single parents. We let these adults know that they and their families are outside the mainstream of traditional family life, and that families disrupted by death or divorce had best make as little commotion as possible in their scramble to reorganize their lives. When single parents choose to remarry, we send them a clear message: that their mistakes are on their own heads—and the heads of their children. As a society, it seems to be all we can do to think about providing for our nation's intact families. In fact, we give so little credence to families formed when single parents remarry, we have not even agreed upon a name to call them.

Currently in vogue for what this text refers to as "combined families" are names such as *blended, reconstituted, remarried,* and *step* families. Unfortunately, there is no societally accepted label that both defines this family type and eliminates the stigma that has become associated with the word *step.* The prefix *step* derives from the Old English word *steop,* which means "to deprive, bereave."[1] Therefore, it seems inappropriate—if not inaccurate—to use the word *step* to define families where divorce, not death, has been the major disrupter of the intact family.

A *combined family* is formed when an adult, with at least one child from a previous union, establishes a household with someone who has no legal ties to that child. Combined families contain people who are blood-related (parents and children, siblings, half siblings), legally related (husbands and wives, adoptive parents, and adoptive children), and/or marriage-related (stepparents and stepchildren, stepsiblings). This is a far different picture than the one presented by nuclear families, where parents and their children hold either blood or adoptive ties to one another.

THE STRUCTURE OF THE NUCLEAR FAMILY

Traditionally, the nuclear family consists of a father, who provides the family income, and a mother, who manages the household while rearing the (couple's) children. There are several structural characteristics that are unique to nuclear families:

The couple bond predates the parent–child bond.[2] The nuclear family is formed when two adults marry, each for the first time. Their union is based on a primary couple bond. As the couple adds children to their family, the adults become parents as well as marital partners.

Generational boundaries between adults and children are clear, distinct, and easily drawn. When couples become parents, wives become mothers and husbands become fathers, but spousal relationships do not change. Couples' roles as parents to their children are added on to their roles as marriage partners.

Parents and children hold symmetrical ties to one another.

Nuclear family members build their sense of continuity and family history through living together. Together they establish traditional ways of celebrating holidays, handing down information, and passing on values and opinions. This family develops its own unique blend of customs, attitudes, and beliefs.

The nuclear family has well-defined boundaries. If we were to build a cocoon[3] around the original couple, and allow that cocoon to expand as the couple adds children to their union, we would find that the nuclear family's solidarity stems from its members' ability to distinguish those on the "inside" from those on the "outside." Like the house they live in, the nuclear family's boundaries hold the family securely within.

Common activities and shared experiences help keep the family fo-

cused inward. The couple and their children usually do not have major external distractions; therefore, authority and affection are contained within the family unit. The nuclear family achieves solidarity because its members have more in common with each other than with anyone else.[4]

When the couple's marriage ends, due to divorce or death, ties within the nuclear family are broken. Gone is the home as the center of authority and economic well-being. There is no solid boundary to envelop and protect the family.[5] The cocoon is ruptured. The parents are no longer together, and there is no common residence. Instead of the old arrangement, there are either two one-parent households, or just one.

THE STRUCTURE OF THE COMBINED FAMILY

The combined family follows a different evolutionary plane than the nuclear family:

The addition of a single adult, or one-parent family, to a preexisting one-parent family creates a combined family. When the head of a one-parent family chooses to marry again,[6] there is no way for that adult to establish a nuclear family with his or her new marital partner: He or she is already a parent to at least one child.

The bond between parent and child predates the bond between the couple.[7] Each combined family is built on a preexisting parent–child base.

Diana thought Brad was the answer to her prayers. He was handsome and caring, and they were madly in love. She never gave much thought to his having been married before because his two children lived with his former spouse all but two weeks out of the year.

Shortly before Diana and Brad were married, Brad's oldest son, Jed, asked his dad if he could come live with him. Brad was ecstatic. Diana was overjoyed that her husband was at last going to have his son living with him.

Diana never gave a second thought to the fact that she was going to have to participate with Brad in raising Jed. She and Brad had made plans for their future lives together, involving only the two of them. It was only when Brad handed Diana his son's activity schedule that Diana realized her husband expected her to take an active part in the rearing of his son.

The hallmark of the combined family is the couple's lack of symmetrical ties to the children. Only the "outside" biological* parent shares the remarried parent's ties to mutual children. Adding a stepparent to a one-parent family unbalances old family ties.

Each combined family begins with the newlyweds holding uneven ties to at least one child who becomes part of their new family unit. The couple forming a combined family have a legal agreement (a marriage contract) binding them together. Children and their parents have blood or adoptive ties to help them remain close. But what is the relationship between stepparents and stepchildren? Who and what are they to one another?

Sometimes a stepparent and stepchild are related, as when a widow or widower marries the brother or sister of a deceased spouse, but most often stepparents and stepchildren have neither the ties of blood nor the bonds of a legal relationship to bind them together. Their ties are affinal. This means that children are related to their parents' new marriage partners solely on the basis of their parents' remarriages.

Couples are often at different stages of their "life cycles."[8] A 55-year-old father of four may be looking forward to his retirement, while his 36-year-old wife may be looking forward to having a child of her own. To satisfy the desires of one is to deny the desires of the other.

Combined families are "born of loss."[9] Children whose parents are free to marry again are children who have experienced either the partial or total loss of a parent. When a parent dies, the remaining parent and children experience total loss. When parents permanently disappear from their children's lives, children are also likely to experience their loss as total. However, when parents separate and divorce, but both stay in contact with their children, the children experience partial loss.

---

*Although inaccurate, for ease in this text, the term *biological* has been used to represent both biologically and legally related families, parents, and/or children. Use of the term *natural*—to refer to parents and children who are biologically related to one another—has been strenuously objected to by some adoptive parents on the grounds that its usage implies that adoptive parents are "unnatural" parents, and their adopted children are "unnatural" children.

It is reasonable to say that everyone in a combined family has experienced loss. Even the adult who joins the child's biological parent in marriage is apt to lose the fantasy of what life will be like in a combined family once he or she gets there.[10] Differences between what stepparents expect and the realities they encounter are likely to shatter many of their hopes and dreams. While all who enter combined families have previous family histories,[11] combined family life may be unlike anything any of them anticipated.

Not all members of a combined family share a common history. The lack of a common history between family members can lead to differences of opinion about how the new family should work. Efforts to develop customs and traditions that are unique to the combined family may put "old" allegiances in conflict with "new" alliances. Finding the right balance between the old and the new is likely to challenge every family member's capacity for growth and change.

Parents who remarry are more likely to choose mates who are less like them than those they chose in their first marriages.[12] Noticeable differences in family members' physical, emotional, cultural, or intellectual make-up can create problems both inside and outside combined families. Faced with significant differences in individual and/or group responses to their new living situation, the task confronting members of a combined family is to develop a cohesive and integrated lifestyle that provides comfort and security for all.

Only the remarried parent is an insider to both new spouse and old children. When a parent remarries, adding a new spouse to a preexisting one-parent family forces a merger of two separate family systems: the one that exists between parent and child(ren), and the one that exists between the couple. Only the remarried parent holds membership in both of these family systems.

Stepparents are expected to function in roles resembling those held by children's outside parents in their original families. Although a stepparent can perform some or all of the outside parent's functions, the stepparent cannot assume the absent parent's role, as that role is not vacant. The role of "parent to the child" is retained by a child's outside biological parent.

There is a "biological parent elsewhere with power and influence."[13] Being that the missing parent is, and always will be, the children's parent, the outside parent remains powerful regardless of whether she or he is known to the children, and regardless of whether she or he is living, deceased, or permanently absent from their lives.

Because original parent–child bonds remain intact, no matter what the marital status of either parent happens to be, outside fathers and mothers are able to find their ways into the bosom of the combined family through their undiminished ties to their children. These outside parents hold power and influence both in the lives of their children and in the lives of those with whom their children live.

When both of their biological parents are living, children may be members of two households.[14]

Neil had lived with his father from the time his parents' marriage ended. When Neil was a toddler, his father, Gordon, married Robin, a young woman who took her role as Neil's stepmother very seriously. Subsequently, the couple enlarged their family by adding three more children of their own.

Gordon had parted on good terms with his former spouse, Georgia, and Neil had spent every other weekend living with his mother since his father and stepmother felt he was old enough to handle living in two households.

Things changed between members of the two households in which Neil lived, however, when Georgia remarried. It was shortly after his mother's remarriage that Neil started running away from home, and from his father, stepmother, and half siblings. The only place Neil ever ran to was his mother's house, but it was dangerous for him to travel there alone, so both remarried parents and their spouses finally agreed that Neil needed to change primary residences. This was difficult because there was really no way Georgia and her new husband could accommodate Neil's living with them on a full-time basis, and there were many changes in their lifestyle that the newlyweds would have to make in order to satisfy Gordon and Robin's fears that Neil be safe and well cared for.

Sad as it was for his combined family, the day did come when Neil left his father and stepmother's house and moved in with his mother and stepfather. Although life became somewhat precarious when his mother and stepfather separated, Neil wanted to stay with his mother, and that was what he ultimately was allowed to do.

Years later, when both couples—father and stepmother, and

mother and stepfather—were all part of his wedding party, they all agreed that they had made the right decision in permitting Neil to follow the path he so obviously needed to travel in order to gain control over his life.[15]

Combined family boundaries must be looser than nuclear family boundaries. For children to be able to travel between their parents' houses, combined family boundaries have to be looser than those associated with nuclear families.[16] The boundary around a combined family needs to be loose enough to permit the movement of the children between the two households in which they live.

Additional pressure on combined family boundaries comes from outsiders who may or may not be related to the children who live in combined families. Courts, schools, social agencies, etc., may be required by law to monitor the well-being of some children who live in combined families. Because combined families are vulnerable to outside interference, their boundaries are considered more "permeable" than those surrounding nuclear families.[17]

Bill and his stepson, Drew, got into an angry fight just as Drew was going off to school one morning. They nearly came to blows. Drew reported his stepfather, Bill, for child abuse when he got to school. Drew's mother, Ellen, and Bill were astonished when, later that afternoon, their household was visited by a representative of a child abuse agency.

There is "no legal relationship between stepparents and stepchildren."[18] While adults in a combined family are bound by a marriage contract, and remarried parents and their children are bound by legal or blood ties, the only tie that binds stepchild and stepparent is the marriage of the child's parent to the stepparent. If the parent's marriage to the stepparent ends, the relationship between the stepchild and stepparent also ends.

A good deal of the strain in relationships between new spouses and old children can be attributed to the lack of a legal relationship between them. Both parties may be unwilling to risk investing in a relationship, fearing it would be lost should the marriage fail.

Lacking reciprocal legal or blood ties, members of a combined family have to find ways to deal with one another—ways that do not rely solely on the bonds of blood, or love. This is no easy task.

Family members are expected to establish relationships with one another even if, in the end, their choice is not to relate. Hopefully, a combination of hard work and good will will enable everyone in the family to reach a satisfactory middle ground—one where all are at least comfortable, if not happy, with one another.

A MODEL FOR THE COMBINED FAMILY

Inasmuch as adding just one adult to a one-parent household creates a combined family, let's explore what really happens when we carry forth the idea of combining a little of this (family) with more or less of that (family). For starters, imagine merging a *canoe* and a *hydrofoil;* if indeed we could manage the task, we could only wonder about how long it would take us to create a stable, sound, and secure structure—that floats!

Canoes are designed to glide through the water, while hydrofoils are designed to ride above the water's surface. The principles upon which these two vessels are build are different; therefore, the people who have arranged their lives to harmonize with these two very different types of water craft are likely to have had two very different types of life experience—both with water, and with the vessels that sail on or in it.

Using this illustration to aid us in our exploration of the inner workings of combined families, let's do some thinking about what would happen if we combined some members of a canoe family with a hydrofoil family, or vice versa.

Life in a one-parent family may have resembled life in the fast lane, with everybody racing around so fast they had to skim the surface of the water in order to accomplish everything needed to keep the family working properly. This hydrofoil family could little afford the luxury of gliding through calmer waters or running the rapids for the thrill of it. They have had to work as hard as they could to keep their heads above water—and they have tailored their lives to meet their needs.

The person (or one-parent family) that joins the one-parent hydrofoil family may be used to paddling his or her (their) own canoe, hauling it across land when necessary, and serenely drifting with the river's current whenever possible. Putting a canoe and a hydrofoil family together may spell nothing but TROUBLE in the early stages of combined family development. The whole idea of building something as makeshift as a "canofoil" or a "hydronoe" with the expectation that the new vessel will function in the same way as either the original canoe or the original hydrofoil is too preposterous for rational people to contemplate. However, people who are combining families are frequently faced with the dilemma of choosing between one lifestyle or another, often creating a unique lifestyle of their own in the process.

Although no one in her or his right mind would think of launching a ship that was built on two so different hulls as a hydrofoil and a canoe, one could easily argue that launching a combined family involves just such a risk.

No matter how difficult the process of establishing a combined family is, day after day, people labor to construct combined families on the basis of adding a single adult to a preexisting one-parent family or merging two one-parent families. It is estimated that more than 1,300 combined families are being established in the United States each day.[19]

The adults and children who form combined families cannot be expected to construct new family units that will meet *all* the needs of *all* of the members of the combined family *all* of the time. However, no family, traditional or otherwise, could be expected to meet such criteria. Compromises need to be found that will allow combined family members to build cohesive family units—using a little of this one's hopes and dreams in combination with a little of that one's wishes and desires; this one's customs combined with that one's traditions. This task is doable, but it cannot be accomplished without the couple's firm commitment to one another.

Before their marriage even takes place, the adults forming a combined family need to realize that *their commitment to one another will be the base upon which their new family unit is built*. However, this base is laid upon another that precedes the development of the combined family, i.e., the preexisting parent–child bond between at least one adult and one child in the combined family. This preexisting parent–child bond challenges the couple bond. How is a combined family to function when the new spouse and the old child or children hold mutually exclusive ties to the remarried parent, and a former spouse shares the remarried parent's ties to the children?

Uneven relationships between family members are inevitable in combined families. Children who live in combined families may be half, whole, or stepsiblings to other children who live in these households (some, most, or all of the time). Differences in surnames, ages, sexes, and eye, skin, and hair colors cannot be explained away to the outside world. Smooth phrases, such as "Mr. and Mrs. John Doe and their children," may be offensive, as well as inaccurate, when it comes to a combined family:

> Bonnie Jean Andrews took her husband's surname when she married John Doe. While the two children who live in their combined family household retain their given and surnames, Jill and Jack Andrews, their father, Tom Andrews, may become incensed when he hears his children referred to as Jill and Jack Doe.
>
> Bonnie Jean Doe may not know what to do about the fact that everyone refers to her children as Jill and Jack Doe, but if she and her new husband do not want to call attention to the fact that their new family is not a nuclear family, they may choose to keep silent on the subject of the children's proper surname.
>
> If John Doe has children of his own who live with their mother in another family unit, his children may resent the fact that their stepsister and stepbrother are sometimes called by *their* family name.
>
> As a matter of fact, John Doe may get so fed up with this whole charade of their combined family masquerading as a nuclear family, he may decide that he does not want his stepchildren to use his last name under any circumstances. This decision on John Doe's part then presents everyone in the combined family with the problem of having to correct *anyone* who mistakenly refers to Jill and Jack Andrews as Jill and Jack Doe.

What is there to do about all this confusion and lack of clarity as to who is what to whom? Telling the truth about combined family relationships will provide a constructive first step in clarifying which members of the combined family are legally related, which ones are related by blood, and which combined family members are related to one another solely on the basis of the marriage tie between the adults.

One thing is for certain: Things will only get easier when people who live in combined families start making their relationships clear to outsiders. People need to be made aware that just because one adult in a combined family is one child's parent, it does not necessarily follow that that adult's mate is also a parent to that child. In combined families, biological, legal, and marital ties often part company.

With the nuclear family still representing the norm in our society, people are frequently unprepared for how combined family life differs from life in a nuclear family. *Different* is the operative word in differentiating nuclear families from combined families; the only way in which these two forms of family are similar lies in the fact that there is an adult couple in both, but there the similarity ends!

CONCLUSION

Combined families are built on unique grounds:

- The addition of a single adult or one-parent family to a preexisting one-parent family creates a combined family.
- The bond between parent and child predates the bond between the couple.
- The hallmark of the combined family is the couple's lack of symmetrical ties to the children.
- Couples are often at different stages of their life cycles.
- All combined families are born of loss. A parent has to be missing in order for there to be room to add a new adult to a preexisting one-parent family.
- Not all members of a combined family share a common history.
- Parents who remarry are more likely to choose mates from markedly different backgrounds than those they chose in their first marriages.
- Only the remarried parent is an insider with both her or his new spouse and old children.
- The stepparent in a combined family is expected to function

in a role that the children's outside parent held in the children's original family.

- The addition of a stepparent does not subtract the children's outside parent.
- The children's outside parent retains power and influence that can penetrate combined family boundaries.
- Combined family boundaries must be looser than nuclear family boundaries.
- When both of their biological parents are living, children may be members of two households.
- There is no legal relationship between stepparent and stepchild.

TWO

Myths and Realities

"When we were first married, I expected our newly formed family to resemble 'The Brady Bunch.' Now, each day I spend with my husband's children makes me feel like I am on the losing end of 'Custer's Last Stand.' Why didn't anybody tell me that it would be so hard to live with another person's children?"

Deeply ingrained in American mythology, the nuclear family continues to be the standard against which we judge all other family types. Ironically, today less than 5 percent of our population live in families that fit the prototype of the nuclear family; where the father is the sole wage earner and the mother stays at home to raise the couple's children and manage the household. While the nuclear family continues to be the standard, it no longer represents the norm.

If we were to ask ourselves why we as a society continue to cling to this "aging, fading norm"[1] that no longer represents the society in which we live, perhaps our best answer would be "nostalgia." In many people's minds, the nuclear family represents a period in our history in which security and stability were embodied in our vision of "home." Home was not only where our hearts were—home represented Mom, greeting us at the door with cookies and milk after school; Dad, taking us on weekend drives; and the familiar faces of "Ozzie and Harriet" and their all-American family (of TV fame in the 1950s), smiling not only at us, but also at one another, as they went about resolving their weekly trials and tribulations. To put it succinctly, the nuclear family embodies the "American dream": home, hearth, and family.

HOW COMBINED FAMILIES STACK UP AGAINST THE AMERICAN DREAM

Those who believe that the combined family can be made to conform to the nuclear family pattern would do well to think about Cinderella's stepsisters. They tried to make their feet small enough to fit into the glass slipper Cinderella lost as she ran from the ballroom, hoping to catch her coach and four before it turned into a pumpkin and mice. As one version of the Cinderella story goes, when the Prince sent his heralds to try the glass slipper on the foot of every young woman in the kingdom, at their mother's bidding, one of Cinderella's stepsisters lopped off her toe and the other cut off a piece of her heel, each in an attempt to stuff her larger foot into the smaller slipper. But their efforts were in vain. Neither stepsister could revamp herself into what she was not, i.e., Cinderella.

In the same way that Cinderella's stepsisters could not make themselves into Cinderella, combined families cannot make themselves into nuclear families. Combined families have a separate and unique structure that cannot be crammed into a nuclear family mold. Those who stubbornly cling to the myth that the combined family can recreate the nuclear family are destined for disappointment. Nothing can make these two distinct forms of family the same—or even equivalent to each other. Combined families and nuclear families are built differently; therefore, they function differently.

In combined families, parent–child bonds predate couple bonds. While the adults forming a combined family share mutual ties to each other, they do not share mutual ties to at least one child who becomes part of their new family. The fact that the remarried parent's children become the stepparent's stepchildren presents every new combined family with a dilemma: The couple cannot bundle their new family into a neat and tidy package, suitable for societal approval.

Combined families are complex and hard to live in—as well as difficult to understand. No one wants to deal with a family unit in which an organizational chart is needed to figure out who is related to whom, and what that relationship implies:

"I'm My Own Grandpaw"[2]

1. Many, many years ago when I was twenty three
   I was married to a widow who was pretty as could be.
   This widow had a grown-up daughter who had hair of red.
   My father fell in love with her and soon they too were wed.
   I'm my own grandpaw,
   I'm my own grandpaw.
   It sounds funny I know
   But it really is so,
   Oh, I'm my own grandpaw.
2. This made my dad my son-in-law
   And changed my very life,
   For my daughter was my mother
   'Cause she was my father's wife.
   To complicate the matter
   Even though it brought me joy,
   I soon became the father
   Of a bouncing baby boy.
3. My little baby then became
   A brother-in-law to dad,
   And so became my uncle
   Though it made me very sad.
   For if he was my uncle
   Then that also made him brother,
   Of the widow's grown-up daughter
   Who, of course, was my step-mother."*

---

*It is interesting to note that the only "step" in this song appears before the word "mother."

4. Father's wife then had a son
   Who kept them on the run,
   And he became my grandchild
   For he was my daughter's son.
   My wife is now my mother's mother
   And it makes me blue,
   Because although she is my wife
   She's my grand-mother too.
5. Oh if my wife is my grand-mother
   Then I'm her grand-child,
   And ev'ry time I think of it,
   It nearly drives me wild.
   For now I have become
   The strangest case you ever saw,
   As husband of my grand-mother
   I am my own grand-paw.

How on earth can we expect the complicated structure of the combined family to become the standard when we already have available to us the sleek classic lines of the nuclear family to guide us in our vision of "what every family should be." Yet how can the nuclear family encompass the variety and dimension that the combined family offers in each new family that is formed?

Comparing the combined family to a nuclear family puts us through the same process Cinderella's stepsisters went through as each tried to alter the shape of her foot to fit a shoe specifically created to fit the foot of another. Although many combined families think that, with a bit of tucking and trimming here and there, they will be able to cram their larger dimensions into the nuclear family's smaller frame, "let's pretend" does not work. Too many adults forming combined families fail to understand just how different these families are from nuclear families. Perhaps when they realize that the odds are that approximately six out of ten remarriages with children will end in divorce,[3] the adults seeking to form combined families will take time to consider the magnitude of their undertaking.

Of course, most couples entering combined families are sure they can beat the statistical averages stacked against them, but for the majority of these couples, their assuredness may amount to little more than wishful thinking. Too few couples plan for success, choosing instead to heed the clarion calls of sea sirens who would lure them to their destruction with a pack of myths spun specifically to deceive them.

"INSTANT LOVE" AND OTHER MYTHS

When a marriage ends, by death or divorce, everything changes. Lives are disrupted; futures are in doubt. Those who survive the end of the two-parent family are forced to reassemble into one or two single-parent families. Time is needed for both adults and children to get their bearings. Some parents and children form cohesive one-parent families. Others remain more fragmented. Some adults complete the task of mourning the end of their previous marriages and go on to remarry. Others do not.

The majority of adults whose first marriages have ended eventually choose to marry again; however, the challenge of adding other adults, with or without children, to their one-parent families is enough to daunt even the most courageous of remarrying parents. Fantasizing about what life will be like with new mates in new marriages may be tantalizing, but couples' expectations need to be realistic for their marriages to succeed. Too often, those adults who are about to join forces deny the magnitude of the challenge they face; they choose instead to put their faith in a collection of myths about combined family life:

Myth #1. Combined Families Are the Same as Nuclear Families. For a full discussion of this subject, see Chapters 1 through 20.

Myth #2. The Myth of "Instant Love."[4] Parents often enter their new marriages with the expectation that their spouses and children will love one another instantly. However, because the stepparent and stepchild in a newly formed combined family are likely to be strangers to one another, it is totally unrealistic to expect a remarried parent's new spouse and old children to like, much less love, one another the instant the combined family is formed.

Myth #3. Both Nuclear and Combined Families Start Out from "Square One."[5] At least one parent and child in the combined family have experienced "square one," i.e., they already are a family. This parent and child have no alternative but to start out from "square two"—even though the remarried parent's new spouse may be entering his or her first marriage.

Myth #4. Children Will Be Happy About Their Parent's Remarriage. Given the almost universal wish of children of divorce—that their parents reunite and recreate their original families—it would be naive for parents to expect their children to be happy about their decisions to remarry. Such decisions often destroy children's lingering hopes for their parents' reunion. Parents would be well advised to accept and respect the fact that children may be mourning the loss of their original families—even as their remarrying parents start new ones.

Myth #5. The Myth of "The Brady Bunch." Based on the old television show of the same name, this myth implies that it will be easy to integrate two or more separate family units into one "great big happy family." Remarried parents may believe that they have found perfect "mothers" or "fathers" for their children, and stepparents may be fooled into thinking they can displace or replace missing (outside) parents. However, reality has its own way of correcting adults' unrealistic expectations.

And That's Not All. Just in case readers think this mention of five of the most insidious myths regarding combined family life completes the amount of misinformation available for couples combining families, here are a few more unrealistic expectations to be aware of:

- The combined family that is formed will be better than the children's original family, and the children will be happier living in it.
- The remarried parent can help to create a closer, tighter, stepparent–stepchild bond by keeping the child away from the outside biological parent.[6]

- By trying hard, a stepmother can beat the myth of the "wicked stepmother."[7]
- Anything negative that happens is the result of being a combined family.[8]

While these adages appear to contain some elements of folk wisdom for both parent and stepparent alike, problems arise when couples attempt to incorporate them into their daily lives. Certainly, everyone entering a combined family has a right to a few expectations; why not? Everyone's future is on the line. However, the closer that couples' expectations are to reality, the better their families' chances for success. Maintaining close touch with reality even helps family members guard against one of the most unanticipated feelings of all—that their new family is not a real family. Few combined family members are ever prepared for this feeling. It is not only unsettling, it is just plain scary.

THE ANTIDOTE: A DOSE OF REALITY

Today, the majority of mothers in America work because they cannot afford not to. Not only are most fathers' salaries insufficient to support the American dream of a home and two-car garage, but approximately one-quarter of all American households are headed by a single parent.

Sociologist Paul Glick estimates that one-third of the population of the United States (i.e., 20 million children and 60 million adults) were involved in a variety of step-situations in 1987. Glick's current calculations regarding the number of people who once were, are now, or eventually will be involved in step-situations lead him to believe that this figure could rise to 50 percent by the year 2000.[9]

It would be a pity if we, as a society, doggedly persisted in trying to model one-parent and combined families after the nuclear family—the norm that is no longer the norm. Doing so would cause us to miss some of the essential realities of combined family life.

Reality #1. Combined Families Resemble Nuclear Families in Only One Way: An Adult Couple is Present in Both Forms of Family; There the Resemblance Ends.

Reality #2. Single Parents Cannot Solve All Their Problems by Remarrying. Remarriage will not necessarily make things better for previously single parents. In taking new spouses, single parents simply exchange the problems of one-parent family life for the even more complex problems of combined family life.

Reality #3. Divorce Does Not Erase Couples' Ties to One Another. Mutual children are the threads that bind parents together—for life.

Reality #4. Everyone Entering a Combined Family Has a Personal Agenda. Not everyone wants to be there; not everyone who is there wants the same thing. Mutual goals cannot be taken for granted in combined families. Couples' joint and personal expectations have to be discussed in advance, and differences have to be resolved. While preliminary goals may need to be modified over time, just hoping that "everything will work out" leaves the choice open—as to whether everything will work out badly or well.

Reality #5. There is No Way of Knowing What You are Getting Into When You Enter a Combined Family. Whenever a collection of strangers is asked to share mutual living space, problems can be anticipated. While some issues can only be dealt with as they arise, preplanning will allow a couple time to come up with some strategies for success prior to their establishing a combined family. Adults who formulate a plan of action prior to their marriage can make the transition to combined family life far easier on their families than it would be were all combined family members simply to come together—and then wait for the first shoe to drop.

As harsh as reality can be for those couples who fail to preplan, couples who work hard can find combined family life to be as rich and rewarding as life in the happiest of first-marriage families. What must be understood, however, is that it will take a great deal of time, patience, effort, and understanding to reach the point where all combined family members are comfortable within their new family structures. This being the case, it is imperative that couples' expectations and goals be as realistic as possible as they begin their long and often arduous journeys "on the road" to combined family formation.

THREE

On the Road

At first, writing a book about the enormously complex subject of combined family living seemed a monumental task. All things considered, to write about family life is to write about life itself. As many have already learned, there is no map laid out for this journey, and it is easy to get lost or detoured along the way.

Yet, much like our twentieth-century roadways and the automobiles that travel them, the combined family is a product of our age. Our patterns of family life in the United States have changed dramatically. No longer can we point to any father, mother, and child and say with certainty: "There is a nuclear family." Current trends suggest that the twenty-first century will be the century of the combined family: a family type that defies simple definitions or easy one-word labels describing how family members are related to one another.

To understand the evolution of combined families we must first understand the fundamentals of nuclear and one-parent family development. Only then can we begin to gain some understanding of the forces that impel couples to merge themselves and/or their one-parent families into combined families. To help us gain insight into combined family development, that most American phenomenon, the automobile, will be used as a metaphor to illustrate the problems involved in assembling a combined family. So, dear readers, fasten your seat belts, as together we begin our journey "on the road" to combined family life.

FIGURE 1. One-parent family convertible.

We begin by comparing the nuclear family to an old family car occupied by two adults and their mutual children. This car is a 1975 sedan that shows its age as it makes its way down the highway: engine knocking, tires bald, and brakes worn thin. After some efforts to repair the old sedan, the couple decides to abandon it and go their separate ways in separate (one-parent family) cars, hopefully continuing to share responsibility for their mutual children and, perhaps, taking turns traveling with them.

When the nuclear family ends, each newly single adult must shift to an entirely different model of car—a convertible (see Figure 1). Unfortunately, these one-parent family convertibles offer little protection from the elements; they leave both parent and child exposed and vulnerable.

Mourning the loss of their original family sedan, however badly it may have worked, the children may find their exposure to the elements in a convertible very frightening. Well-meaning single parents may offer their children their personal assurances that "everything will be all right" in their one-parent convertible. The children, however, may question these assertions. Originally, these children trusted their parents' declarations that all family members would continue traveling together in their old family sedan, but look where that got them; no wonder fresh assurances on this subject sound suspect.

While some adults shift quickly from the nuclear family to the combined family, most find themselves traveling a long stretch of road alone with their children. The lone parent must not only locate the right roads, but she or he must read the map, drive the car, and watch for road hazards—all at the same time. Initially, children are unlikely to trust their single parent's driving. They become constant observers of the conditions of the road, the car, and their parent's ability to drive the car.

Struggling to navigate single-handedly, a solo parent often assigns the position of "secondary road-watch" to one of the children, who may slowly move from the back seat to the front seat. This move signals a change in the child's family standing. Elevated from the position of a child and not quite in the position of an adult, the "parental" child[1] attempts to assume the duties of the missing parent. This child may be expected to read the map, point out road hazards, and pay close attention to the markings on the gas gauge.

As parental children accumulate more responsibilities and privileges "riding shotgun," they may no longer consider themselves children. Instead, they may see themselves as more equal to their single parents than any of their back seat siblings. Many view their positions as indispensable to their parent's well-being.

The longer a solo parent and children drive around in a one-parent family convertible, the more relaxed and secure they are likely to become. Eventually, both the children and their single parent gain confidence in the parent's ability to handle not only their vehicle but the road itself.

If a single parent decides to pull over and pick up a "passenger," however, children's dormant suspicions and fears reawaken. While their parent may know this newcomer, the children do not—at least not within the context of a prolonged journey. Eventually, this passenger may want to navigate and drive alongside the remarried parent. Accommodating the newcomer's desire would require all of the children to occupy the back seat. Neither the new passenger nor the parental child's father or mother may realize that the act of returning the parental child to the back seat can leave that child feeling severely displaced.

Out of place in the back seat, and no longer having a place

alongside Mom or Dad, the parental child faces a rocky road in trying to regain the position of sibling to those who never left the back seat. In those cases where no position in the car feels comfortable or familiar anymore, the displaced child may be tempted to "grow up fast" and leave the car. Outside the family car, the dislocated child could decide to seek shelter elsewhere—with an outside parent, grandparent, relative, friend, or, in extreme cases, on the road itself.

A child's worst fears may be confirmed by a single parent's announcement that he or she and the new co-navigator intend to trade in the old convertible for a new combined family car. Such a declaration forces any and all children to recognize that, unless they want to be left behind, they must move from their now more or less comfortable convertible to a combined family car of unknown size, quality, and durability.

Concerned and anxious, the children may have questions about the make and model of the car they are being moved to and how (and even if) the new family vehicle will work. More important, the children are sure to wonder about the direction the combined family car will take.

Left out of the decision-making process, children fall prey to worrying about such things as whether they will be able to maintain contact with their outside parents. Not knowing just where they stand—or sit—in their present family car, children are likely to keep close watch over the stranger now accompanying their parent. Children cannot help but recognize that somehow or another their parent has been changed by the stranger's presence in their convertible.

Single parents want to believe that moving from one-parent to combined families will enhance their children's future well-being as well as improve their own. However, even the heartiest parental assurances regarding their future may fail to comfort the children. For them, traveling with an unknown navigator in an unfamiliar car over an uncharted course can hold no charms—only concerns.

On the new family's journey, children can be trusted to put both the combined family car and the adults driving it through their paces. An abbreviated test drive will not be enough to satisfy them. The new combined family car will have to endure many cross-country hauls before the children are likely to deem it roadworthy.

The combined family "car" is like no other in the world. Its vast and complex inner workings tend to make this distinctive piece of machinery work better as it ages. Only time and diligence can transform an ailing Edsel into a reliable Rolls. By examining and frequently incorporating family members' previous life experiences, combined families can create custom-built classics—families that are one-of-a-kind.

Although each of these families is custom-built, society does not look upon the combined family as the "family of choice"; however, that is precisely what it is. Unlike those in a nuclear or one-parent family, members of a combined family stay together because they *choose* to stay together. They have managed to integrate themselves and their traditions and value systems into a new and highly sophisticated form of family.

To date, society has not recognized that the combined family may be a more highly evolved type of family than either the one-parent or nuclear family. Far from being appreciated in their own right, combined families are often branded "inferior" or "second-best." Such labels make the rough road to successful combined family development just that much rougher.

By any standard, and even with the most congenial cast of characters, attempting to merge two or more families into a single family unit is a high-risk venture. The groundwork for successful combined family integration must be carefully laid because many of the problems that burden a remarriage grow from unresolved issues, rooted in the past.

"WHAT HAPPENED TO US?"

The first big bump "on the road" that nuclear families face is the disintegration of their two-parent family system. Whether the end comes as a result of death or divorce, this marital disruption leaves its mark on each and every family member. No one can escape the disorienting effects of loss and change that occur as one family structure ends and another takes its place.

How Divorce Affects Adults

Adults seeking to end their unhappy marriages are likely to mourn in advance both their failed marriages and the end of their intact families. Their spouses, however, are not likely to have done this kind of anticipatory grief work. Those who have considered themselves happily married can be left totally bewildered when their spouses announce their intentions to sever their ties and end their marriages. The shock can devastate unsuspecting husbands and wives, leaving their self-esteem and self-confidence in shambles.

Stunned, and left to mourn alone, these (now) single adults must work to disconnect the emotional ties that bind them to their former mates. Failure to achieve an emotional divorce can produce a lingering sense of loss, trapping former spouses in their memories of what used to be. Lost in the past, these adults may not be able to foresee a future for either themselves or their children.

Because Yvonne considered her 17-year marriage to Gerry a happy and secure one, she was shocked and shaken when her husband suddenly announced he wanted a divorce. Yvonne felt as if Gerry had plunged a dagger into her heart when he told her that under no circumstances would he reconsider his decision.

To make matters worse, several months before Gerry dropped this bombshell on Yvonne he had moved her and their three children to a new city, for "business" reasons. Gerry, however, seemed to spend most of his time in their old hometown, leaving Yvonne to deal with their daughter and two severely learning-disabled sons.

After Gerry moved out permanently, Yvonne discovered that he was dating an old girlfriend of hers, whom he would later marry. After his marriage, Gerry sent for the children once a year, but the remainder of his actions only served to confirm Yvonne's firm belief that what Gerry really wanted most was to rid himself of all the problems connected with his former life.

Furious with her former friend and despondent over the loss of a husband she loved, Yvonne shouldered the heavy burden of raising her family alone. She was the one who was left to deal with an enraged teen-aged daughter and two hyperactive sons—all the while nursing her own broken heart.

It took Yvonne years to stop thinking back on all the good times she and Gerry had had together without experiencing a profound sense of loss and regret. Unwilling to accept the cruel blow fate had dealt her, Yvonne never stopped mourning the loss of a husband she could neither give up, nor have.

Struggling to cope with their own losses, newly single adults are likely to suffer a "diminished capacity to parent."[2] Having lost their mates, many adults feel they have lost at least one-half of their ability to parent. Physically, these adults may not have the time or energy to provide for their children in the same way they and their former spouses did before. Emotionally, they may not be able to offer the assurances their children so desperately need to hear because, even to their own blunted sensibilities, such assurances ring hollow.

How Divorce Affects Children

Children may be too young to understand the change in their family's composition, or what caused it. However, those old enough to ask may question why their father or mother left their home, the marriage, and them. Did they do something wrong? Are they in some way responsible for the end of their parents' marriage?

Children are in desperate need of answers as they see their parents struggling with the loss of their intact families. How can soon-to-be single parents come to the aid of their bewildered offspring when they themselves are straining to land on their feet in a world turned upside-down? Faced with having to survive their own personal ordeals as well as having to support their soon-to-be-one-parent families, many parents lack the physical and emotional resources necessary to calm their own, let alone their children's, fears.

The primary challenge in shifting from a nuclear to one-parent family is to maintain children's sense of security. But, just when the children are most desperately in need of strong and steady parental love and support, many find their parents unable to help them. "The particular and paradoxical import of divorce is that the disruption of the child's life itself is initiated by a parent, often by the parent whose inner turmoil renders him or her relatively insensitive to the child's needs at that time."[3]

Too often, parents refuse to deal honestly with their children about the effects of separation and divorce. While these parents may be hoping they can keep their children from going through the agony they themselves are experiencing, their personal denials of pain can create an atmosphere that denies their children the right to *their* own personal sense of loss and pain. As Lillian Messinger and Kenneth Walker advise, "Children must be given permission to vent their shock, grief, anger, and fear. To discuss the separation only in a matter-of-fact way may imply to the child that marriage ties are easily broken."[4]

Caught up in their own grief, parents often fail to appreciate what the loss of their intact families means to their children. No matter how difficult things may have been before, children normally would have preferred staying in their original families to experiencing the pain of disrupting those families.

While parents may fervently believe their children cannot be happy if *they* are not happy, research indicates that only those children who have been continuously subjected to high levels of conflict in their intact families appear to experience relief when their parents' marriages end. Although most divorcing parents are likely to feel they have relieved their children from stressful living situations, these adults may not fully appreciate the secondary effects of their actions: They have ended their children's intact family life.

Making the transition from nuclear to one-parent family life involves loss and change. Members of a one-parent family must redefine themselves while living within a family structure that is at the same time both contracting and evolving. Confronted with heading their own one-parent families, newly single parents are often astonished to find themselves faced with undiminished responsibilities and significantly depleted emotional reserves. At this stressful period in their lives, frazzled single parents may unwittingly send their children a message that roughly translates into: "Don't bother me, I can't cope."

ON THEIR OWN

Sometimes one-parent families function as way stations between the end of two-parent families and the beginning of combined families. However, to increasing numbers of single parents with children, the one-parent family represents the final stage in their family's development. For them, the one-parent family becomes a permanent state rather than a transitional phase in their family's evolution. This is particularly true for women who head one-parent families.

Research suggests that women are less marriageable with children than without them. In fact, most children entering one-parent families will not again live in two-parent families during their childhood.[5]

In reporting that three-fourths of separating white women and less than one-half of separating black women "are likely to remarry," researchers Larry Bumpass, James Sweet, and Teresa Castro Martin indicate that the median time it may take women with children to remarry is approximately five years.[6] It appears that separated women's opportunities to remarry are limited by the number of children they have. About 25 percent of mothers with one or two children and 40 percent of those with three or more children will not marry again. Of those mothers who have one or two children at the time they separate, one-half are likely to take seven years to remarry. Women with three or more children at the time of separation may take 14 years to marry again.[7]

When their nuclear families end, many single mothers are left to raise their children alone, with little or no financial assistance from errant fathers. In 1985, Harvard professor Lenore Weitzman found that, on average, divorced women with minor children experience a 73 percent decline in standard of living in the first year after divorce, whereas their husbands experience a 42 percent rise in standard of living. Weitzman went further: she predicted a two-tiered society with women and children as the underclass,[8] a trend that was already in plain evidence by 1991.

A recent survey conducted by the Children's Defense Fund found that "children in female-headed households are five times as likely to be poor as those in married couple families." The study further cited that "more than half of all children (and nearly two-thirds of all children younger than six) in families headed by women are poor."[9]

Their drastically changed economic conditions and the loss of their intact families can sometimes be too much for children to bear. In every way, the world in which these children live has suddenly "become less reliable, less predictable, and less likely in their view to provide for their needs and expectations."[10]

Single Parents and Their Children

Because single parents may be uncertain as to the direction in which they should lead their new one-parent families, they frequently assign limited parental authority to one of the children. This creates a parental or parentified child. In the extreme, severely distraught single parents may relinquish all personal authority to any and all children who are willing to accept it. In the face of such unfortunate events, children are left to wonder whether they can ever again rely on the trustworthiness of their parent(s).

Children's Fears of Abandonment

Children may well interpret a parent's inability to function as an abdication of that parent's responsibilities toward them. In such cases, the children's sense of security and faith in their parent can be seriously impaired. To children whose parents have left each other, the unthinkable has already happened. No wonder children worry about whom their parents will leave next!

As much as single parents may scoff at children's fears of betrayal and abandonment, these fears are rooted in reality.[11] Parents' struggles to pick up the pieces of their own lives may temporarily cause them to lose their desire as well as their ability to parent.[12] When single parents find themselves heading their own one-parent households, they may seriously question their own ability to survive, let alone provide for their children. And, if the truth be known, there may be times when single parents secretly wonder what it would be like to leave everything—their children included—and just start over again.

Some parents act out these fantasies of escape by leaving. Those adults who are left behind must then face their own ambivalence about raising and caring for their children—on their own. Throughout the first year or two after a divorce, parents may struggle to redefine themselves as "single." Some do this by running out seven nights a week, measuring their mettle by their social calendar. Others dive into their one-parent families, choosing to become supermoms or superdads to the exclusion of all else. Regardless, parental ambivalence, resulting from the pressures of single parenthood, prompts fears of abandonment in children.

As single parents become more comfortable about managing their one-parent families, children can begin to relax and reestablish some of the trust and confidence they lost when their parents' marriages ended. The longer these adults and children live together, the tighter their bonds become. Having fought together "in the trenches," single parents and their children commonly become "fox hole buddies."[13]

One-parent families develop their own standards of conduct and methods of communicating. The longer parents and children live together, the more entrenched they are likely to become in their own unique culture. There is a special bond, a silent code, between single parents and their children that is closed to outsiders.

A KNOCK AT THE DOOR

When their parents begin to date, children begin to worry. Fearing they will lose their parents' love, children often try to prevent outsiders from getting too close to their parents. Drawing parallels from their past life experience, children fear that if outsiders are allowed inside their one-parent families, their families will again be disrupted.

Children's worst nightmares can involve one or both of their parents revealing remarriage plans. Such news can reawaken memories of the trauma these children experienced the last time their parents changed their marital status. Children who have witnessed the disintegration of one family structure become all too mindful that both marriage and the family offer no long-term guarantees. Experiencing flashbacks and disorientation similar to that which they felt when their original families ended, children can easily begin to wonder, What is going to happen to me now?

To children, a parent's decision to marry again may seem as crazed as building a house on the same geological fault line that destroyed their original home. Everyone knows that a second structure—built on the site of the first—can also be destroyed if a strong enough jolt comes along. No one can predict whether the foundation of a new family can withstand the shock, and aftershocks, that might occur as the result of merging separate family units into a single combined family.

In effect, a parent's announcement of another family reorganization, this time to create a combined family, may register as a 10 on the children's emotional Richter scale. Is it any wonder then that children who have already experienced one family disruption instinctively fear a repeat performance?

FOUR

The Couple

Kathryn arrived late to a singles social where she planned to meet a friend, Walter, who had been released from the hospital earlier that day. When she spotted Walter, she rushed over to find out how he was feeling. As the pace of their conversation slowed, Kathryn noticed that she was the only woman sitting on her side of the room. All the other women were gathering around someone on the other side. Curious, Kathryn moved closer. There, sitting on the sofa, surrounded by all the rest of the women in the room, sat a man. When he spoke, Kathryn knew then and there that what she wanted most in her life was to hear that voice again and again. When they finally did meet and fall in love, neither of them gave much thought to the fact that he had three children and she had two.

In today's world, "single" often fails to translate as "unattached." When two adults find each other, be it across a crowded room or through a casual introduction, they have no way of knowing about each other's previous commitments. If one or both of the adults are tied to prior relationships, the threads that bind them are invisible. Because previous attachments do not show, they often come as a shock to those who learn about them later, rather than sooner.

Previously married parents cannot be identified by the color of their eyes or hair, but all of them have one thing in common that should be of particular significance to potential mates: *They are all single parents!* As early as a first meeting or a first date, even before they become romantically involved, marriage-minded single parents need to inform potential partners of their children's presence in their lives. Unless they make full disclosure of their parental status, these adults are being dishonest, with themselves, their potential partners, and their children as well.

As they begin thinking about marriage, single parents and their future mates need to assess what uniting their separate families entails. Couples must know in advance what they are in for: They need to understand the dynamics of combined family living before they involve others in the process. Couples cannot marry first and then ask questions about combined family life later. They must measure their commitment against the odds that tell us that currently about six out of ten combined families fail, as compared to five out of ten first-marriage families.

The difference between the 50 percent divorce rate in nuclear families and the approximately 60 percent divorce rate in combined families can be explained through an analysis of the many additional burdens placed on remarried and stepparents. Couples in combined families may be forced to reckon with unhappy insiders, innumerable outsiders, and more potential and real obstacles to threaten their relationships than most of us could possibly imagine. The equation in combined families is not a simple $1 + 1 = 2$: it is more on the dizzying scale of $E = mc^2$!

Faced with the potential for so many complicated interactions to occur—between any number of related and unrelated people, both inside and outside their new families—one can only wonder why so many couples fail to recognize the many challenges inherent in combined family life: for children, parents, former spouses and in-laws, and the couples themselves.

WHAT MOTIVATES COUPLES TO FORM COMBINED FAMILIES?

There are many reasons why couples choose combined family life: Some like the idea of having ready-made families, while more than a few are looking for "fathers" or "mothers" for their children.

Some people cannot stand living alone, while others cannot tolerate the thought of being considered a one-, two-, or three-time "loser" in marriage. However, there is one class of couples who rival all the others put together—those who have simply fallen in love. Unable to think of living apart, these individuals seek to unite their lives—regardless of the cost to themselves or others!

Because many readers will not understand why couples would choose to put themselves and their loved ones through what promises to be a great deal of trauma, this author can tell you from personal experience that the nature of a couple's love for each other is no less wondrous in a combined family than it is in a nuclear family. Indeed, love for a new mate in a new marriage may prove far sweeter and more serendipitous than anything that either the previously married parent or his or her new spouse has ever experienced. But who counts previous marriages, or children, when lovers meet and are carried away by magic and moonlight? The love between two adults is not diminished because one or both of them have loved before; indeed, that love may be prized all the more!

For those in love, nothing seems too big or too hard or too daring to undertake. Remarriage? Why, it's a piece of cake! Children? They will live with us, and we will all "live happily ever after!" Former spouses? Oh, they will fade into the woodwork, or oblivion, or a memory!

As soon-to-be wives and husbands eagerly anticipate the joys that lie in store for them in their new marriages, many refuse to acknowledge even the remotest possibility that all may not be smooth sailing in combined family life.

Adults who have experienced one failed marriage do not want to repeat the experience. For many of them, remarriage represents a second chance—an opportunity to wipe the slate clean and begin anew. Herein lies the danger in the mythology surrounding combined family life: In order to successfully wipe the slate clean and begin anew, one would have to erase one's children, as well as one's former marriage(s) and marriage partner(s). This is not an option for remarrying parents, since their children are already members of their current families and will automatically become members of any new families their parents form.

COUPLE ISSUES

The Couple Bond

All combined families have at their base a preexisting bond between at least one adult and one child. While preexisting parent–child bonds underlie all combined family development, the success or failure of any of these new families ultimately depends on the strength of the couple's bond.

Although it is on the basis of the parent–child relationship that the combined family rises, it is likely to be on the weakness of the couple bond that it falls. Given this very important note, it is of crucial importance that remarried parents and their new spouses pay close attention to their interpersonal relationships. As a couple nurture and reinforce their commitments to each other, they strengthen their primary couple bond.

The Remarried Parent's Ties to the Children

As a couple works to strengthen their union to the point where their couple bond is primary, any number of obstacles are likely to get in the way. Chief among these may be the remarried parent's unwillingness to make a wholehearted commitment to a new spouse for fear of alienating a child or children. Ultimately this failure to acknowledge the importance of the couple bond may result in the weakening of the couple's ties to each other, which in turn can cripple or totally collapse the combined family itself.

The Couple in a Complex Combined Family

When both adults bring children from previous marriages into their new union, they may shy away from making a full commitment to each other for fear of putting their children at risk. If the couple prioritizes blood or legal ties to their children over their marriage ties to each other, their household may well divide along biological lines. As combined family statistics prove: "A house divided against itself cannot stand."[1]

The Couple's Background

As the combined family is formed, new family members arrive with their previous family histories intact. While the newlyweds may never have given much thought to differences in their family backgrounds, the strength of their commitments to one another is influenced by each adult's previous family life experiences. The way the parents of each of these adults interacted—as a couple and as parents—is bound to have some bearing on the way this couple interacts.

If the parents of both of these adults had strong couple bonds, both adults are likely to set this same goal for themselves. When the adults come from different backgrounds, however, they may find their personal goals for their marriage at odds: One may be seeking close couple ties while the other seeks to reinforce strong parent–child bonds.

Discrepancies between what people expect and what they get once their combined families are formed can leave various family members open to feelings ranging from disappointment to despair. When adults are unrealistic in their expectations of combined family life, they are stacking the deck, not only against themselves but against the children who follow them into their unions.

Asymmetrical Ties to the Children

The couple forming a combined family do not share symmetrical ties to at least one child. While a parent may have remarried, in part, to find a mother or father for his or her children, this parent needs to understand that the stepparent cannot be expected to fill the missing parent's role. Unless parents marry persons who are already related to their children (e.g., aunts or uncles, etc.), the only tie between a stepparent and stepchild comes about as a result of a marriage tie between the remarried parent and his or her new spouse.

Relationships

By their very nature, parent–child relationships are different from stepparent–stepchild relationships. Remarried parents need to understand from the outset that they and their spouses are bound to have different feelings about the same children. To say that feelings are different makes these feelings neither good nor bad; they are simply, and very understandably, different.

The Combined Family's Expanded Family Network

While couples in nuclear families have to deal with their children, in-laws, and extended family, as well as one another, couples in combined families face a dramatically expanded network of people that directly impact the families that are formed by their unions. Adult couples become remarried and stepparents; children become stepchildren; unrelated children become stepsiblings; former and current spouses vie with one another over children and sometimes over remarried parents themselves; grandparents spar with stepgrandparents over those prized possessions—grandchildren; old in-laws take potshots at new in-laws. Additionally, with little or no warning, schools, courts, and other societal agencies can intrude on combined family functioning. There is no way for combined family members to prevent at least some of these forces from impinging on their lives or their privacy. Outside interference finds its way into combined families via the invisible bonds of family kinship networks and/or the collective clout of society's institutions.

The sheer impact of these inside and outside forces is enough to dampen the ardor of any couple seeking to form a combined family. If only couples would allow themselves to fully comprehend just how complicated combined family life can get, there might be a great many more adults pausing to reconsider their anticipated unions, rather than rushing off to consolidate them:

> Ian and Hillary's marriage ended when their son, Seth, suffered brain damage after being thrown from a horse. Unwilling, or unable, to cope with the catastrophic consequences of her son's injury, Hillary divorced Ian, leaving him alone to deal with the trauma of Seth's accident. She took their other son, Collin, and moved "out west."
>
> When Seth regained consciousness, he was prone to wild

mood swings and erratic behavior. Ian found him very hard to handle, but he was determined that his son would have a life and a home with him.

Around the same time Ian and Hillary were going through their trauma with Seth, another couple, Melanie and her husband Giles, had decided to end their marriage. Melanie and Giles had two children, Oliver and Beth. She had legal custody of the children during the school year, while Giles had custody during Christmas and summer vacations.

After the divorce, Melanie, Oliver, and Beth moved to Chicago, where she found work teaching handicapped children. It was in Melanie's capacity as Seth's teacher that she and Ian met and fell in love.

Just as Melanie and Ian were about to marry, Ian was transferred out of the country. Melanie and her children accompanied him abroad. Melanie did not take time to get Giles' permission to take the children along with her; she assumed Giles would not make a fuss about it, especially since she still planned to send the children back to him for Christmas and summer vacations.

Once abroad, Seth became almost impossible for Melanie to handle. His mood swings often led to violent behavior, and the couple finally agreed to place him in a special school. The school was some distance from their new home, however, and Melanie and Ian found themselves—and their relationship—wearing thin as they traveled back and forth visiting the boy.

When summer came, Melanie sent her children back to Giles. At precisely the same time, Ian's former wife, Hillary, sent his son Collin to live with the newlyweds. Pinned to Collin's sweater was a note telling Ian and Melanie to keep him.

The climax of the couple's troubles came when Melanie learned that her former husband, Giles, had gone back to court and gained custody of their children. Because Melanie had taken the children out of the country without his permission, Giles did not allow Melanie to see her children again for years.

Instead of living with her own children, Oliver and Beth, Melanie found herself living with Ian and his two sons: Seth, whom she could no longer handle, and Collin, who felt bitterly rejected by his mother and angry about being "tossed out" like the rubbish. To drown any thinking about the loss of her children, Melanie started drinking heavily.

When Ian was finally transferred back to the United States,

Seth had to be taken out of school. Finding the proper placement for Seth was always a problem.

Although Melanie had gradually built up the courage necessary for her to control Seth, Seth himself absolutely refused to accept her authority. As Seth was now too big for Melanie to handle, Ian and Melanie agreed that Ian would take over sole responsibility for dealing with his son, while Melanie would try to conquer her drinking problem by joining Alcoholics Anonymous.

As she gradually gained control over her drinking, Melanie begged Giles to let her see her children again. Inasmuch as the children were now of an age where they could make a choice, Oliver and Beth came to live with Ian and Melanie for a trial period over the summer. While Oliver eventually returned to his father's residence, Beth chose to stay with her mother and stepfather. By this time, Seth was in a new school, and Collin had returned to live near his mother, who really did not want him around as she had become addicted to drugs.

Conversely, Melanie was overjoyed to have her daughter, Beth, living with her once again. But, Beth had changed! The 15-year-old had been so unsettled by her parents' divorce and her father's decision to keep her from seeing her mother, she was desperate to have something that no one could take away from her. To accomplish this end, Beth became pregnant, and she asked the child's biological father to relinquish all legal rights to the baby prior to its birth—which he did.

Beth was overjoyed at the arrival of her son, but when the baby cried and needed constant attention, Beth became angry; she felt tied down. Ian did not want Melanie to rescue Beth, but seeing her daughter at a dead end at 15 was too much for Melanie. She took over her grandson's care so Beth could return to high school.[2]

Without the clear goal of maintaining their commitments to one another, couples such as Ian and Melanie would never be able to weather the emotional storms that so often cloud the combined family landscape, especially during the early stages of development. The couple's relationship is the force that keeps the combined family from faltering and falling apart in a deluge. The adults heading a combined family must do all they can to protect and preserve their union; they can use no half measures in meeting their commitments. The full measure of their love and devotion is what the couple owes to their union, and all those who are dependent upon it.

With so much hinging upon their efforts, couples heading combined families may find that their time and energy have run out before they have been able to be together in any meaningful kind of way. Too often, couples use the time they have set aside for themselves to instead work on issues that arise both inside and outside their new family units. When couples ignore their marital ties for too long, they may find they no longer have the relationships they have been taking for granted.

The complex interplay between the two adults and all the forces that impinge on them creates a situation whereby it is necessary for the couple to erect clear boundaries to protect their marital relationship. To accomplish this, the couple needs to become, figuratively speaking, like a double-yolked egg (see Figure 2).

When two egg yolks are encased in a single shell, the relationship between them is well defined, yet there is a secure boundary holding them together. In order to preserve their union, the couple founding a combined family needs to "tuck into an eggshell." They need an explicit boundary around their relationship to protect the sanctity of their union. Inside the shell of a double-yolked egg, each individual yolk has its own separate boundary. These internal boundaries serve as reminders to the couple that while it is necessary to reinforce their commitment to one another, the adults need not encroach on each other's needs for personal space.

Throughout their relationship, the adults heading a combined family must fight the odds in order to hold together. Without some

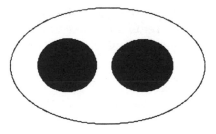

FIGURE 2. Double-yolked egg.

protection (their shell), the newlyweds may find that the preexisting bond between parent and child can exert so much strain on their couple bond that their union is at risk (of cracking).

If couples do not constantly reinforce their unions, old ties to preexisting children are likely to pull remarried parents away from their new mates—sometimes with such force as to shatter their couple bond. If this is allowed to happen, new spouses are left unprotected and alone. When remarried parents fail to support their new spouses, the bonds which cause these couples to hold tightly to one another can be severely weakened or irreparably damaged.

Knowing that so much is dependent on the strength of their relationship, couples have to take care to avoid the hazards that befell Humpty Dumpty, lest they find their lives in pieces all around them. It is in everyone's best interest that couples establishing combined families work diligently to protect the unions they create.

When couples' commitments to each other remain intact, and the adults stay mindful of the importance of their relationships to each other as well as to those who are dependent on them, the unions they have forged can withstand almost any pressure. With the passage of time and the continued growth of relationships, ties between all combined family members are expanded and strengthened. Bonds of affection and loyalty extend throughout individual combined families and beyond to include new, as well as old, family members.

The people who support all this good will and well-being are the couple whose love and affection causes the formation of the combined family in the first place. Each step they take becomes the foundation for future steps. But one of the most crucial and delicate steps that remarrying parents must take immediately follows their decisions to marry again.[3] They must tell their children of their remarriage plans.

FIVE

Telling the Children

Daphne, 12, had lived alone with her mom, Erica, for ten years before her mom remarried Jim. Jim's wife had died, leaving him with two young sons, Mike, 9, and Todd, 6. About six weeks after his wife died, Jim met Erica. After dating for a year, they decided to marry, and they told the children about their plans. Mike felt it was too soon. What about their mom? Todd liked things the way they were. Meanwhile, Daphne felt like she was going to lose her mother. Disregarding their children's questions and objections, Jim and Erica were married.

After the ceremony, Todd's father informed him that he was being moved upstairs to make room for Daphne. To Todd this demonstrated his loss of importance to his father, even though his brother Mike's room was also upstairs. When Daphne was moved into Todd's old room, she felt all alone; her mom had Jim, Mike and Todd had each other, and Daphne had lost all that was comfortable and familiar in her former family life, where she and her mother had been everything to one another.

Three years later, Jim and Erica demonstrate how the children's issues have divided them. Each parent sits with his or her biological offspring. They make no move toward one another. The couple feels that the two big mistakes they made were in not properly informing the children of their remarriage plans and in not paying enough attention to their children's feedback regarding their decision. Currently, Erica and Jim are not sure their union will survive.

When parents decide to marry again, they have to broaden the focus of their thinking to include the new roles and responsibilities they will be undertaking as remarried parents. As these adults shift their focus from their roles in one-parent families to their roles in combined families, the role of the remarried parent emerges. *The point at which a parent decides to remarry marks the beginning of the remarried parent's role.*

Telling their children of their decisions to marry again is likely to be far more challenging to remarrying parents than most of them ever anticipated. A remarrying parent cannot simply say to her or his children: "Oh, by the way, _____ and I are getting married next _____." Too much is at stake for parents to be casual about making lifestyle changes of such magnitude.

The challenge parents face in telling their children of their remarriage plans is but a prelude to a much greater challenge—living together as part of a combined family. If remarrying parents have not given the subjects of remarriage and combined family formation careful consideration prior to talking to their children, how can these adults answer their children's questions or address their concerns?

When parents do tell their children of their remarriage plans, it is important for them to be as specific as possible. Children's fears may be diminished by their parents giving them as much substantive information as possible about what to expect once their combined families are formed. Remarrying parents have to be honest about the amount of information they do and do not have available to share; they cannot know everything their children will want to know. What most remarrying parents do believe, however, is that their children will benefit from the changes in family structure they are proposing.

Who Should Tell the Children?

Unquestionably, the parent who plans to remarry is the one who needs to tell the children of her or his impending nuptials. The discussion should not be left to an outsider, even if that outsider is the remarrying parent's former spouse—the children's other parent.

After their divorce, Steven and Jennifer worked hard to coordinate their efforts to raise their children. Their two boys lived with Jennifer and her new husband during the week and with Steven on the weekends. Because the boys did not get along with their stepfather, they asked their father to "swear" that he would never remarry and provide them with a stepmother. Since Steven had never considered remarrying, he hastily agreed.

That was before Steven met Darcy. After only a ten-week courtship, Steven summoned the courage to ask Darcy to marry him and she said yes. It was only 24 hours later that Steven realized he had another even more nerve-racking task to perform: He had to tell his sons about his remarriage plans.

Steven took his sons out on several occasions, but each time he was unable to break the news. As the weeks passed, Steven's anxiety deepened, particularly since Darcy and the boys had not spent any significant amount of time together. Finally, because she had been told in advance, Steven's former wife, Jennifer, took it upon herself to tell the boys about Steven and Darcy's plans.

Shocked and shaken at receiving such important news secondhand, Steven's sons were outraged by what they saw as their father's double betrayal of them: Steven had failed to keep the promise he had made his sons about staying single, and he had failed in his duty to tell them of his remarriage plans.

Learning of a parent's plans to remarry from any person other than that parent can be a devastating blow to a child. This is one message children need to hear directly from the source—the remarrying parent. If the remarrying parent refuses to accept this responsibility, he or she is giving up control over not only the message the children receive, but also the way in which that message is delivered. When remarrying parents are not the bearers of their own glad tidings, they have no way of knowing how, where, when, what, or even if their children are told; they also have no way of knowing how their children actually respond to the news (if they do hear it).

Children need to learn of their parents' plans to remarry firsthand. This task cannot be delegated because it is too delicate and to important to deliver into the hands of a third party.

When to Tell the Children

Children need to be told of a parent's plans to marry again as soon as possible after the decision has been made by the couple. Unless the wedding date has been set so far in advance as to be beyond a child's comprehension, the children need as much time as the adults do to adjust to the changes that are about to take place in their lives.

How to Tell the Children

If you are a single parent who is planning to remarry, and you have only one child, the problem of telling that child is easily managed. Sit down and discuss your plans with your child. Your daughter or son needs to comprehend the full meaning of what you are telling her or him; deliver your message in terms your child can understand.

If there are two or more children in your one-parent family, it is probably best to inform all of them at the same time of your plans to remarry—unless you have children with special needs who require your individual attention. Children who live elsewhere, near or far, and those who can only be reached by phone or letter, etc., also need to be told of your plans to remarry. Your message needs to be delivered personally, as soon as possible after your plans have been formulated.

However you tell your children, as the parent responsible for their well-being, you must find or make time to talk to each child individually. If some of the children do not understand what a remarriage entails, take the time to explain what it is you plan on doing—and how your plans are likely to impact their lives. When you do speak with your children, be sure you set aside enough time to respond adequately to their most pressing concerns.

What to Tell the Children

Remarrying parents have to tell their children such things as when their weddings will take place, where they will be held, and what the children can expect to happen in their lives as a result. For example: The children will or will not have to change households, change neighborhoods, change schools, live with and/or share rooms with stepsiblings, etc. Remarrying parents must do a great deal of soul-searching before telling their children of their decisions to marry again, because there is much they will need to have considered thoroughly in order to give their children a reasonable picture of what kind of life each of them can expect to lead in a combined family.

Parents need to be as realistic as possible about what they tell their children. No parent should ever try to "sell" his or her child on the idea that remarriage will be the answer to everyone's prayers. In the first place, most children are praying that their original parents will get back together again. Therefore, painting a portrait of a perfect family can lead parents and their children into a reality with which none of them may want to deal—with children wanting to go back while their parents want to go forward.

If remarrying parents can reassure their children that they will be taken care of and provided for in their new living situations, a great many of their children's questions will disappear. Parents must bear in mind, however, that all children in one-parent families have experienced loss. Sensitivity to a child's concerns over abandonment, safety, and security can make this time one of increased closeness between parent and child.

Finding a special time and place to tell the children can provide remarrying parents with their greatest opportunities to discover just what it is that each of their children is thinking and feeling. Meanwhile the children gain a much-needed opportunity to tell their parents as much as they can about what they are thinking and feeling.

Children's thoughts and feelings cannot be discounted in a parent's mad rush to find happiness. Children can feel disrupted and out of sorts when they learn of their parent's plans to remarry, and they are likely to be concerned about just what kinds of adjustments they will be expected to make as a result of the changes that will be taking place in their lives. Therefore, the subject of a parent's remarriage has to be explored in detail, as frequently as necessary to allow children's ambivalent feelings to surface. Remarrying parents have to make sure they set aside sufficient time to deal with their children's reactions to their news.

Children's Reactions

No matter how well a remarrying parent knows his or her children, and no matter how well the children may get along with their parent's intended spouse, there is simply no way of telling how children will react to news of a parent's remarriage. Children's emotions are likely to range widely, from fear to eager anticipation. While some children may ask endless questions, others may feel too overwhelmed to articulate their feelings for fear of alienating their parent. Some children simply do not know, or cannot put into words, just what it is they are feeling when they learn of their parent's remarriage plans. Others just say whatever it is that pops into their minds at the time, and often that response is not exactly what their remarrying parent wants, or expects, to hear.

Children can feel overwhelmed by a parent's news that their entire one-parent family will soon become part of a larger, combined family. Children are certain to be wondering about the kinds of adjustments they will be expected to make when their parents marry persons other than their "outside" parents. That is why remarrying parents have to give their children time to doubt, puzzle, ponder, question, query, acknowledge, accept, and get ready for the momentous changes that are about to take place in their lives.

When Children Object

Children cannot be expected to keep all their doubts to themselves. When children voice their objections to their parents' remarriage plans, remarrying parents need to sit down with them and listen to what they are saying. Remarrying parents must listen very carefully to their children's remarks for clues as to what the children really mean. Parents need to pay attention to their children's tone of voice and body language, as well as to the words they use to express their feelings. Worries or concerns expressed over a variety of subjects may all come back to children's primary concerns: What is going to happen to me? Will I be protected, cared for, and loved? If parents can reassure their children that their needs will be met, no matter what their family structure, a great many of the children's objections are likely to disappear.

When one or several of the remarrying parent's children have persistent and violent objections to the addition of a stepfather or stepmother to their lives, it would serve the remarrying mother or father well to pay attention to the children's concerns. Children sometimes pick up on clues that their parents overlook. Following up on these clues may lead remarrying parents to the uncovering of obstacles to their proposed unions which may prove formidable, if not insurmountable. Therefore, in a sincere effort to clear away any personal doubts about forming a combined family, remarrying parents will have to invest the time and the energy necessary to explore those issues their children raise as problems, both with their children and with their prospective mates.

When Parents See Their Children as Threats to Their Unions

When it is the children themselves who seem likely to pose major threats to remarrying parents' new unions, it would be wise for couples not to go full speed ahead with their wedding plans. Putting their plans on hold allows remarrying parents time to explore what it is about their proposed new mates or new marriages that their children see as objectionable. As children become familiar with prospective living arrangements, their objections may fade. If they remain adamant in their protests, however, couples need time to make alternative plans or to prepare for dealing with children's hostility within the framework of their new family structures.

The above approach allows adults time to make realistic appraisals of their future living situations. It also gives a parent insight into what his or her children are thinking and feeling. The children might have reasons that they have never mentioned for not wanting their parent to enter this marriage. It may be because of the timing. It may be because of the person the parent has chosen. It may be because the children are mourning the total or partial loss of their outside parent. These children may need more time to do their own personal grief work before being put into the position of seeing one of their parents acting in a very happy and perhaps overtly sexual way with an "other" who is taking their outside parent's place. It is far easier to give children some additional time to adjust to the idea of merging families—and gaining stepparents—than to give children cause to build resentments right from the start of their relationships with their new stepparents. These resentments have a tendency to grow over time.

> Although Nina had met her father's lady friend any number of times, she never gave any thought to the possibility that her dad might actually marry Connie. There was no reason for him to do so. Nina had been taking care of the family ever since her mom died, several years earlier. Everything was under control and running smoothly. Therefore, when her dad informed the family of his plans to remarry, Nina could hardly believe her ears. Convinced she was being thrown over for another woman, Nina swore her revenge. Nina vowed that she would never make a place for Connie in her life. She never did.

Adults' Choices in the Face of Children's Objections

Faced with their children's violent objections, remarrying parents would be foolish to believe that everything will work out all right once they are wed. There are many avenues adults can take in dealing with their children's objections. Some couples decide to abandon marriage plans and wait until all the children are in college or out of the house, while others decide to remain engaged until such time as the children become more receptive to the idea of their union.

> Carla was left with three young daughters when her husband took off with a woman half her age, leaving not only Carla and their marriage but their three children as well.
> Carla had been a single parent for several years when she met George, himself the father of two. George's children were out of the house by the time Carla came into his life, so the couple focused their attention on making Carla's children comfortable about their marriage plans.
> As Carla and the girls had lived more like sorority sisters than as parent and children, the proposed shift in their mother's

status made the girls very uncomfortable. They caused one up-
roar after another as the couple tried to set a date for their wedding.

When Carla and George finally realized that they would only
have to wait 4 years for her youngest daughter to graduate from
college, they decided to stay engaged until they could set up
housekeeping without upsetting anyone else's lifestyle.

It was ten years after they began dating that George and
Carla were married. With all of their children fairly well settled,
the couple was able to live their life the way it suited them. They
never regretted waiting because the peace and harmony of their
lives together was, according to them, "well worth the wait."

A Slower Walk to the Altar

If the couple is committed to their union, waiting often becomes part of that commitment. During the interim the couple has
even more time to evaluate their positions relative to one another
and any children involved. The strength and knowledge they gain
from this can only add to their union. If the relationship between
the adults fails to hold up under this kind of testing, one could
reasonably assume that a marriage between them would have
failed as well.

Many couples initiate a campaign designed to integrate all the
individuals into a cohesive family unit before they actually establish a combined family. Others decide to go ahead with their plans
regardless of their children's objections. Many of those who believed that love would "conquer all" have ended their marriages in
despair because the issues between the adults and children were
too substantial to overcome while everyone was living in the same
family unit.

Conclusions

Children often need help understanding in what ways their
lives will change as a result of remarriage. If children are helped to
understand what is going to happen to them as a result of their
mom's or dad's remarriage, there is likely to be less resistance to
the new union. Children will know that they have been included in

their parent's plans, and they will recognize the fact that their needs have been made an integral part of those plans. This has to make children feel good about themselves and good about the parent who has taken their needs into such careful consideration.

Parents who are remarrying need not fear telling their children; however, they must be adequately prepared to receive both the feedback and the fallout that telling their children is likely to produce. When remarrying parents have done their jobs, and their children have been properly informed about what is going to be taking place in their lives, couples thrive, children understand and eventually grow to accept their new life situations, and all stand a far better chance of attaining satisfaction once their combined families are formed.

SIX

The Wedding Ceremony

Teresa and her brother came in from out of town for their dad's wedding. It was being held in the bride's family home, and they knew no one except their uncle. After the ceremony, an elderly, gray-haired man came over, kissed Teresa, and said: "I suppose I am your new stepgrandfather." The man never introduced himself to Teresa's brother, who was standing right beside her.

People use ceremonies to mark the importance of an event. In today's world, some couples choose to live together in committed relationships while others choose to mark the importance of joining their lives together with wedding ceremonies. While society merely tolerates cohabitation, it celebrates the ritual blending of the lives of two adults in a legally sanctioned union.

This ritual blending of two lives works very well in the formation of a nuclear family, but what happens when one or both of the adults bring children to their union? Do children belong at a parent's wedding? Should children be informed of a parent's remarriage beforehand, or should they be informed of the event afterwards? Is it appropriate for children to attend their parent's wedding? If the children are invited, is it proper for them to participate in the wedding ceremony? To date, society has provided no answers to these questions. Without any established protocol, marrying couples are responsible for making their own decisions as to the place of children at their weddings.

For a couple to reach a decision of such magnitude, the adults must balance their needs as a couple against what they perceive to be the needs of the children, and they have to agree on what role, if any, the children will play in their wedding celebration.

In a strange way, the question of whether to include the children serves as a good barometer of the couple's relationship. If, when they are engaged, the couple cannot resolve their disagreements over he children's participation in their wedding celebration, how then are these adults going to resolve the countless other conflicts that are sure to arise over the course of their union?

On a scale ranging from not telling the children until after their marriage to having the children participate in their wedding ceremony, the challenge to the couple lies not so much in the outcome as in the process they must go through to make their decision.

When Children Are Asked to Attend the Celebration

Once a couple decides to invite the children to attend their wedding, it is the remarrying parent who must talk to the children about their role at the celebration. Basically, the children have to know what they are being asked to do—to just be there, to "stand up" for their parent, etc.—and what their options are. When the children are too young to make their own decisions about what it is they want to do about being involved in their parent's wedding, all the adults involved in their lives have to reach some kind of agreement on this issue.

The Role of the Outside Parent

The couple is not always alone in determining whether the remarrying parent's children will be in attendance at their wedding. The children's outside parent holds a good deal of power—to implement, or sabotage, any decision the couple makes regarding the children's presence at the ceremony. In light of the power the outside parent holds, it only makes sense for the remarrying parent to enlist the cooperation and support of this former spouse—for the benefit of their mutual children.

In cases where outside parents are likely to create havoc in their children's lives just to keep them from attending their par-

ents' weddings, remarrying parents may want to consider letting go of the idea of having children present at their nuptials, if only to spare them the anguish of witnessing a full-fledged battle between their parents. Under such circumstances, remarrying parents need to make sure their children understand that, although their parents very much want them to be present at their weddings, they will understand if their children cannot, or feel they should not, attend. Of course, some remarrying parents find it difficult to let go of their own desires and resort to darker means of assuring their children's attendance:

> Sally and Kyle were afraid to inform his children of the actual day they were getting married. Kyle believed his former spouse to be a spiteful and vindictive woman. He would not even put it past her to take the children out of town if she knew the date of their wedding. As a precaution against his former wife's interference, Kyle decided to tell his children that he and Sally were going to be married some time during the summer. In that way, Kyle could deal with his children's questions and possible objections to the marriage beforehand, reassure them that they would be okay, buy them suitable clothing, and only tell them of the actual wedding day on the very weekend the wedding was taking place—when they were already in his custody.

These lessons in deception are probably not at all what Kyle wanted to teach his children, but his situation exemplifies the desperation some remarrying parents feel—and the lengths to which they will go—to get around difficult former spouses.

In reviewing their options, parents need to remember that their children learn from their actions as well as their words. When remarrying parents "hijack" their children—just to have them present at their weddings—it can only antagonize the children's outside parents. In the long run, such actions harm children by undermining the development of workable relationships between the two households in which they live.

In looking at the whole subject of remarriage celebrations, what becomes abundantly clear is that the remarrying parent does not always have either the power or the control to assure the presence of his or her children at the wedding. While the cooperation of an outside parent is necessary for getting the children to the

wedding on time, such cooperation is not always to be expected, because it is not always given. However, thoughtful planning can prevent snags in wedding plans. For example, making sure that their children have the proper clothing to wear at their weddings can prevent remarrying parents from becoming outraged when their former spouses send the children to them with only worn-out sneakers and torn jeans.

Sometimes remarrying parents invite their children to "stand up" for them as part of their marriage celebration. Even if children are happy about a parent's remarriage, they are still likely to feel conflicted about becoming members of the wedding party. These children may be worrying about what their outside parent would think or feel about their being anything more than just witnesses to their parent's remarriage.

Children are likely to experience great difficulty in figuring out what to do about participating in a parent's remarriage ceremony. This ceremony is not a reenactment of their parents' original marriage; quite the contrary. One parent's marriage to another person simply confirms what children already know in their hearts—that their parents are not going to get back together again.

Expect Children to Have Mixed Reactions to a Parent's Remarriage

When children know that all of the important adults in their lives are amenable to whatever decisions they make regarding their remarrying parent's wedding, children are free to exercise their own judgment. However, when there is major disagreement between children's parents, with one parent strongly objecting to the children witnessing the ceremony while the other strongly encourages them to attend, children are put in a double bind. No matter what they decide, they will be hurting someone—most often themselves.

When children decide not to attend their parent's wedding, their decisions must be respected. Children's decisions may not be based solely on what one or the other of their parents wishes. They themselves may feel poorly equipped to handle the strain of watching one parent marrying somebody other than their other parent.

No matter what their ages, children can be expected to have

mixed reactions to a parent's remarriage. At the very time remarrying parents are experiencing their greatest happiness, their children may be reexperiencing loss. No one can really predict how the children will react to the remarriage itself. While these children are witnessing the beginning of one kind of life, they are experiencing the end of another. Therefore, they may appear happy or sad, animated or mournful, etc., and no one may be able to tell for sure what these reactions mean. At best, this is a difficult time for children.

> Alan's mom was working two jobs to support herself and two children. When his dad insisted that his children attend his wedding, he bought Alan and his sister very expensive new clothes to wear to the ceremony. Alan knew that his mom had not bought herself any new clothes since she and his dad were divorced several years earlier. Alan also knew that his mom was very sad about his dad's remarriage; she had even cried as she sent the children off with their dad that weekend. Both children wished they could stay home with their mom to keep her from feeling so lonely.

Allow Children to Be in Touch with Their Feelings

Parents and their new spouses have to be prepared for the children to exhibit a variety of moods. How a child experiences a parent's remarriage is strictly personal and unique to that child. The couple must understand that children cannot help feeling the way they feel; no one can. As long as the children do not act out their feelings through inappropriate behavior, parents should not push them to "be happy."

Children Need to Feel Valued Enough to Be Informed of an Impending Remarriage

When parents are realistic about what they can expect from their children, they free themselves to enjoy their own participation in the wedding celebration. It is likely to be a long time before the children will be able to share with their parents how they experienced the wedding. Most children would probably agree, however, that it is better to have their parents ask them to attend their weddings than to experience the alternative—exclusion!

Provide Support for the Children

Couples are likely to be very busy with dozens of last-minute details on the actual day of their weddings. Therefore, it is very important for them to provide support for all the children attending the ceremony. Remarrying parents need to make sure that friends or relatives are available as supports for the children—to introduce them to people, to keep them informed of what is going on, and to let them know what is expected of them. These adults will also need to keep track of the children. If the couple plans to take a honeymoon, arrangements have to be made to have the children taken home after the party is over. The couple can expect to have their minds on their wedding; making sure the children's needs are attended to in advance will free them to do so.

Have Contingency Plans in Place

It is during the actual ceremony that careful prearrangements can deter catastrophe. Ceremonies can be ruined and parents left brokenhearted by a child's last-minute refusal to participate in the ceremony as planned. Parents who allow their children's participation to be optional avoid this pitfall.

> Gina attended her father's remarriage with a great many reservations. Her dad was marrying a woman with whom he had been having an affair while still married to her mom. Gina's mother reached her by phone before the wedding ceremony began. She reminded her daughter of the part her dad's new bride played in destroying their original family. When Gina's mom insisted that she come home immediately, Gina complied. Her sudden departure left everyone in the wedding party stunned.

Build in Flexibility

Last-minute worries, fears and doubts, or private grief can paralyze a child—even at the point he or she is walking down an aisle or standing alongside a parent. Building in flexibility by giving a child options prevents unanticipated disappointment for the adults. It also alleviates a child's guilt over disappointing a parent. Whatever the reason a child balks or becomes immobilized, contingency plans must be in place to cover a distressed child's reaction.

Make Family Wedding Pictures Optional

Alternative planning must also apply to family pictures on the wedding day. Any photographs taken at this ceremony will reflect a new family constellation. A parent's remarriage expands a child's family network. Children can gain a whole new array of marriage-related kin as a result of this wedding. The marriage vows change not only the parent's status, but the status of the children as well. The children may not be prepared to acknowledge these changes. They may refuse to be in the pictures. They may need more time to absorb the fact that these "strangers" are now "family." This is the time children most need the adults' compassion and understanding.

> Ann was a widow for several years before she decided to marry Greg. Her daughters, ages 15 and 17, objected vociferously to the union. They liked Greg, but they felt their mom should wait until they were out of the house to remarry. They did not want to have to share their house with Greg's two sons. After much deliberation, Ann and Greg decided to go ahead with their wedding plans, but they left the children's attendance optional. The newlyweds informed a group later that both girls not only came to the ceremony, but they also joined in the new family photographs as well.

Children may not be able to put their feelings into words. They might find it difficult, or even impossible, to tell the remarrying parent that they do not feel the same way toward this celebration as the parent and the parent's new mate do. Even if the children wish the parent great happiness and hope they themselves will benefit from the parent's remarriage, the children are bound to feel the loss of their original family.

Children Will Appreciate Parents' Respecting Their Feelings

Most children have fantasies about what their parents' marriage was like. This ceremony is not a celebration of that union.

This wedding signals the end to fantasies that their parents will reunite. How can children tell their remarrying parent that they are mourning the loss of their original family? The children may not even be aware of what is troubling them; they may just be too emotionally overwhelmed to participate. Ultimately those children who choose not to attend the ceremony or participate in the wedding may regret their decisions. They will, however, always appreciate the fact that their participation was not forced and their feelings were respected.

What children seem to be least able to accept is not being informed of their parent's remarriage until after it has taken place. Parents may feel they have valid reasons for such decisions, such as not wanting the former spouse to learn of the event or fearing the children's reactions. Whatever rationale a parent has for making such a choice, it is a poor decision. Children who learn of a parent's remarriage after the fact are dismayed. Subsequently, many of them have trouble living in the newly formed household. Making the children part of the new family unit from the start can facilitate combined family development.

> Kelly remembers her dad's introducing her and her brothers and sister to their "new mother." It was the first time she ever laid eyes on the woman. Kelly never felt a part of the household her father and stepmother established together. She felt her father never really considered his children's feelings. As far as Kelly was concerned, the woman her father married came from nowhere. How could the family they formed work out? As the years passed, Kelly never stopped resenting her father's utter disregard for her feelings.

Whatever remarriage plans the adults make, it is the wedding ceremony itself that changes the couple's relationship to one another, and it changes the status of the children, the family, and the extended family as well. Paying careful attention to feelings, as well as details, can lead a couple to derive all the joy they expect from their wedding celebration. The ceremony clearly marks the beginning of a new life together for all concerned.

At the joining of this couple, a new family is formed. Because this family can contain blood-related, legally related, and marriage-related individuals, it is called a combined family. The combined family comes into existence because the two adults love one another and want to live together in a committed relationship. It is that love and that commitment that results in the blending of more than two people's lives. What happens subsequently, when the combined family comes together, is the subject of the next chapter.

Helpful Points to Remember

1. Ceremonies mark the importance of an event.
2. Children need to feel valued enough by their parents to be informed of an impending remarriage.
3. When children are expected to attend wedding celebrations, former spouses often exhibit unpredictable behavior. Make contingency plans.
4. Expect children to have mixed feelings about their attendance at or participation in the wedding ceremony.
5. Allow children the freedom to be in touch with their emotions—as long as their behavior remains appropriate to the occasion.
6. The children will appreciate your respecting their feelings.
7. The children are bound to feel the loss of their original family. Do not expect the children to be "happy for you."
8. Provide support for the children during the wedding. You will be busy.
9. When children are participating in the wedding, have contingency plans in place—in case the children develop "cold feet."
10. Build in flexibility by giving children options.
11. Make family wedding pictures optional. The children are not used to thinking of this grouping of people as their family.
12. Wedding ceremonies not only change the couple's relationship to one another, they change the status of the children, the family, and the extended family as well.

SEVEN

Homecoming

I remember the first time our separate
families got together, right after our parents'
remarriage. All the children were so gloomy,
you would have thought we had just come
from a funeral instead of a wedding.

"YOU CAN'T GO HOME AGAIN"

When he penned this sage advice, Thomas Wolfe[1] was not talking about combined family living, but he could have been. At no time do his words ring truer than when used to describe the tumultuous beginning of combined family life, when nobody, not even the couple who heads the household, enjoys a steadfast sense of comfort and security.

If, as the saying goes, "home is where the heart is," then it is important to know where the hearts and minds of individual family members are in this first stage of combined family development. What are these individuals thinking, and how do they feel? While newlyweds may be thinking that their home is with one another, children may perceive home as a memory of days gone by, when they lived with their original parents in intact families. Haunted by mixed emotions and conflicting expectations, some children long for what might have been, while others await with trepidation that which lies ahead of them. No one escapes: Every single member of the combined family household can at some point expect to face times when she or he wonders, What have I gotten myself into?

Home Sweet _____

Marriage vows affect not only the lives of two adults who commit themselves to each other, but also the lives of any and all children who become members of their combined family. As the couple's wedding day begins, members of the remarrying parent's family know their places in their one-parent family, but they may have no idea where they are going to fit into the family that is about to be formed. The couple too know their places, as they prepare to exchange vows that will unite them "from this day forward." Nonetheless, although all may leave for the ceremony knowing where they belong, none are likely to return that way.

Every person "going home" to a combined family is entering uncharted territory. The adults' union brings forth a brand new family; most who enter it do so without any clear idea of exactly what changes have taken place in their lives. Old family roles either no longer apply or have undergone some kind of vague, ambiguous change. None can say for sure what their new roles are, or will be. Previously single parents take on new roles as remarried parents, while their new spouses become stepparents and, in the process, remarried parents' children become stepchildren. Upon becoming a member of a combined family, every single person takes on least one new role. This sudden role ambiguity can be distressing for all concerned.

Coming home to a combined family household involves all new family members in a massive restructuring of their lives. Although the remarried parent's children and new spouse are usually strangers to one another, these individuals are immediately thrown into an intimate living situation. Is it any wonder then that an eerie sense of unconnectedness prevails as combined family members search for ways to integrate themselves into something resembling a family, in a living situation that in no way resembles home? That which was home before is gone, and that which is to be home remains in the future. To members of a newly created combined family, "homecoming" may not feel like "coming home" at all. In fact, the experience may leave some, if not all, combined family members feeling like displaced persons.

Even a parent and a child who have lived together for years, in the same familiar home, are likely to react differently to each other now that the parent has taken a new spouse. Likewise, the couple's relationship will undoubtedly undergo change in response to the presence of the remarried parent's children. All combined family members will eventually find themselves challenged by what can only be considered a major task: They must construct their new family on a preexisting parent–child base.

Spurred by their mutual love, the couple may be anxious to get on with the business of becoming a family; however, these adults must proceed cautiously in the long and often painful process of integrating their separate families. Not only will old allegiances interfere in this process, but new alliances will take time to build. In the beginning, the couple's union is likely to be the only force holding family members together.

Where Is "Home" for the Holidays?

Children who become part of a combined family need time to mourn the losses they have suffered in making the move from at least one—and oftentimes more than one—previous family. For most parents, even the suggestion that their children are in mourning is beyond belief. These adults may have worked long and hard to find new marriage partners so they could recreate their children's families, and their children now act as if they are being offered as human sacrifices to their parents' whims. Not only is this conflict between their own and their children's attitudes difficult for parents to accept, most do not get the point, which is that what remarried parents consider a significant gain may only translate into one more loss, in a series of losses, to their children.

Parents cannot expect their children to be grateful for becoming members of a household headed by two adults, unless both of those adults are the children's original parents. Children who have experienced the end of one family are often reluctant to settle into a new family living situation. If children have experienced the death of a parent, they know that nothing lasts forever, and if they have lived through a divorce, they know that if one marriage can end, so can another. And, if they trust, and are disappointed again, could they bear the pain?

WHEN WORLDS COLLIDE

Imagine what would happen if Earth and Mars, by forces natural or supernatural, joined orbits and subsequently collided like a couple of mudballs. There would be total devastation, havoc, and upheaval; nothing would ever be the same again. Yet, after the dust cleared, the merger of the two planets could create a new world whose sum might be greater than its parts.

Those who undertake the challenge of joining their separate families into one combined family are, in effect, attempting to merge two entirely different worlds into one. The reverberations caused by their actions are likely to create some unsettling and perhaps "earth-shattering" changes.

Combined family members have traded, or been forced to trade, all that is familiar and comfortable to them for the uncertainties of combined family life. As individuals, combined family members do not know how their lives will change, or what new customs and traditions they will be expected to adopt. Strangers who happen to be living in the same household cannot know what (if anything) they will come to mean to one another. That is the future; coming home to a house full of strangers is "now."

Establishing a New World Order

In the beginning, combined families do not look or feel like "real" families, and why should they? Family members do not share a common history or a mutually agreed-upon definition of family. Usually, there is not even enough of a sense of "we" among family members for any of them to be able to ask—or answer—this one simple question: Who are "we" to "us"?

Becoming a member of a combined family can be profoundly disorienting. By the end of the first day, family members' common past has begun.[2] It is only in the act of sorting through old memories,[3] however, that combined family members can develop their own authentic family identity.[4] Figuring out the little things about one another is likely to prove a crucial first step in transforming a collection of strangers into a functional family unit. Establishing physical boundaries in the present will help in establishing more complex psychological boundaries later on:

> Bathroom habits, food preferences, sleep rituals—the most private, primitive aspects of being human provide material for the interpersonal encounters out of which individual identity and family structure develop. To borrow a concept from anthropology, families transform physical facts (like walking, eating and elimination), into social and psychological realities. They transform nature into culture.[5]

Essentially strangers to one another, stepparents and stepchildren suddenly become privy to intimate details of one another's lives; however, there is no context in which to place this information. There are no rules or guidelines to help them organize their "intimate family system," and it takes time to transform "nature into culture."[6] However, a well thought out plan of action, set up in advance and implemented from the time the combined family is assembled, may help jump-start the process of establishing a family identity.

The New Family Pattern

While everyone wants to know what to expect from the new combined family pattern, few have a reasonable idea of what its design will be, and fewer still have done much thinking about how and where new family members will fit into the scheme of things. This is why the adults have to do a great deal of advance thinking and planning before assembling everyone under a single roof. To the greatest extent possible, the children need to be involved in this sorting-out process:

> Bev and Del thought they had all of their housing arrangements settled until they were about to move into a new house together and Del informed Bev that his daughters, who were to live with them two days a week, were to have the larger of the

two extra bedrooms. Del felt Bev's two boys would do just fine sharing the smaller, less desirable, but adequately sized bedroom.

Even though Bev did not understand Del's decision, she felt she did not have the right to protest it because Del was contributing a larger amount of money to the purchase of the house than she was. Thus, when the couple were married and the children were shown their rooms, Bev's sons complained bitterly to their mother over what they believed was a totally unfair allotment of space.

Bev's sons could not see why Del's daughters should have the larger bedroom when the girls lived with their mother five days a week, while they, who were to live in the household all of the time, had to squeeze their possessions into a much smaller space.

Although Bev did speak with him, Del remained adamant about his daughters' having the bigger bedroom. The beginning of this combined family's ultimate failure was eventually traced back to the precise moment when Del revealed his total unwillingness to give "anything" to Bev's children.

While adults and children alike may understand that there will be changes in their lives as a result of merging families, few can answer questions like: Who determines the new family pattern? Who has a say in changing it? What happens when the pattern no longer fits the family's needs? If the design that is ultimately chosen requires children to share space, who determines who sleeps with whom, shares what bathroom, gets which dresser, what shelf, which side of the closet? Who says which child must give up what in order to live with whom, and under what circumstances?

Who settles boundary disputes when there are strangers in the house? Territorial boundaries may eventually get worked out between the children who live in the household all of the time, but what happens when nonresidential children come to spend a few days? Do they get any space of their own, or are they expected to take over someone else's territory when they arrive?

Perhaps some permanent household residents will think it unnecessary or even unfair for occasional residents to have any space of their own. Are these nonresidential children to be treated as guests, or are they to have space—a closet, a drawer, a shelf— that is theirs and theirs alone year-round? While it is hard for parents and their children to keep up their relationships when the children live in the combined family household intermittently and for brief periods of time, it is almost impossible for children to think their parents really care about their well-being when they are required to sleep in some makeshift accommodation, with nary a corner to call their own. Who decides what provisions will be made for these children? Whose rules apply? Who makes the choice? What is fair between siblings, stepsiblings, and half siblings, and who determines this?

The adults need to answer these questions before they move on to tougher ones. As important as it is for couples to legislate and enforce household rules and regulations, there is also a pressing need for them to establish guidelines for common courtesy, so their families do not self-destruct in debates over who gets to use the bathroom first, etc. Couples need to remember that just as civilizations only prosper in times of peace so too do combined families.

It is only by setting limits—i.e., establishing rules and enforcing the consequences for any infractions of those rules—that the adults heading combined families can hope to bring order out of chaos.

Family Conferences

As couples prepare and plan for their marriages and the combined families their unions will form, remarrying parents must make certain that their children are an intrinsic part of their plans. Children need to be as well prepared as the adults themselves for the changes that are about to take place in their lives.

To gain a solid sense of where children stand on family issues, it is imperative that couples host family conferences early on—prior to their unions, if possible. Since adults heading combined families will need to make decisions about a wide variety of issues, understanding other family members' thoughts and feelings can be of great benefit in helping them to find reasonable solutions to complex combined family problems.

Family conferences have a way of "leveling the playing field" between adults and children in combined families. For example: While adults have the ability to make rules and establish consequences for any infringements upon those rules, children have a right to object to those rules and consequences they think unreasonable. An appeals process can be incorporated into the structure of a family conference.

Children need to know how to take exception to decisions that are not to their liking—and under what circumstances appeals can be made. Family members need to agree on how changes in rules are to be made and implemented even if, in the end, the adults reserve the right to have the final say on a particular issue. Whatever that final say happens to be, it is best arrived at in the privacy of the couple's bedroom or at a local coffee shop after the children have gone to bed. Major policy decisions are best rendered without undue influence from "lobbyists."

Begin at the Beginning

Because there are so many unknown factors built into the combined family equation, it only makes sense that soon-to-be-wed couples seriously consider and plan for that which *is* known about coming home to a combined family household. For example: There is no such thing as a combined family pattern. Through family members' interactions, each combined family weaves its own design.

The more that adults are prepared for the little things that are known about establishing a combined family, the less likely they are to be thrown by the bigger questions such as, "How on earth can we get this collection of strangers to the point where they 'feel like family' to one another?" That is not a question for a chapter on homecoming; rather, it is the subject of this entire book.

EIGHT

Insiders and Outsiders

Bobbie's mother married Dorie's father when both Bobbie and Dorie were adults. Since Bobbie never had siblings, she alternately referred to Dorie as her "sister," her "stepsister," or her "mother's stepdaughter," depending on how she was feeling about Dorie, or Dorie's father, at the time.

As the nuclear family dissolves, it leaves in its wake family structures that have multiplied through dividing, while contracting because one parent is missing from each new family equation. The one-parent families that remain must struggle to cope with resulting loss and change. Strangely enough, combined families also experience loss and change, but for opposite reasons. Although combined families expand by adding adults to preexisting one-parent families, fluctuations in family structure are bound to produce feelings of disorientation and discomfort in all who experience them.

As family members struggle to find their balance in families that are either contracting or expanding, feelings of loss and change are an inevitable part of the process. In a 1984 article, social scientists Pauline Boss and Jan Greenberg mention the concept of *boundary ambiguity* as a term useful in describing and predicting "the effects of family membership loss and change over time."[1]

Boundary ambiguity is the perfect term to describe one of the most perplexing problems in combined families: membership. The answer to what appears to be a relatively simple question—i.e.,

Who is, and who is not a member of the family?—seems to depend on who you ask, and at what point in the family's history you ask it. One combined family member may "perceive a physically absent member as psychologically present" while another combined family member may regard a "physically present member as psychologically absent. In either case, the family boundary is ambiguous."[2]

The children who become part of a combined family may stubbornly attempt to keep the boundary around their old one-parent family intact, while the remarried parent's new spouse may be struggling to maintain the cozy intimacy that was the hallmark of the couple's courtship period. Meanwhile, the remarried parent may be wondering when everyone is going to "shape up" and start acting like a "regular family."

Essentially, the problem with combined family living lies in each individual's perception of who is "in" and who is "out" of the family. In their commentary on this problem, Boss and Greenberg state: "If a family cannot clarify who is in and who is out of the family system . . . it cannot reorganize."[3]

A parent's remarriage reshuffles the deck. No one—not even the remarried parent—can say for sure who is inside and who is outside the family's boundaries. The formation of the combined family blurs that once clear vision of who "belongs" inside the family circle. Opinions as to whether someone *is* or *is not* a member of the combined family household are likely to vary from person to person and subject to subject. Take, for example, the situation in which some of the remarried parent's children never live inside the combined family household at all. It is likely that both the remarried parent and full siblings of these nonresidential children still consider them to be family members; however, it is just as likely that the stepparent and stepsiblings of these same children do not consider them, in any way, as part of *their* family.

This relationship gap can work both ways, however. Children often consider their outside parent as part of their family, while refusing to recognize the stepparent with whom they live as being in any way connected to them.

As we look at the vastly expanded dimensions of the combined family, we can see that who is included in it is as important as who is excluded from it.

Ginny and Craig used to argue a great deal about who was and was not a member of their family. They had been stepsiblings for seven years, but their prior family histories were markedly different: Ginny's father had been killed in a motorcycle accident three months before she was born, whereas Craig's mother and sisters were alive and well. In fact, Craig spent every summer with them.

Ginny insisted that their family consisted of only those who lived in their combined family household (i.e., Ginny and her mother, and Craig and his father) while Craig refuted her statements by saying that the only members of his family were those who were biologically related to him (i.e., his mother, father, and sisters).

Jockeying for inside positions while the combined family is in flux, insiders and outsiders begin their race as the wedding ceremony ends. While the children and the soon-to-be spouse have gone to the ceremony as insiders, none but the remarried parent returns from the nuptials in the same condition. The stepparent, stepchildren, and stepsiblings, if there are any, leave the wedding celebration as outsiders—each struggling against the newly established family order that has made step-relatives of them all.

The stepparent is an outsider to his or her stepchildren, every bit as much as these stepchildren are outsiders to their new stepparent. Stepsiblings are likely to consider one another outsiders from the outset. Each of these outsiders can be expected to vie for status and power within the framework of his or her newly expanded family network. Each new family member is likely to be very protective of his or her sphere of influence with the one person who, initially, is the only insider to them all—the remarried parent.

To understand the nature of combined family development, it is important to first gain an understanding of how at least three distinct groups of insider–outsider relationships work.

Insiders: Remarried Parents and Their Children

The base upon which any combined family is founded is the preexisting relationship between at least one parent and one child. From the beginning, parents and children are insiders to one another, not necessarily because they share the same gene pool, but because they share the same family history.

Within their original families, parents and children develop complex patterns of thinking, feeling, and behaving. As complex as parent–child interactions can be within the confines of the nuclear family, the parent–child bond can become even more intense inside the one-parent family—especially when the outside parent ceases to be part of the family picture.

When the parent heading a one-parent family decides to remarry, her or his children may make every conceivable effort to monopolize their parent in an attempt to guard against the intrusion of the outsider who is threatening to become their stepparent. Even as the combined family is formed, these children can be expected to work to consolidate their old parent–child code of communication and conduct. In their book *Second Chances*, Judith Wallerstein and Sandra Blakeslee write, "Children are the self-appointed guardians of family history. They do not want to forget act one of the play, and they are suspicious of the new character in act two."[4]

Given children's preexisting relationships with their parents, even if the remarried parent's children spend little or no time in the combined family household, they still remain insiders to their remarried parents. "Old" children can pose a real threat to a "new" spouse who expects to have no dealings with these children.

> When Louise was 24, she married Art, a man nearly twice her age with two college-aged children who made their home base with their mother some two thousand miles away. Art rarely saw his children, and when he did he visited them at college or at his former wife's home.
>
> Louise and Art had been married eight years when Art's older son called, wanting to know if he could stay at his father's house for about a week so he could attend his high school reunion and visit some old friends. The prospect terrified Louise to the point that she sought professional counseling.
>
> In her opening comments to the therapist, Louise said she felt happy and secure in her marriage and she was certain Art felt the same way. Louise even admitted that she did not feel Art's son's presence would pose any kind of threat to her marriage.

When the therapist then asked, "So, what brings you here to-day?" Louise responded haltingly: "My husband and I have always been very close. Until his son called and wanted to stay with us, I never came to grips with the fact that my husband really did have another life, prior to our marriage. I am finding it very hard to have 'a child' of that former union come to stay in the 'love nest' my husband and I built for two."

Insiders: The Remarried Parent and the New Spouse

Act Two: Enter the stepparent. Much to the distress of some children, when their parent remarries, it may suddenly become very clear to them that their parent and his or her new spouse are insiders to each other. The children may feel like bystanders as they watch their parent and stepparent work to expand the context of their own interpersonal relationship. Thus, in the opening scene of Act Two, the children are placed in the position of being witnesses not only to their remarried parent's bonding with a stranger but also to the new couple taking a honeymoon in their midst.

As they witness the couple's partnership blossoming before their eyes, the remarried parent's children can become all too aware of their uncomfortable new status as outsiders in the couple's deepening relationship. Seeing their parent in this new light can be extremely distressing to children of all ages. They can easily interpret their parent's new need for privacy as a loss of their parent's love. Children can also experience the inclusion of a new spouse in their parent's life as a direct threat to that portion of their parent's heart that, until now, they had believed to be exclusively theirs.

Insiders: Remarried Parents

Remarried parents belong in a group by themselves. In the complex equation known as the combined family, remarried parents are the common denominator. They are insiders with their children and insiders with their new spouses. Only remarried parents can traverse the distance between stepparents and step-children; only they start out in comfortable positions with both groups in their new families. Unfortunately, these adults are often unaware that their old children and new spouses do not hold similarly privileged positions in relation to one another.

> From the moment he first heard of her existence, Cary absolutely hated his father's future wife, Ruth. Cary felt Ruth was in the way of his original parents' ever getting back together. Once the couple was married, Cary repeatedly begged his father, Hal, to divorce Ruth.
>
> Hal's response to Cary's protests was firm but loving. Hal loved Cary, but he also loved his wife. Hal assured his son that things were not going to change, so Cary had just better get used to the idea of having a stepmother.
>
> While Ruth's presence in his life always irritated Cary, he was livid when he found out that Ruth was pregnant. When his stepmother gave birth to a daughter who looked exactly like Cary, there was no longer a way Cary could deny his connection to his father's wife. Cary's half sister's birth linked him to his stepmother, forever.

Complex Combined Families

When both adults have children present in their lives prior to their remarriage, the structure of the combined family becomes infinitely more complex. While children may have lived in two households ever since their parents' marriage ended, stepsiblings may find themselves rotating in and out of the combined family household they share—to go to live with those outside parents they do not share.

As if it were not confusing enough for unrelated children to share a common residence, these children may enter and leave their combined family household on varying schedules. And, to complicate matters further, when either or both remarried parents bring children from more than one union along with them into their new family unit, combined family logistics can become a center for mass confusion—or mass transit.

When adults, with children from more than one previous union, decide to add a mutual child to their combined family, everybody becomes connected; however, it may take some family members years to comprehend the full scope of these interconnections:

Listening to a 6-year-old give her family history can be a poignant experience, especially when the child tells you that she is from Mommy's first marriage, and that her infant half sister is from her mommy's marriage to Ken, and that Ken's children live in their new house with them certain days each week; and you know that as soon as she draws her next breath, she will have to tell you about her biological father who has children from several marriages—all of whom are her half siblings, some of whom she has never met.

The Status of the Outside Parent

The question of whether an outside parent is an insider or an outsider in the combined family has any number of answers. The short answer is no if you ask one of the adults, and most likely yes if that outside parent happens to be the parent of the child you are asking. As any family member is likely to attest, the lines of differentiation become dangerously thin when it comes to assessing the status of the outside parent/former spouse from within the combined family household.

The children may regard their outside parent as a permanent insider, regardless of whether that parent is living or dead. It is through their children that outside parents so often seem to penetrate to the core of combined families. Although many means are at their disposal, perhaps the easiest way for outside parents to permeate combined family boundaries is for them to pump their children for any and all information regarding the inner workings of the combined families in which their children live.

With outsiders being able to gain access to a great deal of information about their children's lives as well as access to the children themselves, what goes on inside combined family households is not necessarily private. Through the travels of the children into and out of combined family households, outside parents may become privy to information that might otherwise never have come to light had children's original families remained intact.

Combined family members may become irate upon discovering that outsiders have direct knowledge about strictly personal matters, such as the idiosyncratic behavior of individual combined family members or the interpersonal tensions and squabbles that might crop up now and then between various individuals within their households. Combined family members are not likely to be prepared for the shifts away from the *int*imacies of the nuclear family to the "*out*imacies" of combined family life. Individual adjustments to this lack of privacy are not only hard to make, but family members can find them very "hard to take."

Tensions between Insiders and Outsiders

If the combined family were a static, never-changing system, it would be easy for members to determine their family's parameters. Everyone would have a place, and individual family members could gradually adjust to their family positions. Outsiders such as outside parents would definitely remain outside the combined family's boundaries. However, combined families are progressive and constantly evolving systems. Try as they may, family members may find that they are not able to influence the system under which they now live nearly as much as the system is able to influence them. That is why there is often so much squabbling about who is inside, or outside, the combined family. No one likes to feel out of control, and a lack of agreement between family members about who is in the family definitely contributes to general feelings of frustration and powerlessness.

As combined families struggle to draw clear lines between insiders and outsiders, there are likely to be many occasions when family members feel like shouting, both at each other and to the world: "We have seen the enemy, and it is us!" However, such intense frustrations must be handled in order for members of a newly formed combined family to reach the point where they feel like family to one another.

For everyone to gain a sense of family, the needs and expectations of all combined family members have to be carefully balanced so that, over time, the notion of insiders and outsiders will be replaced by a genuine sense that everyone in the family belongs there. However, this cannot be expected to happen the instant the combined family is formed. Indeed, it cannot necessarily be expected to happen at all.

NINE

The Remarried Parent

Cara worried about her father's love for his new wife and her children. She felt his loving them was taking love away from her. When she finally discussed her feelings with her father, Cara's dad took her on his lap and gently whispered, "Don't you know that love doesn't know how to divide? Love only multiplies!"[1] Cara felt much better when her dad assured her that he could never run out of his love for her, no matter how many people he added to his life.

Headlining most discussions on combined families are the fragile and often problematic relationships that develop between stepparents and stepchildren. Many experts have written and talked about the subject of remarriage and stepparenting; however, most have failed to identify the most powerful person in the combined family: the remarried parent!

From the earliest stages of combined family development, the remarried parent is the bridge between his or her children and new spouse. Mutual love for the remarried parent gives both the new spouse and old children a reason to endure all the upheaval and uncertainty connected with forming a combined family. Skillful remarried parents use this mutual love as balm for the many bumps and bruises family members are likely to suffer along the way, especially during the early stages of combined family development. During these stages, the functions the remarried parent is called upon to perform are essential to the combined family's survival—and success.

THE CENTRAL NATURE OF THE REMARRIED
PARENT'S ROLE

Combined families result from the joining of groups: remarried parents and their children and remarried parents and their new spouses. As the common denominator, remarried parents are insiders in both groups. The central positioning of remarried parents between both these groups affords them the power to establish connections between their new spouses and old children. With proper handling of the remarried parent's role, each new combined family becomes greater than the sum of its parts.

Cohesive, well-integrated combined families result from the efforts of remarried parents. Remarried parents' positions remain central until the functions they perform evolve into a network of interrelationships that connect all family members to one another. The establishment of these interrelationships is by no means a foregone conclusion, however. If these connections are made, they take place in a seemingly endless series of transactions—over a period of years.

When Scott married Adele, he never saw himself having to have much to do with her teen-aged children. However, Adele purposely selected Scott from among her various suitors because she thought he would be the perfect man to help her through what she had correctly assumed would be difficult years with her teen-agers.

When Scott and Adele returned from their honeymoon, a hurricane was brewing in their combined family household. Adele went to Scott for his advice and help in any situation that she felt was beyond her control. Although willing to support his wife, Scott told Adele he had no idea what to do with her children. When Scott did try to intervene on his wife's behalf, the children's misbehavior would escalate to the point where the couple feared the whole house would come crashing down.

After two months, Scott and Adele sought professional counseling for the problems they were having in their new family.

Adele learned that she would have to take responsibility for putting an end to her children's disruptive behavior. Scott had no personal authority with her children, and putting him in the role of a disciplinarian had only made Scott the "heavy."

As the children's mother, Adele already possessed all the authority she needed to set limits on her children's behavior. Her parental authority confirmed, Adele sat down with Scott to formulate four to six household rules to regulate her children's behavior. For example, one rule read: "There is to be no use of tobacco or alcohol in this household." The consequence for breaking this rule was listed right beside it: "No friends allowed over to the house for a week."

After everyone had discussed and agreed upon a list of rules and resulting consequences, the list was posted on the refrigerator. Adele's children were now sure that their mother was in charge. However, they also understood that their stepfather could enforce the consequences for any infractions of the limits that had been set for them.

Remarried parents and their new spouses must respond to many situations for which they may be unprepared; however, they are not without resources. Remarried parents hold great power in combined families; unfortunately, most do not understand the nature or source of their power. That is why the remarried parent's expanded role in a combined family must be defined. Remarried parents need to know in advance what tools they will have available to them to deal with those problems only they can control.

THE EXPANDED ROLE OF THE REMARRIED PARENT

The Changing Roles of Parents

As parents change their marital roles, their parenting roles change as well. Parents remain responsible for their children's health and safety, but the manner in which they fulfill their responsibilities differs dramatically, depending on where individual parents are in their own life cycles.[2] A nuclear family has two biological parents who provide for their children's needs. Single parents do not have the luxury of two adults in the household, so they alone care for their children. In both cases, parenting is done by adults who are legally or blood-related to the children. This is not the case in a combined family. The marriage tie between the two adults heading the combined family household is the only link between at least one child and one adult.

> When Marla and Mitch married, Marla envisioned becoming another mother to Mitch's delightful 4-year-old daughter, Alicia. She was eager to share a happy and loving relationship with Mitch and Alicia.
>
> Mitch saw no real reason for Marla to get involved in Alica's upbringing since he and his former spouse had an excellent co-parenting relationship. All Mitch expected was that Marla be kind to his daughter.
>
> It did not take long before Marla became angry about being closed out of any kind of real relationship with Mitch's daughter. Marla felt insecure and "second-class" in her relationship with both Mitch's daughter and his former spouse. Eventually, Marla started taking out her frustration on Alicia.
>
> Alicia started complaining to her father about Marla's treatment of her, and at that point Marla finally vocalized how she felt. Marla told Mitch that being left out of his relationship with his daughter caused her great pain. Mitch gradually became aware that shielding Alicia from Marla had prevented his daughter and his new wife from working out a relationship of their own.

Shifts take place in biological parents' roles as they move from nuclear to one-parent to combined families. Unfortunately, these shifts and the many other changes that are altering the shape and structure of today's families seem to be taking place in a vacuum; they often go unnoticed.

Falling in a Vacuum

In a thought-provoking article written in 1978, sociologist Andrew Cherlin depicts "Remarriage as an Incomplete Institution."[3] He writes: "The institution of the family provides social control of reproduction and child rearing. It also provides family members with guidelines for proper behavior in everyday family life, and, presumably, these guidelines contribute to the unity and stability of families."[4] Cherlin concludes that "the difficulties of couples in remarriages after divorce stem from a lack of institutionalized guidelines for solving many common problems of their remarried life."[5]

An interpretation connecting clinical findings with theoretical studies might conclude that because combined family members do not have definite roles to perform, they operate in a vacuum. Thus it would seem only natural for remarried parents to be confused about their roles in combined families—their roles have yet to be defined! Society prescribes parental roles; however, society does not seem to have a prescription for the role of a remarried parent in a combined family. This leaves remarried parents at a loss to know how to act once their combined families form.

Lacking prescribed roles of their own, remarried parents all too often fall back on the well-defined rules regulating the behavior of parents in nuclear families. However, these roles are not suitable for the two adults heading a combined family—the remarried parent and her or his new spouse. In a combined family, the role of the remarried parent is expanded far beyond that of either parent in a nuclear family in three important ways.

Remarried parents must:

1. Make sure that their new spouses become members of their preexisting one-parent families by becoming "gate-keepers"[6];
2. "Mediate" conflict between stepparents and stepchildren without getting caught up or caught in the middle of it; and
3. Know how to prevent, or break up, the "triangles" that so often trap them, and others, in three-way conflict.

Combined families need these functions performed, and remarried parents are the only ones who can perform them.

THE REMARRIED PARENT AS GATEKEEPER

The Function of the Gatekeeper

A gate, built to control the passage of people from one side of a barrier to the other, necessitates the appointment of someone to regulate who gets through and who does not. The gatekeeper is the person who is charged with regulating such movements, allowing either outsiders in, or insiders out.

As the combined family forms, there is a natural barrier between the remarried parent's new spouse and old children that only the remarried parent can cross. This right of passage is granted to the remarried parent by the new spouse and the old children, but these individuals do not grant similar rights to each other. Because of their mutual mistrust, both sides can be expected to look around for someone to safeguard the barrier between them. The remarried parent is the only person everyone trusts; therefore, the function of the gatekeeper automatically falls to the remarried parent.

In an enlightening discussion,[7] Elizabeth Carter described several areas in which it is crucial for remarried parents to function as gatekeepers:

1. New spouses should not be left to fight their way into preexisting one-parent families.
2. It is the responsibility of remarried parents to make a place at their side for their new spouses.
3. Remarried parents can introduce their new spouses by delivering a message to their children that reads something like: "This is my new spouse; therefore, you (the children) must be respectful." Its meaning: "Treat my spouse well, or answer to me."
4. Remarried parents have to hold their children accountable for children's behavior toward their new spouses. If remarried parents do not, their children may well escalate their role in combined family conflict.

Carter recommends that new spouses should not be made to fight their way into preexisting one-parent families. She feels it is up to remarried parents to ease the entrance of new stepparents into their old one-parent families.[8]

In practice, preexisting one-parent families act much like guarded palaces: sanctuaries fortified against invasion by high walls, sturdy gates, and retractable drawbridges spanning their moats.

Who Goes There?

Most children do not want any strangers intruding on their lives. Imagine then the surprise of children in one-parent families when their parents find "special someones" they want to add to their lives—permanently! When faced with such an unwelcome development, it is not uncommon for children to attempt to erect barriers that effectively bar the entrance of their parents' new spouses into their old one-parent families.

When children barricade themselves against the entry of new spouses, their parents must respond appropriately. It is the responsibility of remarried parents to bring their new spouses into their old families. If introductions are not made, and stepparents are left to battle their way in, there will be casualties.

Initially, stepparents have no authority with their stepchildren; they are the outsiders. Only parents have the authority to do such things as set limits on their children's behavior and discipline them for misbehavior. Society grants parents this authority, but stepparents have no such permission. Only remarried parents can legitimize their new spouses' entry into their children's lives.

While new spouses may be permitted to enter children's old parent–child families, this does not automatically make these newcomers parents to their spouses' children; it does, however, make them stepparents. Remarried parents can expect their children to be respectful toward their new spouses and to treat them well, but parents cannot demand that their children love, or even like, their new stepparents. Children have a right to their feelings, whatever those feelings happen to be. All that parents can require of their children is that they not act on or act out any negative feelings they may have toward their parents' new spouses.

Children must be held accountable. If they are not held accountable, children are inclined to test their parents to see how far they can push them. Sometimes they will stop at nothing to get things back to the way they were before their new family was formed. A child who feels he or she has nothing to lose can create conflicts that yield devastating results.

Obstacles to Remarried Parents' Functioning as Gatekeepers

Gatekeeping is a crucial function of the remarried parent's role. However, when remarried parents first attempt gatekeeping, they are faced with a couple of notable obstacles: old allegiances and divided loyalties. Unprepared for all the hard work involved in tackling these obstacles, many remarried parents begin to doubt the wisdom of their decisions to remarry.

Old Allegiances versus New Alliances. Unable to deal with their own internal conflicts about their remarriages, many parents feel so guilty about once again disrupting their children's lives that they cannot even contemplate bringing their new spouses into their old one-parent families. Over time, these remarried parents are likely to feel guilty about a number of things, including:

1. Breaking up their children's original families;
2. Marrying and living with new spouses, who automatically become stepparents to their children;
3. Causing biological children to become stepchildren;
4. Burdening their children with stepsiblings; and
5. Creating a situation in which newborn children become half siblings to preexisting children.

Divided Loyalties. Remarried parents frequently encounter situations in which their old loyalties are at odds with their new ones. What could be worse than suddenly being called on to protect one set of loved ones from the other? Remarried parents may never have believed that they would find themselves having to protect either their old children from their new spouses or their new spouses from their old children. Sometimes their divided loyalties compel remarried parents to choose between loved ones. They can either renege on bringing their new spouses into their old families or alienate their children by siding with their new spouses.

Undoubtedly, remarried parents face a gut-wrenching dilemma: To whom should they remain loyal—their old children or their new spouses? Both sides demand allegiance.

All family systems have needs, and remarried parents' loyalties make them feel obliged to provide for the needs of each system. This means that remarried parents must simultaneously balance the needs of their old one-parent family systems, their new couple systems, and their combined family systems. This is why gatekeeping is an enormously challenging function: success depends on endurance and creativity.

What Happens When Remarried Parents Fail to Meet Their Gatekeeping Responsibilities?

When remarried parents fail to meet their gatekeeping responsibilities, they give up their power to control what goes on in their new family units. Nonperformance of their gatekeeping functions is likely to result in either a power struggle or a power vacuum. Power struggles take place when stepparents and stepchildren are left to "slug it out" with each other from the moment their combined families form. Power vacuums occur when remarried parents are unwilling or unable to assume any kind of control over what goes on in their new families. When power vacuums are present in combined families, one of two things happens: either the children jump in to fill them or their stepparents do.

> Alcoholism had played a major role in the breakup of his original family, so it came as no surprise to Dean that his alcoholic mother, Gayle, would choose another alcoholic husband, Elmo. What Dean could not have known was that his new stepfather abused more than alcohol.
>
> When Dean's mother took no part in defending her son against her new husband's tirades, Dean's stepfather knew he had the upper hand. One night when he was in a drunken rage, Elmo battered Dean so badly that Dean's spleen ruptured and had to be removed. When his mother continued to live with Elmo, Dean tried to get relatives to take him in. His relatives had their own problems, though, and did not want to get involved in the "goings-on" at Deans' house.

Dean was 9 when his mother married his stepfather; he was 14 when his stepfather decided to move out of town. Dean was not invited to come along. Elmo gave Dean's mother, Gayle, a choice: she could come with him or she could stay with her son, but as far as Elmo was concerned, Dean was out. He would not be allowed to come along.

Gayle chose: She told Dean that he was now on his own. She was too old to get herself another husband.

Gatekeeping in Complex Combined Families

The concept that applies to a simple combined family remains essentially the same in a complex combined family: the remarried parent has to bring the new spouse into her or his old one-parent family. The complication in a complex combined family is that each adult is already head of an existing one-parent family. These adults have to figure out ways to bring each other into their old biological families—and consolidate their couple bond—simultaneously.

In complex combined families, both adults have to give their children clear direction as to what is expected of them regarding their behavior toward their new stepparents and stepsiblings. Remarried parents in complex combined families must make exactly the same demands on their children as remarried parents in simple combined families: the children must be respectful of their new spouses and treat them well. Stepsiblings also must be held to this standard of accountability toward one another.

When the adults forming a complex combined family have difficulty in merging their individual family units, conflict between the pair seems inevitable. How can remarried adults reinforce their couple bond and accommodate each other when each adult's children keep urging a return to their old biological family? With their allegiances divided, it is likely that the couple's relationship will be damaged. Stepsiblings who do not pull their parents apart individually may band together to break up the couple's marriage. When the situation in a combined family household gets this far out of control, everyone loses. Such goings-on highlight the second most crucial aspect of the remarried parent's role: the remarried parent must function as a mediator.

THE REMARRIED PARENT AS MEDIATOR

The purpose of a mediator is to "reconcile (opposing forces), to settle (a dispute), or effect an agreement between others."[9] In a combined family, the "others" in the conflict are usually the remarried parent's new spouse and old children. A second major challenge in the remarried parent's role involves his or her mediating conflict between stepparent and stepchildren without getting caught up or caught in the middle of it.

Mediators are expected to negotiate solutions between opposing forces. They do no one any good, themselves in particular, if they take sides in the controversy.

To illustrate the mediating role of the remarried parent, it would be helpful to imagine a seesaw or teeter-totter, such as the one depicted in Figure 3. On this seesaw, there is a stepparent on one end, a stepchild or stepchildren on the other end, and a remarried parent in the middle.

The reason it is important to keep this picture in mind is because, in the early stages of development, the combined family seems to be on just such a seesaw, with the remarried parent's child or children on one side of the plank and the remarried parent's new spouse on the other. Poised on the center mount of this seesaw, ready at a moment's notice to shift his or her weight in one direction or the other, is the remarried parent. By maintaining a central stance, the remarried parent hopes to create a balance of power between the new spouse and old children. With the remarried parent strategically located and in control of the teeter-totter's momentum, neither the new spouse nor the old children can over-

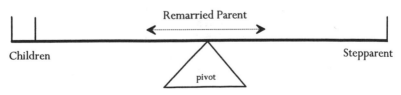

FIGURE 3. Combined family seesaw.

power the person or persons at the opposite end of the teeter-totter, and there is balance.

Using the power and authority implicit in the mediating role, remarried parents need to gauge where they can best shift their weight to correct for any imbalances. For example, to mediate a dispute between her old children and new spouse, the remarried parent needs to examine all issues relevant to the conflict:

> Both my children and my new spouse have told me that one day of the weekend should be a family day, but they cannot agree on which day it will be.

Having identified one central area of disagreement, the remarried parent can look for ways to find some "give" on each side. Mediators need working room. Their goal is to find a starting point from which to begin negotiations which, hopefully, will end in a successful compromise.

Continuing with this example, the remarried parent might next consider the issues and individual positions involved in the conflict:

> My children really want to spend the whole weekend with me. My husband, Sandy, might be willing to spend all day Sunday as a family day, but only if we can have an exclusive Saturday night date.

Aware of the impasse, the remarried parent begins to seek solutions that both sides might accept. Normally this is accomplished through negotiation. In our example, as mediator, the remarried parent might say to her children:

> "Sunday can be a family day, but Sandy wants an exclusive date with me on Saturday night." The children's response now may be to tell their mother that they do not want to have a baby sitter, and they do not want to stay alone Saturday night.

Mediation is a simple, yet painstaking process. It involves a search for workable solutions—arrived at through clear communication, negotiation, and compromise. The main focus of mediation is to end up with solutions that are acceptable to all parties involved in a dispute.

In the example we are working with, the remarried parent

must seek solutions that create harmony, not dissonance, among family members:

> Having obtained her children's response to Sandy's request for an exclusive Saturday night date with her, the remarried parent goes back to her new spouse and says, "The children do not want to have a baby sitter, and they do not want to stay alone on Saturday night."
>
> The remarried parent can then propose an alternative solution: that the children's minds might rest a great deal easier about having a sitter Saturday night if she (their remarried parent) and the children could do something exclusively on their own during the day on Saturday.
>
> Sandy's response is quick and to the point. "That sounds like a really good idea to me. I have been wanting to spend some time with my friends, and a group of them are getting together for poker Saturday afternoon. I would like to join them."
>
> With the new compromise formulated, the remarried parent can go back to the children and say, "If you consent to having a baby sitter Saturday evening, we can have all day Saturday to ourselves, and Sunday will be our family day. What do you think?"
>
> The children wanted most of all to have exclusive time with their remarried parent; therefore, they readily agree to having a baby sitter Saturday evening. Now all are free to relax, because their combined family (seesaw) is in balance.

The mediator is the one who finds ways to establish a comfortable middle ground between individuals or groups in the combined family. When the old children and new spouse feel that they are being heard by the one person most significant to them all, the remarried parent, resolving issues becomes much easier. As solutions are found, battles end, and harmony prevails.

In Search of Equilibrium

Most remarried parents are unprepared for functioning as mediators. Some may be afraid of hurting either their new spouses or their old children. Others do not realize how crucial it is for them to maintain a central stance. Many remarried parents may never have known equilibrium in their previous family structures—and wonder how can it be achieved in their new ones.

Each person entering a combined family has been part of at least one other family, but there is no context for this new family's assembly and no pattern for its design. Combined family members quickly learn that life can never go back to being the way it was. They are living in a brand-new family.

Establishing a sense of balance in a family system feverishly sorting itself out requires extraordinary effort—and a real knowledge of how the system works. Therefore, it is important for remarried parents to understand how the balance of power in their new families would likely be weighted if they remained completely neutral during the combined family formation process. On the teeter-totter, the balance tips in favor of remarried parents' old, well-established, parent–child relationships (see Figure 4).

Stepparents enter combined families with no identifiable power bases of their own, other than the strength of their relationships with their new husbands or wives. Because stepparents enter combined families in the least powerful positions of all, remarried parents need to devise ways to empower their new spouses—using some of their own authority with their children as the basis for lending credibility to their new mates.

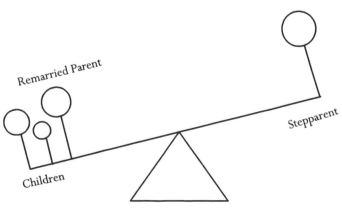

FIGURE 4. Initial weighing.

Figuring out where they should throw their support remains a constant challenge to remarried parents. If remarried parents shift their support away from their old children and toward their new spouses, their children may feel powerless, unsupported, and even abandoned by the very persons they count on to protect and defend them. Of course, any shift in the other direction can cause the same problems for new spouses. In either case, equilibrium will not be achieved.

However much they fear the consequences, remarried parents cannot refuse to get involved in balancing the needs of their children along with the needs of their new spouses. Their efforts are essential in stabilizing combined family teeter-totters (see Figure 5).

Even the tiniest shift in the remarried parent's position on the combined family teeter-totter can cause fluctuations in combined family equilibrium. The remarried parent has to be careful not to make abrupt shifts in the balance of power away from her or his old children and toward her or his new spouse, or vice versa. Shifts in support have to be gradual to prevent disruption of both sides' ties to the remarried parent. Care must also be taken to avoid damaging whatever stability has developed between stepparent and stepchildren within the combined family household.

Obstacles to Remarried Parents' Functioning as Mediators

No Mediation. When remarried parents fail to recognize the essential nature of their function as mediators in combined families, they themselves can become embroiled in family conflict. For

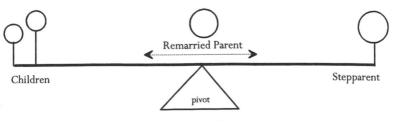

FIGURE 5. Equilibrium.

example: Children can convince their parents that their new spouses have become "wicked stepparents." In such cases, remarried parents' long-standing allegiances to their children may cause them to abandon their mediating positions and rush to aid their children. When this happens, their new spouses are left totally unsupported. Feeling maligned and isolated, these now "wicked" stepparents come to know what it feels like to be outcasts as well as outsiders, and that is likely to make them feel insecure. Over time, this insecurity creates anger in stepparents.

The balance on the combined family seesaw is not always in favor of the children, however. New spouses can dominate when remarried parents side with them against their children (see Figure 6). Equally as destructive as favoring children, making children the victims does nothing to restore combined family equilibrium. Remarried parents who take sides in stepparent–stepchild conflict cease to function as mediators.

Stepparents' and stepchildren's frustrations with each other may result from remarried parents' failure to function as mediators. However, neither stepparents nor stepchildren are likely to feel comfortable directing any of their hostile emotions toward the one person both parties consider an ally, the remarried parent. There are safer targets at which to vent their anger—each other. Their anger deliberately misses the remarried parent, thereby leaving stepchildren and stepparent free to target each other directly. The irony of this situation is that remarried parents may not even

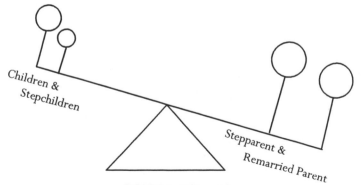

FIGURE 6. Taking sides.

recognize tensions between their old children and their new spouses because both parties are insulating them; they are on neutral ground in the middle of an undeclared war.

Remarried parents may be completely unaware of just how detrimental their failure to function as mediators may be; the harm to all family members can be profound. Unfortunately, once negative cycles of interaction between stepparents and stepchildren are established, they are very hard to reverse, and essentially, they do not change over time.

Mediation in Complex Combined Families. If finding a balance in a simple combined family (one with only one remarried parent) is this difficult, imagine how tricky it becomes to find that balance when both adults bring children into their remarriage. In a complex combined family, each adult is not only a remarried parent but a stepparent as well. In these families, no one individual can assume a single, central position to balance the needs of the children against the needs of a spouse.

The couple's position in a complex combined family presents each of the adults with an extraordinarily difficult set of problems to resolve. As a gatekeeper, each remarried parent must facilitate the entrance of his or her new spouse into his or her old one-parent family. As a stepparent, however, each of these same adults is an outsider to the other's parent–child relationship. The structure of a complex combined family is very complicated and can, at times, produce choking tension.

The adults in complex combined families normally find themselves in strong, central, "remarried parent" positions with their own children, and in weak, powerless, "stepparent" positions with their stepchildren. The ambiguity of their dual roles leaves both adults with difficult choices. Seesaws do not work well as analogies for complex combined families. In such families, both parents have to find their own ways to mediate conflict, especially while bringing their new spouses/stepparents into each other's old one-parent families.

There are no easy answers for the adults heading complex combined families. However, there are a few suggestions that can be made regarding their complicated roles:

1. Adults in complex combined families must work diligently to keep their couple bonds intact. It was on the strength of their couple bonds that their new families were formed, and it will be on the strength of those bonds that their combined families will survive.
2. Each remarried parent must balance his or her own stepchild–stepparent teeter-totter, while both adults must fulfill their gatekeeping responsibilities by bringing their new spouses into their old one-parent families.
3. Both of these adults have to be careful not to get trapped in stepparent–stepchild conflict. Both must hold firm to their mutual commitment to establish a single combined family, with all its members living in peace and harmony.
4. Both remarried parents must mediate conflict within their old one-parent families, while seeking to integrate all family members into a single combined family unit.

Maintaining equilibrium in simple or complex combined families can be extremely difficult for couples to deal with, but the mediating function of remarried parents is larger than one might think. For example, remarried parents may not only be mediating conflict between stepparents and stepchildren but also between former spouses and current spouses. Remarried parents might even be called upon to mediate conflict between their own parents and their new spouses, regarding stepparents' treatment of grandchildren, and so on. There are countless balancing acts that remarried parents can get involved in as their new family units get underway. It is no wonder that remarried parents frequently feel overwhelmed by the challenges that confront them as they attempt to bring together all those they love under one roof.

Personal Risk. Remarried parents who get personally involved in disputes between stepparents and stepchildren fail in their responsibility to maintain the integrity of their mediating positions. When there is no neutral stance, a two-on-one situation can form against either the new spouse or old children. Remarried parents who get caught in the middle of stepparent–stepchild conflicts can no longer be viewed as mediators.

In complex combined families, when there is a failure in mediation efforts, both adults can become trapped. Unsuccessful in their mediation attempts, both remarried parents may witness their new family's plunge into disarray, and their old one-parent families' call to battle. When collapse is imminent, combined families typically divide along biological family lines. In such cases, the damage to the couple bond may be irreparable.

After failing in their mediation efforts, remarried parents usually feel responsible for all that has gone wrong. Seeing the damage that has resulted from their failure to maintain equilibrium, guilt-stricken remarried parents often try to "make it up" to both parties. They do this by becoming intermediaries in those conflicts they cannot settle through negotiation.

There is a fundamental difference between a remarried parent functioning as a mediator and as an intermediary. The mediating parent is a free agent in negotiating various individuals' needs, while an intermediary is a go-between. This is true for both simple and complex families.

To illustrate the change in the remarried parent's position, from mediator to someone "caught in the middle," imagine that the seesaw that has balanced the remarried parent's old children and new spouse begins to collapse. While watching her or his family's collapse, the remarried parent tries to get under the central mount that supports the teeter-totter—to give additional support to its shaky foundation (see Figure 7). This yields the configuration shown in Figure 8. Then the seesaw collapses around the remar-

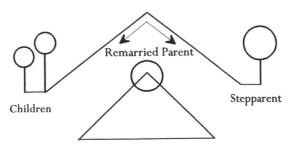

FIGURE 7. Collapse of the seesaw.

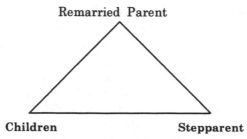

FIGURE 8. The combined family triangle.

ried parent, trapping that parent in a new structure—a triangle. A triangle is an accurate representation of the new family structure for two reasons. First, remarried parents, unable to resolve the conflict between their new spouses and old children, effectively vacate their central positions on combined family seesaws. Also, remarried parents have loyalties to each party involved in these triangles, and accordingly, a connection to each party in the conflict.

TRIANGLES

Triangles can occur almost anywhere within the immediate or extended combined family network. This discussion will be confined to those triangles in which remarried parents have been trapped. While all triangles are based on loyalty conflicts, they have their roots in power issues.

Power, in a family, amounts to being able to get something done "the way you want it done."[10] Remarried parents are the only ones who enter combined families with power, but others seem to want it as well. At issue are two individuals, or sets of individuals, that want something from each other—or somebody else. Instead of directly involving each other in their struggle for power, these individuals involve a third party as an intermediary.

The lack of communication between two parties to a conflict requires the presence of a third party to create the illusion of a relationship between the warring parties. Remarried parents who

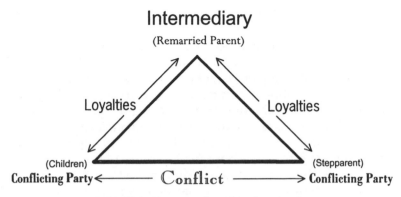

FIGURE 9. The struggle within the triangle.

have lost their balance as mediators are often "triangled in" as intermediaries (see Figure 9).

Once fixed in this middle position, intermediaries find it extremely difficult to break out of the vicious cycles of interaction that produced their triangles in the first place. Their loyalties to each side remain, yet they are unable to mediate the conflicts that keep them locked in place. Triangles have a tendency to become fixed over time. When remarried parents choose sides, they cannot win. They become caught in a power struggle in which they themselves are the prize.

If remarried parents consistently allow themselves to be put in the middle, the other parties to the conflict may never have to deal with each other again. For them, the solution is simple: Remarried parents will function as the switchboards through which all their communications are channeled.

Dismantling Triangles

In simple or complex combined families, when remarried parents peek out from under the debris of their shattered seesaws, they have to take a good look around. If these parents want out, they must say to themselves—as well as to their new mates and old children, "This simply will not do. I refuse to carry messages between the two of you; figure out ways to resolve your problems without me."

To break up a triangle, someone must eliminate an angle by getting out. In the early stages of combined family development, remarried parents who are caught between their children and new spouses can get out by returning to the teeter-totter analogy: new spouses on one end, children on the other end, and the remarried parent poised in the center—ready to negotiate a balance. In the middle and later stages of combined family development, other factors intervene to make remarried parents less necessary and inevitably less functional in this central position.

The actual dismantling of a triangle occurs when the person caught in the middle insists that all parties to the conflict break up into pairs and establish one-on-one communication regarding whatever problems they are having with each other. Each pair of individuals—in this case stepchild and stepparent, stepparent and remarried parent, and remarried parent and child—must have its own separate discussion. As their combined families develop and mature, remarried parents must be prepared to become active and tireless promoters of one-on-one relationships, both within and without their combined families.

Avoiding Triangulation. If a combined or any other kind of family is balanced, there is harmony in the household. This represents a major clue for remarried parents. When a remarried parent lends her or his weight here or there, is the result harmony or havoc? If the answer is harmony and a peaceful calm, the remarried parent is functioning as a mediator and doing a good job at it. However, if the remarried parent has allowed her or himself to become part of the conflict, she or he has become trapped in a triangle.

COMBINED FAMILY LIFE

When strangers first begin to interact, they are bound to misinterpret one another from time to time. In the early stages of combined family development, "time to time" may equate to 20 times a day. However, with all members of the combined family acting in good faith, the fine lines between gatekeeping, mediating, and triangulation become clear.

In each case, the issue boils down to problems between insiders and outsiders. Learning to deal with one another on terms not quite satisfactory to anybody but "good enough" will eventually lead combined family members to the safety and security of knowing that all of their opinions count. Where there is goodwill, there is a way! If remarried parents keep this motto in mind, they may find they will lose their way a good deal less than they thought they would.

TEN

The Stepparent

Lori, a young woman unable to have children, married Craig, a man with custody of his two young children. One was a baby and the other was 3 when Lori assumed her stepparenting role; she relished caring for the children and thinking they were her own. After about a year and a half of the couple's having sole custody, the children's biological mother started calling the house and wanting to see her children. Lori was devastated. Her dream was shattered. She realized that she was not, and never could be, the children's mother because they already had a mother. This thought led her to start distancing herself from the children. Craig was at a loss to understand what had happened, and so were the children!

In a 1956 book on remarriage, Jesse Bernard writes that there is continuing evidence that stepparening is "one of the most difficult of all human assignments."[1] As many a person who has been thrust into "the role of stepparent" can attest, there is no specific role in a combined family that a stepparent can *properly* assume. This chapter helps explain the reasons why.

THE STEPPARENT AS A PARENT

Starting with basics we know that a mother is a mother, a father is a father, and both are parents. But what are stepparents? Stepparents are not mothers or fathers unless they have children of their own. Well, what about parents? Are stepparents parents? The answer is "Yes," "No," and "That depends."

The status of the stepparent is largely dependent upon the parental status of two other people: the remarried parent and the remarried parent's former spouse—the parent outside of the combined family frequently referred to as the other or outside parent. Although they are no longer together, the former spouse and the remarried parent continue to share blood or legal ties to their mutual children. It is their children who become the stepparent's stepchildren once the combined family is formed. Because the outside parent continues to be a parent no matter where or with whom the children live, the role of the stepparent in a combined family is ambiguous; it lacks clarity as well as definition.

What is the Function of a Stepparent in a Combined Family?

When they remarry, single parents add their new marital partners to their old one-parent families. Their marriages change formerly single parents into remarried parents and their new spouses into stepparents. Their unions also change their old parent–child families into a new form of family: the combined family.

Within the context of the combined family, the stepparent can be looked at as:

1. The remarried parent's new spouse,
2. One-half of the adult couple heading the combined family; and
3. Someone who is expected to function in a role formerly occupied by the child(ren)'s outside parent in their original family.

Will Functioning in an Outside Parent's Role Make the Stepparent a Parent?

Clearly it is possible for stepparents to function in roles that were previously occupied by children's original parents, but functioning in these roles does not make stepparents parents in combined families. Stepparents cannot assume roles that would lead them to become parents to their stepchildren because these roles

are not vacant. Unless their parental rights have been legally termi-
nated, deceased or absent parents remain entitled to their roles as
parents to their children.

If stepparents cannot be parents to their stepchildren, what
can they be? What options do they have? What roles are available
for stepparents in combined families, and will defining their roles
make stepparents' jobs any easier? Let us explore these issues fur- ·
ther.

A STEPPARENT BY ANY OTHER NAME
IS STILL A STEPPARENT

The problem with stepparents is that we do not know what to
do with them in our society. Besides not knowing what to call them
(e.g., parents, nonparents, or relatives), we do not know how to
treat this particular group of people. Stepparents' main problem
seems to be that they have fallen in love with another type of
person: parents who have children from previous relationships.
We understand the relationship between remarried parents and
their new spouses, but who and what are stepparents and stepchildren to one another?

If we were to tell stepparents that they could be their stepchildren's parents we would be sending them a mixed message. To
illustrate the point we will examine stepparents' rights to authorize
emergency health care for their stepchildren. In most states, stepparents do not have the right to authorize emergency medical treatment for their stepchildren. Biological and adoptive parents and
legal guardians have this right. Without express permission from
children's parents or legal guardians, stepparents cannot sanction
emergency medical care for their stepchildren. What does this say
about stepparents' roles and responsibilities toward their stepchildren as compared to parents' roles and responsibilities toward
their children?

By not allowing stepparents the right to authorize emergency
medical treatment for their stepchildren, our society is, in effect,
telling stepparents that they are no one and nothing to their stepchildren. The message we are sending stepparents translates into
something like this:

"Yes, we will allow you to function in parental roles, i.e., you can make your stepchildren chicken soup when they are sick. However, do not try to sign for emergency medical care on your own authority when they are injured in car crashes or playground accidents; only 'real' parents can do that!"

By failing to recognize relationships between stepparents and stepchildren, the law seems to be sending stepparents a clear message: "Do not attempt to act as if you were your stepchildren's 'real' parents." Since the law fails to recognize stepparents as parents in something as basic as health emergencies, *our conclusion must be that stepparents cannot be parents to their stepchildren!*

No legal relationship exists between a stepparent and a stepchild. A parent's marriage results in an affinal (marriage-related) tie between stepparent and stepchild, and, because there are only affinal ties between them, there are no well-defined ways for stepparents and stepchildren to relate to one another. Consequently, relationships between stepparents and stepchildren are unclear. Currently, all that we can say for sure is that when the marriage between a remarried parent and a stepparent ends, the relationship between stepparent and stepchild also ends.[2]

In light of these realities, one can understand why being a stepparent is thought to be "one of the most difficult of all human assignments."[3] The stepparent is not a parent and is not "not a parent"—the role of stepparent lacks definition.

PROBLEMS IN THE STEPPARENTING ROLE

In an article by Irene Fast and Albert Cain,[4] the authors refer to the messages society sends to stepparents as "contradictory." Stepparents are being asked to function as "parent, nonparent, and stepparent," yet no one has clearly defined how they are to accomplish this impossible task. Adding to the confusion, we ask the stepparent to share the role with the "previous parent in ways not clearly established in the society."[5]

A stepparent is asked to share his or her role with this previous parent, but we fail to tell the stepparent how this is to be accomplished. Each stepparent has to figure out how to share a role with the child's outside parent. Frequently the stepparent must accomplish this feat without the cooperation of that outside parent and without any real desire on his or her own part to communicate with that parent.

Essentially, stepparents and outside parents have to find their own ways to share the role of parent. Our society does not give these adults adequate information to guide them in sharing their roles and responsibilities. All outside parents and stepparents know is that, whatever problems they have with one another, they must work them out, keeping the best interests of each child/ stepchild clearly in mind. The objective is for the parent and step-parent to work out *how they deal* with one another, not *how they feel* about one another:

> Evan's stepson, Cary, was very athletic. Being athletic him-self, Evan always enjoyed attending Cary's games and sports events. Evan had a problem, though; he did not know how to act when Cary's biological father, Hal, appeared at the same games. Cary too felt awkward each time his stepfather and father showed up to watch him play, but he was always happy to see his dad, and he enjoyed Evan's being there. Neither Evan nor Hal knew what to do when they saw each other, but eventually Evan started talking to Hal about his son's athletic ability. Over time, both men began to feel more at ease with each other, and this made Cary happy. Somehow, Evan and Hal had worked out a way to deal with the ambiguities inherent in their relationship, and every-body felt better about it.

While most stepparents have living, breathing parents to con-tend with, others have to deal with missing or deceased outside parents. Even in situations in which no living outside parent exists, stepparents do not have a clear path to "real" parenthood or to the role of parent. This is because surviving children maintain current relationships with deceased parents.[6] Commonly, these children tell their stepparents that their deceased parents "would not want" stepparents to make any changes in "their households," and that their parents "would object" to many actions stepparents might otherwise take.

Bereaved children frequently have active fantasy lives concern-ing their deceased parents; therefore, they are prone to interpret any changes made by stepparents as disrespectful of their parents' memories. Unaware of their stepchildren's continued involvement with their deceased parents, stepparents quickly find dealing with these "ghosts," or idealized memories of deceased (or unknown) parents, both tricky and taxing.

Whether an outside parent is alive or dead, stepparents acting in parental roles have to accommodate the "parental rights of others." Stepparents who attempt to assume previous parents' roles may find that they function in the "roles of parents" but are looked upon as "nonparents." Consequently, stepparents who assume parenting roles in combined families may be considered "inappropriate" or "disrespectful," depending on the "social norms."[7]

Children are often confused as to what their relationships to their stepparents should be because the stepparent role contains aspects of "parent, nonparent, and stepparent." With all this uncertainty, how are children to know when a stepparent is acting appropriately toward them? How are children to know when stepparents have overstepped their bounds?

A taboo prohibits sexual relationships between parents and their children, but what kind of protection is there for children from their stepparents in combined families? There isn't any! The absence of a clear-cut household incest taboo endangers children.[8] Sociologist Diana Russell found that "17% or one out of approximately every six women who had a stepfather as a principal figure in her childhood years, was sexually abused by him." Additionally, "47% of the cases of sexual abuse by stepfathers were at the *Very Serious* level of violation." The statistics for sexual abuse of women by biological fathers were 2%, with 26% of these cases listed "at the *Very Serious* level of violation."[9]

Without clear sanctions against sexual relationships in other than the primary husband and wife couple, boundaries between combined family members can break down. Stepparents are not just husbands or wives; they are in parenting roles toward their spouses' children.[9a] Parents have developed protective instincts through bonding to and nurturing their children from birth. Stepparents, on the other hand, do not develop the same protective instincts toward their stepchildren because they have no history with them. Without sanctions, stepparents can get confused. In their confusion, the generational boundary between stepparent and stepchild can become blurry, especially to a stepparent sharing the same living space with a budding adolescent of either sex, or with a beautiful stepchild of any age. If we make stepparents non-parents, we then expose the whole problem of incest.

"No clear-cut taboo exists for the situation of 'nonparent'."[10] It is up to us as a society to protect children who live with nonblood-related adults and children. Unrelated individuals who live together in combined families must be made aware of their duties and responsibilities toward everyone who lives in the combined family. Margaret Mead makes a most telling plea in behalf of extending the incest taboo to cover "all members of the household":

> If the incest taboos are seen to make an essential contribution to the rearing of children within a situation where their own immature emotions are respected, and where they are at the same time prepared for both sexual and non-sexual relationships as adults, it is then obvious that the taboo must be extended to include all members of the household. No matter what the size of the household, sex relations must be rigorously limited to the sets of marital couples—parents, grandparents, married aunts and uncles—who live within its confines. When these rigorous limitations are maintained, the children of both sexes can wander freely, sitting on laps, pulling beards, and nestling their heads against comforting breasts—neither tempting nor being tempted beyond their years.[11]

THE MARRIED COUPLE: REMARRIED PARENT AND STEPPARENT

Not everything that is involved in the stepparent's role in a combined family has to do with stepparents' obligations and responsibilities toward their stepchildren. Stepparents also have rights and privileges as one-half of the adult couple heading a combined family. These rights and privileges are conferred upon stepparents as a result of their relationships with remarried parents—their stepchildren's fathers or mothers.

The stepparent joins the remarried parent in a combined family in the position of *consort*. As a consort to her or his new spouse (a person "that shares the company of or is associated with another: as . . . a wife or husband: SPOUSE, MATE"[12]), stepparents are much like those individuals who marry kings or queens.

Consorts are expected to help their mates carry out certain functions in their capacities as consorts to kings or queens, such as attending ceremonies, representing their mates when they have prior commitments, etc. Consorts do a great many things to make their spouses' jobs easier, but that does not entitle them to assume equal positions when it comes to the monarchy. The position of monarch is ascribed: the King or Queen is born to the throne. Although lawfully wedded, a Prince Consort cannot be King to the Queen of the Realm, and the wife of the King may be called Queen, but she does not possess the King's hereditary entitlements. If the King dies, his Queen cannot aspire to his throne—only a legitimate heir to the throne can do that.

Stepparents have problems with their roles primarily because remarried parents and outside parents maintain their hereditary entitlements to their parenting roles. While stepparents can and do carry out many of the functions children's parents are expected to perform, fulfilling these functions does not entitle a stepparent/ consort to an equal position with regard to the remarried parent's children.

A stepparent cannot gain title to the role of parent unless a child's outside parent relinquishes his or her title to that role. *As long as the position is not vacant, a stepparent cannot be a parent to his or her stepchildren.* Even though stepparents may love their stepchildren and function as parents in their care and protection, stepparents cannot pretend to be parents to their stepchildren. Preexisting entitlements guarantee biological or adoptive parents this right.

Stepparents can support the family, car-pool, or cook and clean, so their stepchildren's lives will be balanced and orderly, with two adults to watch over them. However, stepparents' promotion of their stepchildren's welfare does not enable or entitle them to become parents to their stepchildren. Stepparents can only become parents to their stepchildren when biological or adoptive parents formally relinquish their ties,[13] or when children come of age and ask their stepparents to adopt them.

WHERE DOES THIS LEAVE STEPPARENTS?

Thus far, stepparents have been defined as "nonparents" to their stepchildren and "consorts" to remarried parents. These names help define who stepparents are, but names can hinder stepparents too. Specifically, stepparents have been negatively stereotyped by society throughout history. The negative references to stepparents indicate that the stepparenting role is "socially disapproved" of; therefore, stepparents are encouraged to assume a parental role.[14] Jointly these realities comprise the essential dilemma facing stepparents: *Stepparents are asked to assume roles that are not available (parent), not defined (nonparent), or negatively stereotyped (stepparent).* No wonder so many adults are overwhelmed by the role of the stepparent in a combined family. These adults do not have just one role to fill when they become stepparents—they have three, and, as it stands, they cannot succeed at any:

> Lance and Maureen had three children before Maureen was tragically killed in a boating accident. The couple had been separated at the time, but Lance immediately moved back into the family home with his three children; Claude, 13, Renee, 9, and Jon, 5. The accident was never discussed, and life went on.
>
> Lance started dating LeAnn two years after Maureen's death. Although LeAnn had never been married, she took great interest in Lance's children. Within two years, the couple had married and moved the new family unit to a new and larger home some distance away from where the children were raised.
>
> LeAnn was a good stepparent to the children—caring, loving, and interested in their welfare. Believing the children no longer had a mother, LeAnn set herself up to fill the role. But Renee, who had many warm personal memories of her mother, challenged LeAnn. She felt that LeAnn had no right to pretend to the position of mother in the combined family, as Renee's mother maintained her original position, even though she was deceased.
>
> Conversely, Jon willingly accepted LeAnn in the position of mother. Losing his mother at 5 left Jon with almost no memory of her. He was glad that LeAnn took such a keen interest in him, and he became very close to LeAnn, referring to her as his "mother." LeAnn referred to all of the children as "her children." She introduced them as her sons and her daughter, and LeAnn's parents referred to the children as their grandchildren. Claude accepted these labels without any fuss. Jon welcomed them, and Renee resented them.
>
> Claude and Renee had clear memories of their mother. Nei-

ther felt that LeAnn was their mother, but while Claude was not bothered by LeAnn's assumption of a parental role, Renee was. Jon wanted a mother to care for him throughout childhood, and he welcomed the opportunity to "adopt" LeAnn as his mom on purely an emotional basis—without the benefit of legal proceedings.

Difficulties with Jon surfaced when LeAnn gave birth to a son. The new baby robbed Jon of his position as the youngest in the combined family, and also served to remind Jon that his "real" mother was dead.[15]

There is much to be said about children's roles in the acceptance of stepparents in any capacity. Those children who desperately want the warmth and caring a loving stepparent can provide may go along with the fiction that their stepparent is their parent. In effect, these stepparents "replace" deceased, absent, or missing parents. Nonetheless, the place that the outside parent once held remains occupied by that original parent, regardless of the relationship between stepparent and stepchild!

THE ILLUSION

Stepparents sometimes seek to find a place for themselves in their stepchildren's lives through adoption. Adopting a stepchild allows a stepparent to legally assume the position of parent to a former stepchild. There are many good reasons why stepparents might consider adopting their stepchildren, but some stepparents seek to do this just to get around the discomfort of having to explain to outsiders that their spouses' children are not their own biological children. These stepparents hope that by changing the surnames and legal relationships of their stepchildren they will escape detection.

Disenchantment is likely to be swift for those combined families using adoption as a way to make their new families "look like" nuclear families. The problem is that these stepparents become parents to remarried parents' children in name only. The change of names does not supplant the need for former stepparents and stepchildren (now parents and children) to build relationships with one another. There are no shortcuts, nor are there any sure and steady paths for remarried parents, stepparents, and stepchildren to follow in establishing relationships with one another.

It was Byron's practice to drive his son, Dennis, to college at the beginning of each fall quarter. Byron and Nora were married shortly before Dennis was due to go back to school to commence his junior year. They both were delighted when Dennis asked Nora if she would come along on the trip back to his college campus.

Dennis's difficulties in "explaining" Nora started immediately upon their arrival. Byron had dropped Nora and Dennis at the entrance to a popular restaurant in town and then driven off to find a parking place for the car. As soon as Nora and Dennis entered the restaurant, Dennis met up with a middle-aged acquaintance of his. Taken off guard, Dennis stumbled to make an introduction. He introduced Nora as his "friend." When Byron walked in, however, he was introduced as Dennis's dad. Anyone could see that Byron and Nora were close in age. Dennis's hasty introduction of Nora as his friend proved to be embarrassing to them all. All through dinner, Dennis's acquaintance kept glancing at the three of them. Nora, Dennis, and Byron all agreed that Dennis's introducing Nora as his friend just was not going to work.

After dinner, Dennis took Nora and Byron around campus. When they arrived at his residence hall, Dennis introduced Nora and Byron as his parents. Nora was exceedingly uncomfortable when the hall director started making all sorts of admiring comments about her "son" Dennis.

It was obvious to Nora that Dennis was ill-at-ease about having a stepparent. Dennis had managed to place Nora in two very uncomfortable situations by failing to acknowledge their true relationship to each other.

PERCEIVING THE ROLE

Stepparents who do not actually become parents to their stepchildren still can hold positions in combined families similar to those held by biological parents in their children's original families. Remarried parents often ask stepparents to perform all of the functions biological parents might be expected to perform: e.g., ferrying children to and from a party, helping a stepchild with her or his homework, etc. In reality, stepparents may be doing everything for their stepchildren that the children's outside parents could or would have done, and more! This is why the role of stepparent is thought to be so burdensome. Stepparents often get all of the work with little or none of the rewards of parenting.

Stepparents need to clarify with their new spouses what is expected of them in relation to their stepchildren. For example, do the children's remarried parents expect their new spouses to participate in the raising of the children, or are stepparents expected to remain unobtrusive, with no real duties or obligations?

Understanding how their spouses expect them to act once their new families come into being is very important information for stepparents to have in advance. Stepparents who enter combined families as strangers must understand that the role of parent belongs to children's mothers and fathers, whether they are gone forever or living down the street. All too often stepparents pretend to be heirs to previous parents' roles, when all that remarried parents require of them is to talk with the children when the entire combined family sits down for dinner or to be friends to the children when they need them.

Stepparents can be many important things in combined families. They may be welcomed by their spouses and stepchildren as additional parents, or they can be nonparents to their stepchildren in very creative and constructive ways. How stepparents will act toward their stepchildren, and how they will be received by them may not be known when combined families first come into being. However, stepparents need advance knowledge of where they are expected to fit into the combined family picture every bit as much as children need to know what is going to happen to them once a stepparent appears on the scene.

STEPPARENTS AS "PART-PARENTS"

In her book *The Half-Parent*, Brenda Maddox makes the point that the stepparent "has become the person closest to the closest relative a child can have,"[16] the closest relative being the remarried parent. She goes on to write that children may "consider any spouse of their parent to be at least their part-parent."[17] If this is so, who determines the role of part-parent—the stepparent, the stepchildren, the remarried parent, or society? Which part of the stepparent's role is part-parent and which is nonparent? Does the stepparent have to do anything to achieve this status, or does it simply come about as a result of the stepparent's marriage to the children's mother or father? Is the stepparent's status as part-parent purely that of a figurehead, without any substance or meaning, or does the part-parent designation entitle the stepparent to certain power and privileges?

> Edgar and his first wife, Eleanor, were married for 20 years before Eleanor died of a massive heart attack, leaving Edgar and his 15-year-old son, Warren, on their own. Three years after Eleanor's death, Edgar married Rita.
>
> Rita had been Warren's stepmother for almost 20 years when Warren fell victim to a fatal illness and died at the age of 38. Stricken with grief that Warren had come to such an untimely end, Rita could not believe the obituary notice that the family released to the newspapers. It read: "Warren B_____, son of Edgar and the late Eleanor B_____," etc. No mention of Rita was made. Rita was so hurt by this utter disregard of her 20-year relationship with Warren, she did not want to attend the funeral. She did so only under duress.

AS COMBINED FAMILIES FORM

In the early stages of combined family development, two very different relationships can be presumed, the one that exists between the remarried parent and his or her children and the one between the remarried parent and his or her new spouse. The presence of a new adult may cause the remarried parent's children to fear losing their close ties to their parent. Yet, the tie that usually causes the most difficulty in combined families is the one between stepparent and stepchild. What this tie will later become is unknown when the combined family first forms.

Predictably, the new couple's greatest challenge often turns out to be that of finding ways to ease the stepparent's entrance into a formerly one-parent family unit without causing the children to feel displaced. Recognizing that, in the beginning, the only connection between stepparent and stepchild is the remarried parent, one can readily see the potential for conflict between stepparents and stepchildren.

Stepparents and stepchildren vie for remarried parents' attention and affection. A stepparent may only have undertaken the burden of her or his new spouse's children because the remarried parent came as a "package deal"—with children already present. Stepchildren may feel unwanted because they realize they are part of the package that their new stepparent had to accept in order to marry their parent. These are not the most promising grounds on which to found a relationship; however, this is precisely the challenge that faces stepparents and stepchildren. They must establish relationships with one another, even if, in the end, their choice is not to relate.

Each remarrying parent is certain to enter into a remarriage with some expectations as to what the relationship between stepparent and stepchild should be. Sometimes these expectations on the part of the remarried parent are realistic, and sometimes they are not. Until the combined family actually forms, stepparents and stepchildren cannot know how they will feel about one another as members of the same family—living under the same roof.

Usually there is a honeymoon period between new stepparents and stepchildren that may last some days or weeks, but ultimately it is up to them to work out their own relationships. No one can truly predict what these will be; however, everyone about to join a combined family would be well advised to become as knowledgeable as possible about combined family life. Members of a combined family need to know what they are getting into; they need to know what to expect!

WHAT CAN BE EXPECTED OF STEPPARENTS?

Faced with the dilemma of whether "to be or not to be"[18] parents to their stepchildren, stepparents may find themselves feeling like Hamlet, unable to take any kind of positive action. The indefinite nature of stepparenting may indeed be responsible for the frustration experienced by countless stepparents who struggle with a role that causes them to feel hamstrung at every turn. Perhaps an acknowledgment that the actual role of parent is unavailable to them is what needs to be clarified for future stepparents. This would also help to define for society what it can and cannot expect of stepparents.

Establishing norms that do not require the stepparent to be a "parent" would relieve stepparents of the burden of feeling they have to be parents to their spouses' offspring. It might also relieve them of some of the guilt they take on when they feel less than successful in their attempts to parent their stepchildren. This does not mean that all is lost concerning the relationship between stepparents and stepchildren. Stepparents and stepchildren can, and often do, grow to love one another.

In the movie *The Last Emperor*,[19] three scenes relate to the psychological adoption of a child. They are pertinent even though the movie is a fictionalized account of the events that actually occurred.

> When a 3-year-old child is chosen to assume the throne by the dying Empress of China, the child's mother turns the boy over to a wet nurse saying, "I am giving you my son. My son is your son."
>
> In a later scene, the boy is shown as being much older, still suckling at his wet nurse's breast. Shortly thereafter, this woman is pictured as being abducted from her quarters and bundled into a carriage, which then speeds off. The woman begs her abductors: "Let me say good-bye. He is my child." As the carriage whisks her away from the Forbidden City, the woman can be seen looking out its window, straining to get one last glimpse of the boy she looks upon as her child.
>
> Although the original transfer of the child's custody—from mother to wet nurse—presumably had no legal backing, the mother's total relinquishment of her child constituted grounds for the wet nurse to assume a parental role in the raising of the biological mother's child.
>
> When the young emperor realizes that this woman who is so dear to him is being taken away, he forlornly asks, "Why is she

being taken away from me?" When one eunuch makes a reference to the fact that he is now too old for a wet nurse, he angrily proclaims, "She is not my wet nurse!" and then he adds, mournfully, "She is my butterfly." As he runs after her hastily departing carriage, the young emperor can be heard calling her name, over and over and over again. His despair is obvious when, at last, he is forced to deal with the fact that he can neither overtake the carriage nor regain his one great source of comfort.

If, in time, stepparents come to have maternal or paternal feelings toward their stepchildren, and these feelings are reciprocated, everybody wins. Where legitimate barriers to the legal adoption of stepchildren by stepparents do exist, who is to say that stepchildren and stepparents cannot informally choose to adopt one another? Who is to tell these children and adults that their feelings are inappropriate or wrong? One cannot legislate feelings.

One also cannot will loving relationships between stepparents and stepchildren. Instant loathing might be just as feasible as instant love when it comes to relationships between these two sets of individuals. Often, stepparents and stepchildren begin combined family life as strangers, and they are hard-pressed to form any kind of a relationship at all with one another. How can remarried parents expect stepparents, who are relative strangers to their children, to parent those children?

INSIDE COMBINED FAMILIES: STEPPARENTS' ROLES AND RELATIONSHIPS

The position that is being spelled out here is that it is unreasonable to handicap a person entering a stepparenting role by saying to that person, "You have to be a parent to your stepchild(ren)." Stepparents have to find comfortable roles within the combined family; suggestions for models include mentor, camp counselor, favored aunt or uncle, and trusted friend and confidante.

In her book *Stepchild in the Family,* Anne Simon writes: " 'Those who educate children well,' Aristotle said, 'are more to be honored than those who produce them.' He may not have been thinking of

stepmothers when he conferred the ultimate honor, but his words have meaning for them. Stepmothers are educators; their subject— Modern Marriage."[20] Perhaps here is another role for stepparents to model!

If we eliminated the expectation that stepparents be parents, a great deal of the confusion that currently surrounds the role of the stepparent could be eliminated. Relationships outside the combined family also could benefit from the elimination of this expectation. For example, children's outside biological parents might not be as worried about competing with new stepparents if they could be assured that stepparents could not assume their roles.

Currently many of the former spouse's greatest fears revolve around being displaced, or worse yet, replaced, by the stepparent who lives with his or her child(ren) some, most, or all of the time. Alleviating these fears on the part of former spouses should considerably reduce the tensions between these outside parents and stepparents.

> Rhonda, a middle-aged woman whose 15-year-old son, Eric, had just gone to live with his father and stepmother, became hysterical as she reported to her therapist that Eric's father was requiring him to address his stepmother as "Mom." The therapist asked Rhonda if she was Eric's biological mother. Rhonda immediately responded yes. She was asked if anyone else could make that claim, and of course her answer was no.
>
> Rhonda also was aware that no one could replace her, and that her son did not think of this other woman, his stepmother, as his mother. The therapist then asked her: "What is this catastrophe you are fearing? Does your son's being required to use the word 'mom' make this other woman his mother? Can she really replace you, or erase you from your son's memory?"
>
> The response came slowly and thoughtfully. "No," said Rhonda. "She can't replace me or make my son forget me, but it just isn't fair that Eric's father is making him call *that* woman 'Mom.'"

With the knowledge that neither parent can be replaced, remarried parents and their former spouses are more likely to lay down their personal hostilities toward one another and work out a mutually satisfying "parenting coalition."[21] This provides biolog-

ical parents "who are no longer married to each other" the opportunity to create and maintain a "continuing relationship between
the child and both parents . . . so that the child's identity is not
shattered by divorce."[22]

DEFINING THE ROLE OF STEPPARENT

There is a discrepancy between that which is achievable—the
stepparent as nonparent; and the societal ideal—the stepparent as
parent. Repeatedly these discrepancies form shackles that bind
stepparents and prevent them from fulfilling the stepparenting
role. If stepparents know they do not want to be "stepparents,"
those harsh, cruel, and unforgiving villains, and they *cannot* be
parents, they will have only one role available to them, that of
nonparents. Designating the stepparent as "nonparent" leaves us
room to design a role for the stepparent which is far different from
fairy tales and mythology. This should also forever remove stepparents from the second-class status to which they were formerly
consigned.

Since the role of stepparent carries with it no entitlements to
the role of parent to the child, each stepparent's relationship to
each individual stepchild can be defined as nonparent to *nonchild*.
The designation "nonchild" means "not the stepparent's child."
Stepparents have a "duty of care" for the well-being of their stepchildren in their capacities as consorts to their stepchildren's parents, but this duty of care comes as a result of their holding marital
ties to their stepchildren's parents, not as a result of their holding
legal ties to their stepchildren.

> Nancy was only ten years older than her youngest step-
> daughter. She had been able to gain the respect of her three
> young adult stepchildren by not coming into the family as a
> mother figure, and she had not tried to be anything other than
> the soft, sophisticated young woman that she was.
> Being that the age difference between his wife Nancy and his
> children was so small, Vern had decided from the beginning that
> he would keep control over his children. Vern introduced Nancy

to his children as someone from whom they could learn a great deal if they cared to do so. They were to show her respect and consideration. He went on to tell them that Nancy was in no way going to be a substitute or replacement mother, as they already had a perfectly good one living not too far away.

Nancy held back from intruding on her stepchildren's privacy, and she did not get involved in their affairs in any obtrusive way. She always remained interested in the children's well-being and available to them if they felt their father was not hearing them correctly.

Eventually each of her stepchildren turned to Nancy for help with dating problems. They felt that she was closer to them in age, and she would probably have better solutions to their problems than their father might offer. Nancy valued their confidences and took them seriously, giving careful and thoughtful advice on how to handle certain delicate male–female relationships. Slowly, Nancy and each of her stepchildren developed mutually rewarding relationships.

When difficulties arose between Nancy and Vern, some 15 years into the marriage, the relationship between Nancy and her stepchildren held. None of the children took sides against either adult in the couple's dispute. No matter what happened between Nancy and Vern, the children's relationship to each adult remained committed and grounded in mutual respect and love.

MAKING THE ROLE OF NONPARENT WORK

Incest

Determining that stepparents are nonparents creates the clear and present danger of the sexual abuse of a stepchild by a stepparent, or of one stepsibling by another stepsibling. The danger of incest exists because these relationships are ill-defined. For example, there is no role description that specifically precludes sexual relationships with, or among, stepchildren. Therefore, the question, What is incest? must be clarified for everyone concerned prior to the combined family's formation. Inside the combined family, sexual relationships must be specifically confined to married couples. Sexual relations between any other members of the household are taboo—no matter who else happens to be living in the combined family household.[23]

Outside Parents

As people grow to understand combined family dynamics, it will become a matter of common knowledge that neither parent can be replaced by a remarriage. Once this is understood, living parents might be more inclined to stay involved with their children—as they are the only parents their children have. Even when outside biological parents are deceased, stepchildren continue to have two biological parents, and stepparents continue to be nonparents.

In light of the stepparent's nonparent status, former spouses will have to work out satisfactory co-parenting agreements regarding their children. This need for developing a parenting coalition across the dual households in which their children live should prove helpful in keeping noncustodial parents involved with their children. Parents cannot "pass the buck" on this issue of who is a parent! Mothers and fathers are parents, and "the buck stops there."

Making the Fit

Stepparents need to know in advance how they are expected to fit into their new family structures. Keeping in mind that the continuity of relationships is an important factor in child rearing, remarried parents need to find a slot for stepparents in their children's lives. This can be very challenging because it involves taking individuals from outside a family system and putting them into positions that were formerly filled by biological parents.

Conceptually, the combined family represents a tremendous shift from the tight, composite nature of a nuclear family structure to the looser, more ambiguous structure of a nonnuclear, nonbiological family. Maintaining continuity in relationships throughout the transformation process is more than difficult; it is critical.

To facilitate the transformation of one-parent families into combined families, remarried parents have to escort their new spouses into these new families and support them from their gate-keeper positions until stepparents can function in their own right as nonparents. Successful couples also must find ways for step-parents to assume their rightful positions as consorts (to remarried parents) without disrupting important biological relationships be-tween parents and children.

Negotiating the Role of the Stepparent

The part that stepparents are going to play in the lives of their stepchildren has to be negotiated. How much stepparents are ex-pected to contribute to the upbringing of the children, or to their general emotional and psychological well-being, has to be consid-ered *in advance*. Whatever their goals, couples need to reconcile what remarrying parents hope their new spouses will be able to accomplish with what future stepparents believe they can accom-plish. This leaves a great deal of room for negotiation. Whatever their conclusions, however, the one thing that cannot be bargained away is stepparents' need for family positions and roles that are exclusively their own.

Stepparents come to combined families with no space desig-nated for them, with no parental roles open to them, and with no guidelines. In truth, there is little to prevent stepparents from slip-ping into the quagmire of outside beliefs and opinions about what they should be doing. To the uninitiated, the role of the stepparent may appear quite simple. Maybe this is the reason why everyone seems to want to "get into the act" in combined families.

The position of the stepparent is not clear enough for outsiders to assume that the stepparent is performing her or his role proper-ly; as a result, outside interference in the internal workings of the combined family is commonplace. No one can prevent all of the complexities of the role from overwhelming stepparents, primarily because it is impossible to predict all the circumstances stepparents will face upon entering their new families (e.g., too much outside interference, conflicts with or between stepchildren, excessive de-mands on time, energy, resources, or too little time with spouses, friends, own children, etc.).

We can, however, let the stepparent know where he or she fits in! In the past, where the stepparent was supposed to fit in was described in the language of nuclear families (i.e., as a replacement, substitute, or surrogate mother or father), and these references had misleading implications. The language itself masks the stepparent's main problem: *the stepparent cannot fit in.* A position has to be designed for the stepparent. If stepparents have their own roles and their own names, separate and distinct from outside biological parents, all will know that stepparents are not replacement parents. If we then further clarify the role of stepparent by defining it as "nonparent," the stepparent will have an identity and a position in the combined family that is the stepparent's sole province. Giving the stepparent a role of her or his own also serves to assure outside and remarried parents of the inviolability of their own parental roles.

Framing a role that places potential stepparents in the proper context to join preexisting one-parent families has been the essence of this chapter. The next chapter, "Stepmothers and Stepfathers," will provide us with more concrete models for nonparents. Meanwhile, the issues of stepparents and stepchildren in relation to one another can be found in Chapter 13, "Stepparents, Stepchildren, and Remarried Parents."

Isolating the components that will enable us to offer future stepparents a happier entry into the world of living with another person's children has taken an entire chapter in this book, and years of collective thinking in many fields of study. There is no group, however, that more richly deserves the kind of attention that has been paid to them here than stepparents themselves. Past, present, and future stepparents undertake to create new lives with remarried parents and their children, in a new form of family which is created from the moment the couple says, "I do." The least we can do for these brave men and women is give them realistic objectives in feasible roles.

ELEVEN

Stepmothers and Stepfathers

Meg's mother had been dead six years when her father married Sherri. Meg never talked to or otherwise acknowledged Sherri's existence. Sherri tried to make friends with Meg, but she could not.

Several years of this nonassociation had gone by when Meg announced that she was going to marry Lance. Since her dad was not available, it was Sherri who had to help with trousseau shopping, wedding hall deposits, etc., for Meg and Lance. Sherri started to believe that Meg would finally let her be part of her life.

Sherri's joy did not last long. Meg cut her out of any personal role in the wedding ceremony itself. Meg even avoided having Sherri appear in any of the wedding pictures. Sherri felt alienated, mistreated, and duped.

In the preceding chapter the undefined role of the stepparent was given an antidote: the stepparent's role is now defined as that of a nonparent. Let us say that we all agree that the role of nonparent is appropriate for a stepparent and we tell every stepparent, "Your official role in the combined family is that of nonparent to your spouse's child or children." Telling stepparents that their role is that of nonparents contradicts other messages already sent. For years we have told stepparents there are times when they can be parents to their stepchildren.

Some stepparents will not know what to do with this new message, some may be confused by it, and still others may hate it. However, we must look at what we have been doing to stepparents by asking them to assume roles of parents to their spouses' children.

GOOD MOTHER/BAD MOTHER

Perhaps one reason stepmothers have fared so poorly over time is that children can see only good in their own mothers if there are bad mothers available to absorb any negative feelings. A stepmother is a perfect target for a child's negative feelings; in effect she becomes a victim of the phenomenon called *splitting*. To keep the good image of a person uncontaminated, that person can be split into two—one all good and the other all bad. Splitting a person into either all good or all bad can provide a solution for a child who finds a particular relationship too difficult to cope with, or too hard to understand.[1]

Splitting serves to protect the biological parent from a child's anger. Also, splitting allows the child's angry and vengeful fantasies to be directed at someone resembling the parent, but who clearly is not the parent.[2] The stepmother resembles the child's mother in that she married the child's father, but she is not the child's mother. Since she is not the child's mother, it is safe for the child to have hostile feelings about her. The darker the stepmother looks, the better the child's own mother is likely to appear. Splitting allows the stepmother to be cast as the "bad mother," thereby allowing the biological mother to appear all good.

SOCIETY'S ROLE IN THE PLIGHT OF THE STEPMOTHER

Society has prescribed definite roles for mothers and fathers to play such as caregivers, providers, and disciplinarians. Society also has definite functions for them to perform, including homemaking, breadwinning, car-pooling, etc. Mothers and fathers either know, or can find out, what their roles are.

Society, however, does not seem to know what to do with stepmothers who are alive. By neglecting to define the role stepmothers should play, stepmothers have only the biological mother as a role model. This might explain why a woman in the role of stepmother who is not acting like a "good mother" is accused of being a "bad mother."

Ideally, women becoming stepmothers should be told: "Look, you are not your stepchildren's mother, so take it easy and let the father bring you into the old one-parent family. Be congenial, observe quietly, and do not interfere in parent–child interactions." Unfortunately, in reality we give stepmothers the opposite message; we tell them that it is their responsibility to nurture their husbands' children—to assume the role of mother.

Following tradition rather than common sense, our society assumes that we overburden the father by expecting him to take responsibility for his children. Instead, we ask the stepmother to take the "burden" of caring for his children—though as a single parent the father may have been caring for his children for months or years. The problem is that the stepmother is not the mother; she enters the role after the fact, after the children already have (or have had) a mother. The role of mother is already occupied, in reality, memory, or fantasy!

THE STEPFATHER AS FATHER

Similarly, the idea of being or becoming a stepfather has led men to the understanding that they too should become fathers to their stepchildren. Because traditionally men have not nurtured their own or anyone else's children, they are not expected to nurture their stepchildren. Instead stepfathers are seen as breadwinners and disciplinarians.

Although there is less stigma attached to being a stepfather, the father's role still can be split into "good father" and "bad father." With reference to Bettelheim, Michel Radomisli writes, "A displacement figure for a 'bad father' image is probably not as necessary . . . because the father is less involved with the young child and is absent more frequently; therefore, the child's ambivalence for the father is more tolerable and the father's importance is more easily minimized by the child."[3] While stepfathers may have fared better as parents than have stepmothers, clearly neither step-fathers nor stepmothers are their stepchildren's parents.

THE STEPPARENT AS NONPARENT

While designating living stepmothers and stepfathers as non-parents can eliminate stereotypes or splitting into good and bad, there is another crucial issue facing stepparents. We have given the remarried parent's new spouse an identifiable role (nonparent), but we have not given the new spouse/stepparent a name by which he or she can be addressed.

We can now say to a new stepparent, "All right, your role in the combined family is that of a nonparent," but to a brand-new stepmother or stepfather, what does it mean to be a nonparent? Will new stepparents have names they can be called by remarried parents' children? If new stepparents have names of their own, will these names immediately convey their status inside combined families? Can these names be used to introduce stepparents to others? Mothers and fathers have such names in nuclear and one-parent families. When they are introduced, there is no way of confusing them with anyone else.

Have you ever heard a stepparent called by the name "Step-mother" or "Stepfather"? No? Well, it is not likely that you will. Children in combined families are in the position of having to use their stepparents' given names (which sound pretty ridiculous coming out of the mouths of 3- or 4-year-olds). Or, at their remarried parents' requests, children may be asked to call their step-parents by their outside parents' names, e.g., "Mother," "Mom," or "Ma" for women, and "Father," "Dad," or "Pa" for men. This action by remarried parents usually threatens and incenses the rightful holders of those names—the children's outside parents. What is it that has prevented us from devising other names chil-dren can use when relating to, or even referring to, their step-mothers and stepfathers? Stepparents can live in a combined family for 20 years and never be directly addressed by their step-children. An "Ahem" or false throat-clearing may be the only indication a stepparent gets that a stepchild is getting ready to launch some kind of communication in his or her direction.

NAMING: A MEANS FOR ESTABLISHING IDENTITY

In their roles as nonparents, what stepparents need most are identities of their own. We name families of plants and animals; we even name inanimate objects like schools and hospitals. Schools have "teachers" and "principals." Hospitals have "doctors" and "nurses." All these people can be identified by their names. So, how is it then that we have not yet let people know by what names stepmothers and stepfathers are to be addressed? Stepparents need proper names to identify their positions in combined families. Without proper names, stepfathers and stepmothers will continue to lack

1. Roles of their own;
2. Names that belong exclusively to them and identify the roles they play in combined families;
3. Names by which their children can address them; and
4. Names by which their stepchildren and others can refer to them.

With proper names of their own (i.e., ones by which anyone could address and/or refer to them), stepmothers and stepfathers would have identities of their own; they would be free to establish more authentic relationships with those with whom they live, and with everyone else as well.

To give identity and a name to each stepparent, as well as to give all stepparents a chance to establish successful relationships with their spouses' children, this author proposes additions to our vocabulary and language (see Chapter 21). If we were to adopt the names listed therein, children in a combined family could identify their stepmother as their *matu*:

> **Matu(s)** /mȧ´ tü/(s) The wife of my father by a subsequent marriage, or my father's wife.

and their stepfather as their *patu*:

Patu(s) /på´ tü/(s) The husband of my mother by a subsequent
marriage, or my mother's husband.

Above is the rationale for changing the names of stepmother(s) to matu(s) and stepfather(s) to patu(s). Below are the potential benefits of these changes:

1. Children have no socially accepted names to use when calling or referring to their stepmothers or stepfathers. In our society, for a child to call a female stepparent "Stepmother" would be an insult; the word has too many negative connotations. Then again, hearing a child refer to a man as "Stepfather" might suggest that that child fears the man occupying the role.

   Matu and patu have no negative connotations. They are words children could use when referring to their stepmother or stepfather without bringing up every negative association the word *step* carries with it. For example: "Matu, this phone call is for you." "Patu, I'd like you to meet Denise. Denise, this is my patu."

2. Patus and matus are not biological parents to their stepchildren. This is implicit in their names. Children would not have to explain to anyone that their patu or matu is not their biological parent, and stepparents would not have to explain to others their relationships to their stepchildren.

3. A patu would be different and apart from a father, although he may perform some functions fathers perform. Likewise a matu would be different and apart from a mother, although she may perform some functions mothers perform. With names of their own, patus and matus could be clearly differentiated from fathers and mothers; they could at last be seen as distinct people with distinct roles of their own.

4. The names *matu* and *patu* would define the unique positions these individuals hold in combined families. The names would also give those individuals bearing these titles a legitimacy and identity which they currently lack.

Thus, the appropriate use of the names *matu* and *patu* would allow children living in combined families to clarify the exact nature of their relationships with the adults heading those families. *Matu* is the name of a child's father's wife. *Patu* is the name of a mother's husband. Because of their soft "tu" endings, patus and matus sound like they would be a good deal friendlier and easier to be around than stepfathers and stepmothers. "My matu (or patu) can take us to the skating rink, if your mom (or dad) can bring us back."

5. Matus and patus would not be expected to have the same feelings toward their spouses' children as these children's biological parents would be expected to have toward them. Similarly, the children would not be expected to have the same feelings toward their patus or matus as they might be expected to have toward their fathers and mothers. When patus or matus and stepchildren got to know one another, they would be free to develop their own mutual feelings of love or caring. Loving feelings need to be based on people's personal experiences with one another, not on their unrealistic expectations of what their relationships should be.

6. Either a matu or a patu could function as a caregiver in a combined family. What you expect from a caregiver is essentially what you require from a responsible baby sitter: adequate provision for, care of, and concern over the well-being of the children. You would not expect a baby sitter to love the children. However, precisely because that is not a requirement, and the relationship is not forced, love often develops between the children and adult, regardless of their lack of kinship ties.

Putting a patu or matu in the role of caregiver would free that adult from competition with the children's outside parent. If the matu cooked, there would be no requirement that she had to cook like mom. If a patu barbecued hamburgers, there would be no requirement that they tasted like dad's. We would not expect baby sitters to cook like, or be like, the fathers or mothers they baby-sit for; they are themselves, and their roles are separate and apart from those of children's remarried or outside parents.

Just as we allow baby sitters to be free of being fathers or mothers, patus and matus need to be free of comparisons to children's biological parents. By seeking to give patus and matus their own status, we would eliminate unnecessary rivalry with biological mothers and fathers. Stepfathers cannot win against fathers. Stepmothers cannot win against mothers. Patus and matus would not be competitors for those roles; they would have roles of their own.

7. If a person was a matu or a patu, she or he would then become a model for that role, not for the role of mother or father. Matus and patus would not have to compete with children's mothers and fathers. Matus and patus could be evaluated in their own right, without looking to the role of the mother or the father as a model for their behavior.

8. Patus and matus could be attractive, sincere, dedicated, and fun-loving adults who hold roles of their own, somewhere outside children's parents' roles. Potentially, matus and patus could discuss things with children that their parents might become too emotionally involved with to discuss, such as dating. If relationships between these adults and their stepchildren were positive, there is nothing that would bar patus and matus from becoming children's special confidantes, mentors, teachers, or simply favorite adults.

9. Young children are often afraid of getting a stepmother because of the fairy tales they have heard or read. Matu is a new word that should not frighten children. This should make it easier for a man to tell his children that he is planning to remarry. Stepmothers are in fairy tales, but *a matu is a child's father's wife.*

10. Centuries of negative stereotyping make it extremely difficult to change the image of a stepmother into a positive one; stepfathers have not been as maligned. With images of stepmothers as loathsome, abusive creatures, how can we remake them into warm, loving caregivers?

By keeping stepmothers as mythological characters who appear only in fairy tales, we can supply a female character who can bear the "bad mother" label without destroying real lives. The "wicked stepmother" must be confined to the realm of make-believe. Once freed of the myth of the wicked stepmother, the living, breathing matu could go about her business of being a wife to her husband, a mother to her children, and a good matu to her stepchildren. If successful, everyone in the combined family would have a better chance of living "happily ever after."

WHAT IS IN A NAME?

If we do not give stepmothers and stepfathers names, we cannot give them identities. Until we do find names that accurately depict how people in combined families relate to one another, we are going to be stuck with stepmothers in mothering roles, stepfathers in fathering roles, and stepchildren in roles as children to their stepparents. Currently this is what we have, and it simply does not work.

Combined families are likely to be in the majority in the United States by the year 2000. The time is right for combined family members to come out into the open and identify themselves. It is time to eliminate the need to try to pass as a nuclear family. Having a legitimate place of his or her own in society will eliminate the embarrassment caused now when a stepparent has to admit, "Well, Joe (Joan) is not really my child; he (she) is my husband's (or wife's) child."

For people who are nonparents (stepparents), the benefit of having names of their own, clearly identifying their roles and relationships, is the freedom to establish open and honest relationships with their nonchildren (stepchildren). These relationships are not givens; they have to be developed over time. First people have to know who and what they are to one another; only then can they make rational decisions about what they want their future relationships to be.

TWELVE

The Children

"Sometimes I feel like a thumb," sobbed 15-year-old Allison to her father, stepmother, and family counselor. Her father insisted that Allison was an integral part of their new family, but Allison said she had lost her place once her stepmother had children of her own. Through Allison's eyes, the children of her stepmother and father's union were clearly favored over her.

Sorrowfully, Allison described how she interpreted the relationship between the couple and their two children. "The four of them are like fingers; they match and belong together. But I feel like a thumb. I have a place in the family only when the fingers need something."

Allison felt she may have been an integral part of the new family initially, but that the birth of children to her stepmother had radically changed her status. Allison's position had dropped from that of an "insider" to that of an "intimate outsider." This notion at times was simply too much for her to handle.

While each chapter in this book is devoted to a particular aspect of combined family life, there is one central thread that runs its course throughout: What about the children?

LOOK WHO'S TALKING

Let us imagine that we are among the children who have just been told of our parent's plans to remarry. Each of us is going to become a stepchild! Becoming a stepchild means we will be abused, rejected, neglected, or somehow suffer the ill fate of others who have gone before us in fairy tales such as "Hansel and Gretel," "Snow White," or "Cinderella." In thinking about what it is going to be like to become a stepchild, we wonder, What is going to happen to me?

These seven words bring home the essence of our fears about remarriage. We, as children of a remarrying parent, are desperate to know what is going to happen to us—our customs, traditions, values, and feelings. We need to know that those things that are familiar, comforting, and secure will survive our parent's remarriage. Parents need to address our concerns fully—we fear facing the unknown alone.

Frightened, we wonder what it will be like to have a relative stranger living with us: a stranger who will become our stepparent. What happens if I hate this person? Will my relationship with my stepparent affect my relationship with my mom or dad? If my stepparent dislikes me, can he or she change my mom's or dad's feelings toward me?

While we are wondering about the stepparent's influence on our parent, we also might have some questions about other ways our parent's attitude and behavior might change toward us. Will I be important to my parent in the same ways I was important in my nuclear and one-parent families, or will all that change? Have I outlived my usefulness to my parent now that she or he has found another person to protect and care for her or him. Will my mom or dad still love me, or will this stepparent take the love that used to be mine? These questions and others run through a child's head when told of remarriage—and it's very scary.

NO PLACE LIKE HOME

If both parents remarry, children can truly begin to wonder how their lives can ever work out right. The original family of which they were a part no longer exists in anything but their memories.

Children who are about to enter a combined family have many

concerns. Young children worry about being abandoned, while adolescents wonder about fitting into a new family structure just as they are getting ready to strike out on their own. Foremost in the mind of each child whose parent is about to remarry remains the question, What's going to happen to me?

Children who become part of a combined family have undergone a great deal in the way of loss and change. They have a right to wonder about what is going to happen to them. They have lost their original family, and they have experienced either the partial or total loss of a parent. Children must resolve these losses, whether they have been sustained because of a parent's death or their parents' separation and divorce.

Resolving losses can be trying for children since divorced parents commonly do not recognize their children's losses.[1] The difficulties parents have in recognizing their children's losses may be caused by their own guilt about having found happiness in their new marriages. Sometimes it is easier for divorced parents to deny their children's unhappiness rather than recognize that, while divorce may have been good for them, it has not necessarily been good for their children.[2]

RECREATING THE NUCLEAR FAMILY

Many single parents considering remarriage believe that all they need to recreate their children's old families is to find new mates in new marriages. Combined families will replace children's original families, and everyone will be back at "square one,"[3] only this time the whole thing will be done right! This mistaken belief is based on myths that lure parents into thinking that they can recreate the nuclear family by replacing the children's missing parents with stepparents and the children's original families with combined families.

Recreating the nuclear family is a comforting but misleading notion. Parents would love the chance to undo the hurt their children have suffered due to the rupture of their former marriages. Going back to the nuclear family would provide relief for their children's pain, as well as their own. For these parents, remarriage represents a second chance: to find happiness and to recreate their children's original families. Children, however, view this notion differently.

The idea of recreating the nuclear family by adding a step-parent and combining families is *not* what most children desire. Most children want the real thing: their moms and dads back together again. If children have not resolved the partial or total loss of their parents, or their original families, they do not think of remarriage as a blessing—they think of it as a betrayal of both their outside biological parents, and themselves. If remarried parents can so easily replace outside biological parents with stepparents, it might seem to children that they could be replaced just as easily. Otherwise, they figure, things would be left as they were—parents and their children living in one-parent families.

Adopted children, children from unwed mothers, and children who have lost a parent face developmental issues as well. These pertain to their having been given up for adoption by their biological parents, or revolve around their fantasies of their long-lost, or unknown fathers. For these children, losses are compounded by a marital split or the death of a person in a parenting role. A divorce only serves to further complicate the issues.

THE ADDED PSYCHOLOGICAL TASKS OF CHILDREN OF DIVORCE

Children of divorce have to master several preliminary life tasks before they can achieve realistic expectations regarding relationships. In fact, these children may have an *additional* developmental sequence to complete before they can move on to build healthy and solid relationships within the structure of the combined family.[4] Judith Wallerstein suggested that children of divorce need to complete "six coping tasks," in "addition to the usual tasks of growing up."[5] Later, with Sandra Blakeslee, Ms. Wallerstein added a seventh coping task: Taking a chance on love.[6] These preliminary tasks must be fulfilled before children can achieve a sense of closure regarding their former family systems. Without closure children may be unable to face the challenges of their future family systems.

The Tasks

Task I: Acknowledging the reality of the marital rupture.

Task II: Disengaging from parental conflict and distress and resuming customary pursuits.

Task III: Resolution of loss.

Task IV: Resolving anger and self-blame.

Task V: Accepting the permanence of divorce.

Task VI: Achieving realistic hope regarding relationships.[7]

"Understanding the Divorce."[8] At the time of their parents' separation, children need a realistic understanding of what their parents' marital rupture means to their family. They need a clear understanding of what the consequences of their parents' divorce are likely to be. The fears, fantasies, and feelings that children have about divorce and what it will mean to them must be discussed repeatedly to bring them more in line with reality. Doing so will help the children adjust to the actual sequence of events that normally occur.

At a later developmental stage, older adolescents and young adults will be able to look back upon their parents' marital dissolution with more perspective and broader understanding. Then they will have the opportunity to draw more meaningful conclusions about their parents' actions, as well as valuable lessons they themselves can use.[9]

"Strategic Withdrawal."[10] Children need to disengage from parental conflict and distress and resume their customary pursuits as soon as possible.[11] Children and adolescents can be concerned over what is going on within their own families. However, focusing all their concern and care on the well-being of the others in the family sacrifices their own developmental progress, which involves keeping up with their own age-appropriate interests and activities. Put plainly, children must be encouraged by their parents "to remain children."[12]

"Dealing with Loss."[13] Children whose parents have divorced experience not only the end of their intact families, but the loss of

one of their parents, usually their fathers, from their daily lives. "The task of absorbing loss is perhaps the single most difficult task imposed by divorce. [In coping with] . . . the profound sense of rejection, humiliation, unlovability, and powerlessness they feel . . . [with the departure of a parent] . . . children of all ages blame themselves."[14] In blaming themselves for their parents' departures, children conclude that it was some personal failure on their part that caused their parents to leave. In this way, the loss of their parents and their own lowered self-esteem "become intertwined."[15]

In an effort to escape the rejection of having one of their parents leave, children of all ages attempt to "undo the divorce scenario, to bring their parents back together, or to somehow win back the affection of the absent parent."[16] When children come to grips with the finality of the situation, some may use their good relationships with nonresidential parents to grow, while others may decide their nonresidential parents are not good parents for them or good role models for their own future lives. Whatever the path children choose, their task is to "effectively master the loss and get on with their lives."[17]

"Dealing with Anger."[18] Children of parents who divorce can become overwhelmed with anger at their parents' inability to hold their marriages together, particularly if one of the parents has divorced before. Children know divorce is a voluntary decision by at least one parent. Knowing this, children may reason that parents who have failed at marriage may fail them as well. The dilemma that faces these children is that the very persons causing them such distress are charged with the responsibility of protecting and caring for them.[19] Children need to work through their anger with their parents and, ultimately, come to see their mothers and fathers for what they are—human beings who have made mistakes.

If not expressed and dealt with, children's anger can cripple remarriages. Fearful of endangering their alliances with their parents, children often suppress their anger or project it onto their stepparents. Unchecked, such emotions can fuel the fires of combined family conflict.

As children grow to maturity, the tasks of permitting their anger to diminish and forgiving their parents go hand in hand.

When children do accomplish these ends, the relief they experience normally allows them "to put the divorce behind them."[20] In forgiving their parents, children let go of the angry and guilty feelings left over from their inability to reverse their parents' decisions and make their old families whole again. This process allows children the freedom not to identify with either an aggressive parent or the role of the victim.[21]

"*Working Out Guilt.*"[22] Often, children feel guilty over the roles they think they have played in their parents' divorces. Some children, especially young ones, wish they could get rid of one parent so they can have the other one all to themselves. If the parents of these children subsequently divorce, these children can be left feeling guilty. Their guilt comes from the belief that they willed their parents into divorce. Other children may feel guilty because their births have driven wedges between their parents—sometimes this is even true. Whatever the ties of guilt that bind children to parents, it is important that they let go of them, with love and compassion, and get on with their own lives.[23]

"*Accepting the Permanence of the Divorce.*"[24] Children use denial to blunt the reality of their parents' divorce. To cope with this brutal reality, children confront their emotions a little at a time. Years later, many children still refuse to accept the permanence of their parents' divorce, still looking for signs that the process may yet be reversed.

Wallerstein and Blakeslee view facing a divorce as more difficult than facing the death of a parent. Divorce is a matter of choice; death is not. Therefore, it is possible for children to retain fantasies that their parents will reunite up until the time they themselves are able to separate and leave home.[25]

"*Taking a Chance on Love.*"[26] Despite all they have lived through, and the worries and fears that remain, "children of divorce must grow, become open to the possibility of success or failure, and take a chance on love."[27] This may not be easy for them, just as it is not easy for children who have lost parents to death. As all of us ultimately come to know, life does not last forever, and circumstances beyond our control can change our lives at any moment. Children of divorce must ultimately "take a chance on love, knowing realistically that divorce is always possible," yet be willing to make the commitment to love, "marriage, and fidelity."[28] For children of divorce, this idea of love and commitment involves turning away from the models their parents have given them and risking their futures on less familiar models that reflect their own personal beliefs. As they work through adolescence, this last step, "taking a chance on love," ultimately builds on the successful resolution of all the tasks that have preceded it. The reward: "psychological freedom from the past."[29]

Parents Reactions

When children hurt, parents hurt. When children suffer from the loss of their intact families, parents suffer right along with them. Parents may want to know how they can absorb their children's anguish and erase the hurt, but the answer is that they can do neither. The children must do their own mourning; parents cannot do it for them. Parents overwhelmed by the need to do something—anything—can only stand by, vigilant, ready to provide moral support and comfort when their children need it. Parents must be willing to let children work things out by themselves, or with professional guidance, if necessary. Parents foster their children's recovery by providing an environment that is as stable and free from stress as possible.

Providing a positive environment can start with parents comforting their children by assuring and reassuring them that the divorce was not their fault. Children need to know that even though their parents no longer love each other, their love for their children continues undiminished. Remarrying parents also can help by simply providing their children with sufficient time, space, and encouragement to mourn and recover.

How Parents Can Hurt. It is in the nature of children to remain loyal to both parents, and be unable to choose between them. Many children have not only witnessed battles between their parents but they have been pressed into service as couriers across enemy lines. Children caught in this kind of warfare are not free to grow up. Too often children are used not only as pawns in their parents' conflicts, but as spies, scapegoats, messengers, informers, co-conspirators, and so forth. While parents may use the children to hurt one another, the hurt they can cause their children by this is far worse.

The finalizing of a divorce does not necessarily signal the end of hostilities between warring biological parents. Therefore, if harmonious relationships with former spouses cannot be achieved, parents need to create boundaries around their relationships to protect the children from their bitterness. They must take their children out of the crossfire on the post-marital battlefield.

How Parents Can Help. This battlefield is mined with many potential conflicts, and children should not be made witnesses to or participants in any of them. Besides biological parental conflicts, children should be isolated from disagreements between

1. Their outside parents and their stepparents;
2. Their remarried parents and their outside parents;
3. New spouses of their outside parents regarding the children who live in both households;
4. The *parents* of outside parents, remarried parents, and stepparents concerning their grandchildren/stepgrandchildren; and
5. Any set of grandparents, the adult couple, or outside parents concerning any issue that involves the children.

Children's Reactions

To children, entering a combined family may feel like just another loss in a string of losses over which they have no control. Whether or not children want to become members of combined families, they automatically do so when one or both of their parents remarry. Children do not ask for their parents' marriages to end, nor do they ask for stepparents to intrude on their relationships with their single parents.

When one looks at children's issues such as "the three L's—

Loss, Loyalty, and Lack of control,"[30] it is much easier to empathize with their positions. Children are asked to adjust to loss, such as the loss of their original families, and to adjust to loyalty conflicts, within themselves, between their original parents, or between their stepparents and outside parents, etc.; and all the while, they lack the power to control what happens to them.

When marriages end, children need time to adjust, but they are not usually allowed this adjustment period. Therefore, *children's dilemmas* and their parents' responses to their predicaments often differ.

1. *The children now live in two households;* Children are so adaptable, they will learn to adjust.
2. *The children have to change locations, attend new schools, and make new friends;* Children make friends easily, and they will quickly adjust to living in two different environments.
3. *Children's biological parents fight, and the children feel pulled to pieces;* Children will have to learn not to take sides in conflicts between their parents.
4. *One parent remarries, and the other one stays single;* Children will learn to adjust to living in two different family structures with differing rules and regulations.
5. *Parents fight each other in court for changes in the children's primary residence;* Whatever the outcome, the children will be expected to adapt.
6. *Children have to share their remarried parents with stepparents;* They will learn to love their new stepparents.
7. *Children have to share space with stepsiblings;* They will learn to adjust and enjoy their new brothers and sisters.
8. *Children need time alone with their parents;* They will adjust to the fact that now there are more demands on their parents' time.
9. *Children have to wait in line to gain access to their remarried parents;* They will learn to accept and appreciate quality (less?) time with their parents.
10. *Children's parents leave their stepparents in charge;* Children have to get used to accepting their stepparents' authority over them.

11. *Children object;* They are being bad, unruly, and unsympathetic to all their remarried parents and stepparents have been trying to do for them.

One can only wonder how children survive, let alone adapt to all these changes. Parents and stepparents alike have to develop an appreciation for the changes children are expected to make. When one considers all of the shifts children are required to make in the process of going from their original families to combined families, it is easy to see the amount of loss and change they experience. Everyone needs time to mourn losses, and, for the most part, the reality for children is that they have not had time to mourn their losses, adapt to the changes that have taken place in their lives, or adjust to the fact that their parents have brought "strangers" to live with them. When "strangers" occupy roles in combined families that were formerly held by these children's outside parents in their original families, is it any wonder that children react? If they did not, there *would* be something wrong with them.

The mere presence of stepparents in their lives signifies loss and change to children: they are no longer the sole recipients of their parents' love. Their parents have made room in their lives for significant others. Thus, even though it is imperative for the existence of combined families that couples form primary bonds, the very act of their parents' adding new spouses to their old one-parent families can be perceived as disloyalty, or even abandonment, by remarried parents' children.

CHILDREN IN THE MIDDLE

When children are "caught in the middle," they may "act out" (become aggressive or disruptive), or "act in" (become withdrawn or depressed) in their efforts to cope with their feelings of helplessness. They can become paralyzed and unable to act, or they can take advantage of being intermediaries and pit one parent against the other in an attempt to gain control over their feelings of helplessness. Children can become more dependent, to allay their fears of abandonment, or they can manipulate their parents into continuing their conflicts, thereby prolonging their parents' involvement with each other. They deal with their divided loyalties in a variety of ways.

Children who avoid the realities of their home life may pursue behaviors leading to problems in school, loss of friends, etc. Their difficulties in school or in their social adjustments may cause radical changes. If not properly addressed, these difficulties can turn into delinquent behavior, drug use, or the onset of psychosomatic[31] complaints or illness. How children relate to their parents' behavior toward them, or each other, is largely dependent on how emotionally healthy or vulnerable they are.

Without adults' guidance toward open emotional expression of feelings, children will likely choose whatever course of action seems appropriate to them at the time, regardless of whether their choices are good or bad.

PARENTS AND CHILDREN FROM ONE-PARENT HOUSEHOLDS

Parents and children who reside together in one-parent families usually form tightly knit groups, with close ties and solid boundaries to protect them from outside interference. Due to mutual dependencies between single parents and their children, one-parent households seem to foster greater equality between family members.[32]

When residential parents find "strangers" to replace children's outside parents, children may consider these new additions as threats to their own personal well-being. Children can only wonder why parents, the very people who profess to love them, would choose to make them stepchildren by adding stepparents to their lives.

When single parents leave the closeness they have developed with their children to meet their own personal needs—needs most children do not comprehend—how are children to interpret their actions? It is unreasonable to expect children to understand what lures unmarried parents from the unity of their one-parent families to seek the addition of new marital partners. Parents cannot explain the urgency of their unmet physical and emotional needs to their children.

On the other hand, how are the children to have their own needs met in the face of their parents' mad grabs at personal happiness? Children who have not completed mourning the loss of their original families are now being asked to give up their remaining parents. Children's greatest fears center around the loss of these incredibly significant adults. And now they must trust some stranger to protect them after their own two parents could not protect them from the pain of separation, divorce, or death!

WHERE THE POWER LIES

Power and control are more often at issue between adults and children in combined families than in nuclear families. In large part, this struggle is nourished by children's desire to retain the power they had in their old one-parent families. Typically the additional power children have in one-parent families is the result of their partial assumption of the role of their missing parent. When stepparents come on the scene, a power struggle frequently develops as these "parental" children try to retain the power they were awarded in their one-parent families. In the end, children in combined families are generally more powerful than children in nuclear families. Once children have been awarded extra power and privileges, they will not return them without a fight.

Children want power to exclude stepparents and maintain their intimate one-parent family relationships. Additionally, some children want to keep or build upon the power bases they established as parental children within their old one-parent families. Even young children know enough to realize that when their parents remarry, there will be another series of changes to endure. Children figure they have a better chance of enduring these changes *with* power than without it.

Children may employ several tactics to seize the reigns of control, but often the basic strategy is elegantly simple: divide and conquer. In this way, children can capitalize on the unusually close ties that have developed between them and their single parents and "close ranks," effectively shutting out any prospective or new stepparents. An element of the strategy involves children keeping their parents involved with them, making sure that couples have no time to strengthen their alliances with one another. Children almost instinctively sense that interference in a couple's opportunity to bond may be all that is needed to keep a stranger at bay.

The divide and conquer strategy is not limited to potential stepparents though. For example, children frequently try to get their way with one biological parent by boasting of how well their other biological parent treats them. Claims of differing treatment are just one technique that children can exploit with some effort. There are easier targets. Perhaps the easiest of all are parents who fail to make joint decisions, or parents and stepparents who fail to act in unison because confusion is already present.

Oftentimes, children can be unmerciful as they vie for power. The most sensitive issues are not beyond exploitation, including the tender insecurities of noncustodial parents. Noncustodial parents are particularly vulnerable because they already have fears relating to their relationships with their children (e.g., fear of losing visitation rights), making manipulation that much easier.

Children manipulate their parents, reasoning that if they cannot control their environment, they will seek to control those who do. Through manipulation, children can keep their parents off-balance and their stepparents disadvantaged. They may even succeed in gaining more power than one or more of the adults.

> Doug and his new wife, Tammy, had custody of Doug's son and daughter from Thursday after school until Monday morning. Tammy's two sons and daughter lived with them full-time, except every other weekend when they went to their dad's house.
>
> After Doug and Tammy were married, trouble broke out among the children almost immediately. There was fighting over sharing rooms, games, and the television set, as well as over who was to do what chores. Eventually Tammy and Doug got caught up in their children's bickering. Nothing made sense anymore.
>
> One thing was obvious to Tammy: her children hated it when Doug's children came to stay with them. Doug ignored her children, and his children were trying everything in their power to get their dad to give up his remarriage.

Doug reminded Tammy that getting joint custody of his children had been extremely difficult. He was convinced that he would lose custody unless he went out of his way to please his kids. As far as Doug was concerned, Tammy's children would just have to adjust.

Doug and Tammy were at an impasse. All they could agree on was that it was time to get a counselor. The counseling led to the creation of, and adherence to, a carefully considered regimen of rules and regulations governing the entire household. Only then did Tammy and Doug regain the power to control themselves and their children.

Gaining power over adults is not healthy for the development of children. When the balance between parents and their children is upset, with children gaining inordinate amounts of power over their parents, who remains to parent the children? It is imperative for parents to maintain their rightful authority. For example, children have to accept their parents' decisions to remarry. Parental decisions that have such profound effects on children's lives may cause heightened feelings of helplessness in the children. Yet, it is the right of adults to make such decisions; it is not up to the children to dictate what their parents can and cannot do.

Of course, the power to influence children does not mean parents shouldn't consider and respond to their children's concerns. Concerns ranging from impending remarriages to fears of imminent lifestyle changes should be addressed in an appropriate fashion. Otherwise, remarrying parents are likely to find that their children's concerns will be voiced, or acted out, after their combined families are formed.

WHAT CHILDREN STAND TO LOSE

Children stand to lose their remarrying parents as they have come to know them, as heads of one-parent families. Children accompanying their remarried parents into combined families can lose both the close ties developed with their parents and their former roles in their one-parent families.

Frequently, children in one-parent households have been

lifted out of the position of "child" and pressed into service as mom's or dad's "confidant" or "special helper." These children become the ones on whom their parent relies. When new stepparents appear on the scene, these children, who have been elevated out of their positions as children and made almost coequal to their parent, are then expected to go back to being children. Seldom is any consideration given by parents, or their new marital partners, to their loss of status, or to the idea that they may no longer feel like children.

> Danny, now 11, had been the "man in the family" since his father left when he was 7. He had taken on all the "manly" tasks assigned to him by his mother since then, and he considered himself her protector. The arrangement worked very well until his mom met Ed. To Danny's astonishment, his mom started turning to Ed whenever she needed "manly" things done around the house. His mom started telling Danny not to act so grown-up and to go play when he tried to resume some of his old roles in the house. Danny was feeling displaced. Not only wasn't he the man of the house; he wasn't a child either. Confused, he then wondered if he belonged any place at all!

The Tension of Change

Tight parent–child bonds can prevent stepparents from forming solid relationships with remarried parents. If a functional combined family is to result, these bonds must be loosened. There must be some relaxation of the parent–child bond to permit entry of the stepparent. To achieve this, parental children must be returned to their age-appropriate positions in the family. But when they are removed from their previously privileged positions, they may become ostracized by siblings who have been jealous of them in their one-parent families. Siblings also may be joined by stepsiblings in picking on these displaced, demoted children. Demotion, resulting from the addition of stepparents, usually causes "resentment against stepparent and stepsiblings alike for such a loss of status."[33]

When both adults bring their children with them into their new family units, children's fears of being replaced or becoming unimportant can escalate. Invariably they will have questions, whether voiced or not. Will stepsiblings be competitors or will they become friends? Will they add resources, or will they take them away? Resources include *space* (my room, or my house), *possessions* (that are, or should be, mine), *money* (that would otherwise have been spent on me or my family), *time* (that my parent would have spent with me), and *attention* (that my parent would have paid to me).

Living with stepsiblings entails sharing more than just resources. Because there is no biological relationship between stepsiblings, it is possible for them to share the same given name, or be of the same age. Even the birth order may be subject to revision.

> When Jacky married Paul, both adults knew they were in for problems between their children. Each had a son named John, and their daughters were the same age. Jacky's son John was losing his identity as an eldest child, and Paul's daughter, Katie, was losing her favored position as baby. Both became middle children because of their parents' remarriage.
>
> Siblings and stepsiblings alike felt disoriented with the shift from one-parent families to a combined family. Yet it was the parents who went looking for help when it came time to figure out who was to sleep in which of their three bedrooms, and with whom!
>
> Jacky and Paul did not know how to allocate the bedrooms to the children. Should siblings be kept together, or should children be placed together because of their ages? The couple could find no reasonable solution.
>
> When they presented their dilemma to a counselor, Jacky and Paul were asked to bring their children along with them to the office. The children themselves were the ones who ultimately decided how the space available to them was to be allocated. On their own, they also figured out how to differentiate between the two Johns. Working out the solutions to these problems was an important first step in building their combined family history.

Although birth order does not change, the changing of the age order or age interval within the context of the new family may cause children to feel resentment.[34] Harmony is elusive among stepsiblings. Along with what can be defined as traditional sibling rivalry, stepsiblings compete for such things as space, possessions, money, gifts, vacations, time, and attention. This competition is real rather than symbolic, as is frequently true between biological siblings.

Space is at a premium in most combined families containing two sets of children. The territory of one set may be deemed to have been invaded by stepsiblings. Things that were of significance to one group of children before their combined family came into existence may become disputed items of possession between stepsiblings. This gives rise to the issue of what is "fair" between them. There is no easy way to find an agreed-upon definition of what is fair. Due to their different origins, the children's "claims are not seen to have the same legitimacy."[35]

Children frequently view their parents as their personal possessions. Thus, when stepsiblings appear to be winning their parent's affection, children can feel threatened. After all, "blood" is supposed to be "thicker than water," which is why so often blood-based coalitions are the basis for divisions within combined families. Ideally, stepsiblings should form age-based or sex-based groupings, thereby avoiding division into family camps, with one set of siblings against the other.

> When Pamela and Bruce were dating, Pam noticed that Bruce paid a great deal of attention to his children, and very little to hers. She had some concerns that the household would divide into "separate camps" once they were married. Bruce assured Pam that he cared for her children and would give them the same entitlements and privileges as his own in their new family.
>
> Pamela worked very hard to make friends with Bruce's children, and she succeeded in establishing friendly relationships with all of them. Her children, however, felt that she was neglecting them in favor of their stepsiblings. While Pamela had been diligent and successful in her efforts to win over her stepchildren, Bruce neglected Pamela's children completely. He was very critical of them, their behavior, etc., and he kept a watchful eye so that Pamela's children did not get anything at his children's expense.
>
> After a year of marriage, Bruce scolded Pamela for trying to take his children's love away from him. He was mistrustful of her positive relationships with them. Pamela felt Bruce's actions were harming her and her children, and she began to withdraw her

attention from Bruce's children to pay more attention to her own. Her children had felt deprived of her attention throughout her entire marriage to Bruce. They had complained of her lack of loyalty to them, and thought that she favored her stepchildren over them. Nonetheless, they welcomed their mother's return to the fold.

With Pamela and her children closing ranks, and Bruce and his children still within their closed ranks, the household divided into two armed camps. Eventually the split along biological lines led to two one-parent families living in separate households, as the couple divorced.

If blood ties between parents and their children are stronger than couples' bonds to one another, combined families are endangered. However, it is difficult for blood-related parents and children to relinquish their loyalties to one another. This blood-related bias is best combatted by impartial and equitable treatment of stepsiblings by both adults.

This issue of equity carries over to the treatment of stepsiblings by noncustodial parents. When there are large discrepancies in the amounts of "goodies" provided by one outside parent versus the other outside parent, or between grandparents and step-grandparents, jealousies between stepsiblings may grow to be very ugly.

Jealousies are not all one worries about between stepsiblings. Many other issues can arise between unrelated children living under the same roof in combined families. For example: What happens when stepsiblings are sexually attracted to one another, or teen-aged stepchildren are sexually attracted to stepparents who are close in age?

There is no clear-cut incest taboo for adults and children who live under same roof and are not biologically related. This leaves children in combined families at risk. In order for children to properly develop, they must live in an atmosphere "where their immature emotions are respected, and where they are at the same time prepared for both sexual and non-sexual relationships as adults."[36] Margaret Mead tells us that unless sexual intercourse is strictly prohibited, except between marital pairs, there is danger to the children. The danger is that stepsiblings may be tempted beyond their years, which can create a situation that is destructive both for combined family functioning and for the children's development.[37]

When stepsiblings are attracted to one another, they are more likely to fight and pretend indifference than they are to indulge in overt sexual relations.[38] This problem is much more common to teen-agers in newly combined families than it is to children who are raised together from early years; however, this issue presents itself as something for remarrying couples to reckon with in setting up "house rules." When adults are clear on what is and is not permissible between stepsiblings, children are free to set up warm and close ties without the danger of uncontrolled eroticism taking over and disrupting the entire family.

"But It Was a Tradition"

Combining families necessitates combining lifestyles. To children this creates all kinds of personal losses, especially in the area of sometimes sacred traditions. Each former one-parent family had established its own set of customs, attitudes, and beliefs. Changing these to create new combined family traditions can precipitate mourning among all members of newly combined families. They are mourning the loss of a former way of life, one that had given comfort in the past.

> When Abby and Gus were married, they had hoped Christmas celebrations would be a unifying force in their combined family. It had seemed a perfect opportunity because Gus's children lived with them during Christmas and summer vacations only.
>
> When it came time to decorate the Christmas tree, Abby and Gus realized that her children were used to decorating the tree with treasured family ornaments, whereas Gus's children made their decorations out of popcorn, paper, and prizes. They had not planned for the differences in tree-trimming customs and traditions. Their first Christmas together was a disaster.
>
> In an effort not to have a repeat of the tree-trimming fiasco, a family meeting was called. Everyone was asked to contribute ideas as to what could be done to ensure that the sadness that had filled the household during their first Christmas together

would not be repeated. Through great effort and personal sacrifice, original family conventions were forsaken and new ways of combining traditions were found for decorating the tree and celebrating the holiday.

Christmas the following year was a compromise, and a success, but all the members admitted feeling some degree of loss and nostalgia for the missing pieces. Pieces of their old family traditions had to be sacrificed to forge a successful compromise.

What Next?

Besides trying to integrate old traditions while acquiring new ones, children in combined families may experience an even more direct challenge. When couples add children of their own to combined families, the preexisting children's blood ties to their remarried parents are no longer unique or exclusive.

Each child born into a combined family will have the same claim to a remarried parent as the parent's original children have. But possibly more painful yet, the new child has two biological parents in the home, while children who predate the remarriage have only one. Further, the birth of a mutual child to their remarried and stepparents forever connects the original children to their stepparent. Their new half sibling is blood-related to everyone in the combined family.

For children who would like to see their remarried parent's marriage to their stepparent dissolved, this new child's birth confounds their chances of coming away from this remarriage unscathed. If a child chooses to view it as such, this half sibling's birth may seem like the remarried parent's ultimate inconstancy toward his or her old children.

WHAT CHILDREN STAND TO GAIN

To children who wish to live in a bona fide family unit, the birth of a mutual child may come to symbolize the "rebirth" of hope that they will again live in a "real family."[39] This baby is their blood relative, and together they make a real family.

Since a mutual child is perceived as living proof of the adults' commitment to one another, this baby's birth may be hailed as a bond that will hold this new family together forever. This expectation of combined family members puts the mutual child in a unique and often overly responsible position. The new child "carries the hopes of this new family on his or her little shoulders."[40]

For children who seek "legitimate ties," the mutual child gives life and meaning to the combined family. However, for some children, just living in a two-parent household represents a gain. Consider those who have lost a parent early and may not remember their two-parent family, or those with mothers who did not marry their fathers. The idea of having a second adult around to help out is appealing to many. To these children the thinking can be as simple as, Other kids live in a two-parent family, why can't I?

Children need not come from a home where two parents were a rarity to feel a sense of gain when another adult is added. Children left without a support system after their parents' marriage ended may want more people to turn to for support, comfort, and understanding. After losing parental role models, children may then seek new role models or objects of identification in the form of stepparents. Fairy tales never mention the children who want or need stepparents to be "in their corner" or "on their side." For these children, remarrying parents' announcements of forthcoming marriages may signal an answer to their prayers. In their minds, these children may see the arrival of an ally, not an ogre.

When stepparents actually arrive on the scene, they are sometimes accompanied by others: their own children. Even when stepparents enter combined families alone, these new adults also have family. Stepparents' extended families may become yet another source for knowledge development, role identification, support, and understanding for remarried parents' children. These new people expand children's relationship networks, as do stepsiblings, who may or may not accompany stepparents into combined families.

Steprelatives can be very important in stepchildren's lives. For example: When stepsiblings are close in age, they can provide much in the way of mutual support and understanding for one another. When stepsiblings are of the same sex, exchanging information on sex-related issues can be tremendously informative. Children in stepsibling groups often provide more support for one another than do biological siblings. Biological siblings normally cannot fill the same roles, due to differences in their birth intervals or their gender.

Growing up in unrelated families often provides stepsiblings with a greater pool of information than they might have had in their families of origin. There are also more role models available for them to identify with; they can decide for themselves who they do or do not want to pattern themselves after.

Living in combined families often challenges individuals to grow and change. To children whose parents are deceased, growing up in a happy combined family can clearly demonstrate that life is worth living, even after the death of a loved one. For children whose parents have been divorced, or who have always lived in a one-parent household, witnessing a happy marriage can provide a model on which to base their own future relationships.

WHEN CHILDREN LIVE IN TWO HOUSEHOLDS

Combined family events are only part of what goes on in the lives of children who live in two households. When children live in two households, they are required to make physical and psychological adjustments in going back and forth between the two residences in which they live. While one household holds a combined family, the other might contain a one-parent family, another combined family, or it might well be the household of relatives or "others."

Transactional Anxiety

Children's shifts between residences produce emotional drains on them, on those who must let them go, and on those who wait to receive them. Adults should plan and anticipate that children going back and forth between two households will experience what can be called *transactional anxiety* any time they have to make one of these transfers. The transaction is the changing of households; the anxiety is a normal part of going from the known to the unknown.

Imagine how it would feel to be lifted (sometimes against your will) out of one ongoing household routine, only to be transported and plunked down in the midst of another ongoing household routine. How do you think you would feel being required to make this shift? How do you think you might feel having to make the shift once or twice a week, a month, a year? Do you think normal people might experience some anxiety in readying themselves to make this kind of shift, however often it would be necessary to do so? Further, wouldn't it make sense that everyone in each of those two households would also be experiencing some form of anxiety about the shift?

Even if children were just living in their Mom's household earlier in the week, emotional energy is used to anticipate what will be needed in the way of clothing, supplies, etc., at Dad's household—all of which must be brought from Mom's place. Parents and children alike can get caught up in these activities.

Shifting also means catching up on what has been going on in the household the children are going to next, just as they must leave behind whatever has been going on in the household they are leaving. The adults also have to adjust to the comings and goings of the children, stretching or shrinking their individual family boundaries to include or let go of the children who live there some of the time!

However often children make the journey, one can expect certain behavioral changes before they make a shift between households. Generally, children tend to become a bit edgier and a little more agitated or withdrawn than they were before they started thinking about making a residential shift. They also may be "off the wall" as the time nears for them to change households. It can take a good deal of "settling in" time for them to prepare for saying their good-byes to one household, before saying their hellos to the next!

If things are not "bad" in either household, what causes children to be anxious about their moves? Children who live in two households are expected to handle whatever differences exist between the two households in which they live. Although the differences may not be great, there are bound to be two sets of rules and regulations, specific ways of doing things, and unique expectations of how the children should think, feel, and act, etc. Differences come from the fact that different people live in each of the two households. There may even be varying numbers of people in each household each time the children live there.

It can take quite some time for children to learn each family's routine and remember it for the next time they live there. Once children get one household routine down pat, they may be uprooted and transplanted to the other household in which they live.

Although some children's biological parents may try to match one another's values and standards of behavior for the children, others may throw out old values and adopt new ones. Children who come into these households expecting familiarity often experience culture shock as they are greeted with a set of rules and regulations that they have never before encountered. Sometimes they encounter a value system that is far different from that to which they were previously accustomed. It is not easy for the children; they have to adapt continuously to these new standards of behavior and ways of life. Then they have to remember which behavior fits what standard, and where. In the midst of all this change, they have to mourn the loss of their original family—the one in which both parents lived—in which there was only one set of rules.

If children live in two households, they need to feel they are part of both. They need to have a place of their own in each household, even if it is in a corner of a room. They also need an exclusive space in which to store their possessions, even if it is simply a drawer in a dresser. No matter which parent they are with, children need to locate themselves in space and time in the household of each parent. Parents also must allow their children to be free to make their transitions, change their mindsets, and live their own lives in peace.

Cross-Household Rivalries

Children can feel torn to pieces by being made messengers, spies, co-conspirators, etc., between the two households in which they live. They cannot be expected to tell Mom what happened at

Dad's house, or vice versa. For children to be realistic in their expectations regarding relationships and for them to develop meaningful ties in each family unit, they must be kept out of their parents' cross-household rivalries.

It is difficult for parents who are emotionally "stuck" in their past relationships to allow their children the freedom to grow and develop, yet it is imperative for children to have this freedom. These children must be allowed sufficient privacy to think their own thoughts, feel their own feelings, and learn to deal with what is going on in their own lives. Children's rights extend across household boundaries.

Pertinent information as to hours of departures and arrivals, travel times between locations, and clothing or supplies necessary are the kinds of information parents need to share. What a step-mother makes for dinner, or what Mom is doing with the money Dad gives her is not subject to discussion between households. Unless there is suspected physical, psychological, or sexual abuse, neither parent has to give the other a report about what is going on in the other household.

Children must have freedom to work out their own relation-ships with each parent, stepparent, stepsibling, and half sibling, as long as these others are involved in their lives. Children have a right to live in peace and harmony wherever they live. Gaining control of their lives, regardless of which household they are in, is essential for children's well-being during this very challenging phase of their development.

Children are resourceful and adaptable; however, they need all the help they can get in learning to adjust to living in two households, or in just one combined family. Help does not mean interference by one parent in the internal functioning of the house-hold of the other parent. The help children need comes in the form of household rules and regulations and parental guidelines for behavior and functioning. Certainly love, caring, nurturing, and understanding are welcome in large portions. With all of this, chil-dren have a great deal to gain, and so does everyone else that participates in making their lives worthwhile.

In accepting the 1988 Academy Award for Best Actor, Michael Douglas thanked both his mother and his stepfather, his father

Kirk Douglas, and his stepmother for all they had done for him in helping him attain this high achievement. In his own words, he thanked all four adults for helping him to grow up successfully!

THE DEVELOPMENT OF CHILDREN

As hard as it is for children to undergo all the changes that take place as they go from nuclear family to one-parent household to combined family, it can become more difficult. At some point they have to realize that their parents, or stepparents, may disappoint them! Sometimes, parents are not all their children hoped they would be. If adults let them down, children must learn to cope with, adapt to, or simply make do in situations they are unable to change.[41] Children cannot take responsibility for their parents' behavior; they can only take responsibility for their own.

Taking responsibility begins with accepting that life within the combined family is different. This new family is not as snug or invulnerable to outside interference as an intact nuclear family might be, but there are still many advantages. Children are able to see that there are many ways to look at life, and there is more than just one way of doing things. Knowledge of these different ways comes from living in new family structures with new people. Children gain flexibility by learning to deal with the differences between themselves and those others with whom they live. Accepting their living situations and looking for alternative solutions to problems they encounter between combined family members can provide good training for children. Reality-testing and decision-making processes are likely to be enhanced in such environments. However, what these children may ultimately learn best is how to use the positive power of negotiation to get what they want out of life, while developing strategies for handling disappointments.

Seeing their parents strive for, and achieve, new and positive goals in their remarried lives is important. It represents hope for children that they too will be able to achieve growth and personal change as they mature. If their parents have been able to live more fulfilling lives because of the changes they have made, children see positive models of behavior with which they can identify and which they can adopt if they so choose.

There *are* choices, and children learn this lesson well in a combined family. This realization can lead children to attain greater autonomy and establish stronger personal identities[42] as they discover that the agents for change can be themselves.

Moving On

When adults and children alike are able to get on with their lives, they will find that combined family life can be challenging, diversified, and enriching. When children grow and prosper because of the new and exciting dimensions added to their lives, parents will find that they are able to let go of their guilt. The end of a marriage does not spell the end to the lives of the children born into it—far from it. It merely spells another beginning of another chapter!

THIRTEEN

Stepparents, Stepchildren, and Remarried Parents

Over the course of Claire and Brian's four-year courtship, Claire had developed a "testy" relationship with Brian's teen-aged daughter, Sheila, and what she believed to be "a marvelous relationship" with his 10- and 12-year-old children, Gere and Nicole. Once Brian and Claire decided to marry, however, each of them faced new concerns.

Brian worried that, even though Claire assured him that she was comfortable with the idea of not adding biological children to their union, the issue would resurface once the couple was married. Brian was 17 years Claire's senior, and he hated cheating his soon-to-be wife out of the fulfillment he believed she would derive from having children of her own. However, with children from two marriages already, Brian was firm in his conviction that he would father no more children.

Claire had come to terms with not having children. She focused instead on her relationships with Brian's children. Could her relationship with Brian's younger children continue to be as positive once Brian's second wife, Renee, learned that Brian was going to marry again and that Claire was going to be her children's stepmother? Would Renee attempt to undermine Claire's relationship with Gere and Nicole, and if she did, would she succeed? Claire was also concerned that her difficult relationship with Sheila might color Gere's and Nicole's attitudes toward her once they all were members of the same family.

Earlier chapters on "The Remarried Parent," "The Stepparent," "Stepmothers and Stepfathers," and "The Children" gave detailed descriptions of combined family members. What has not been detailed in preceding chapters are the many different levels on which combined family members must relate to one another. Historically, the interconnections between stepparents, stepchildren, and remarried parents have been notoriously ambiguous, and they are not much clearer in modern-day combined family life. This chapter attempts to clarify some of the murkier aspects of combined family relationships.

To help you gain perspective on these relationships, eight captions follow. If you are already a member of a combined family, this list should be familiar. These captions represent just a few of the issues that confront stepparents, stepchildren, and remarried parents.

- Unrealistic Expectations
- Life Cycle Differences
- Failures in Role Complementarity
- Divided Loyalties
- Insiders and Outsiders
- Power . . . Conflict
- Boundary Problems
- Closeness and Distance[1]

Combined family troubles begin with the lack of clarity and definition in family members' roles. Without the needed societal support, many combined families become unstable—some quake and fall. Each time a combined family falls, the pervasive myth that combined families are somehow less than equal to "real" families is furthered. The myth is a distortion of a sobering reality: combined family members' roles *do not* complement one another; in truth, they are inherently different. Combined family failure is not a foregone conclusion, but to prosper, family members must work diligently to cope with the ill-defined roles and stereotypes that comprise their legacy.

UNREALISTIC EXPECTATIONS

Adults and children come to combined families with expectations developed from their previous family life experiences. Essentially, what they expect is what they have known before. These expectations may have been appropriate for their previous families, but they may be totally inappropriate for their new ones. In the face of discrepancies between what individuals expect and the realities they encounter, disappointment appears inevitable. Few are prepared for the realities of combined family life.

Remarried parents and their children usually have lived together before entering combined families. They are familiar with one another's routines and unique ways of behaving. In a sense, they have established protocols for living together. Stepparents and stepchildren are not so lucky; not only do they lack protocols for living together, but they also lack credible formulas to help them develop successful patterns of interaction. The difficulties these individuals experience in living with one another are both expectable and predictable.

At first, stepparents and stepchildren are likely to relate to one another as strangers because most have shared very little history prior to becoming members of the same families. Their relationships are new and their experiences in living with one another untested. They start out on "page one" of their combined family history and go forward from there. Stepparents and stepchildren learn of one another from very different vantage points than do parents and their offspring.

Parents and children are conditioned to one another's ways, dating back to the births of the children. They understand one another. Fewer parents and children are likely to misinterpret one another than are stepparents and stepchildren. Remarried parents and their children share values and traditions; each understands the other's perspective. Stepparents and stepchildren do not share the same values, traditions, and beliefs because they do not share a lifelong history. They are missing the common denominator that allows them to make sense of one another. For example: When a child makes a remark that might be offensive, a biological parent looks for meaning in the remark rather than responding instantly with criticism or punishment. Biological parents are likely to attribute wayward remarks or actions to their children's having had a bad day, showing off in front of friends, or coming down with an illness, etc. Parents give this leeway based on their experience and history with their children. Meanwhile, stepparents, who have no previous knowledge of these same children, may respond to the contents of their stepchildren's messages—without ever comprehending their real meaning.

Mixed signals account for a great many of the difficulties experienced by both stepparents and stepchildren. Neither knows what the other means by his or her actions or words; however, each holds the other strictly accountable for anything that is said or done between them.

LIFE CYCLE DIFFERENCES

Stepparents, stepchildren, and remarried parents all come to the combined family with different histories and life experiences, and they arrive at varying stages of their lives. If there is to be harmony, each family member has to adjust for discrepancies in individual, marital, and family life cycles. Life cycles are defined as "predictable developmental stages of American middle-class families in the second half of the twentieth century."[2] These developmental stages vary from family to family depending on the adults' backgrounds, marriage histories, number of children and when they were born, etc.

While one parent and one child in each combined family can be expected to share some individual and family developmental stages, others enter with all the earmarks of their own unique backgrounds and life experiences. However, all of these individuals will need to find ways to reconcile where they are in their own life cycles with where all of the other combined family members happen to be in theirs. Some of these accommodations are easier to make than others.

Some family members may be completely out of sync due to their former family functioning or their differing ages or stages of development. When the gap in stage synchronization is small, adjustments are also small. In cases where there are large gaps in family members' developmental stages, there will need to be many interpersonal adjustments and plenty of time allowed for such. Learning to live together in the face of differing expectations and incongruent life cycle stages becomes a primary task for all combined family members.

FAILURES IN ROLE COMPLEMENTARITY

From the start, remarried parents can give their new spouses precisely the wrong impression of what they are supposed to be doing in their new families. In their haste to make combined families feel like "real" families, some remarried parents insist that stepparents assume their stepchildren's absent or missing parents' roles. When this occurs, these stepparents have been set up to fail. Simply bringing a new spouse and an old child together does not mean that either will accept the other's role in their combined family. Frequently, there is a pronounced failure in role complementarity between stepparents and stepchildren. Differences in how these individuals are likely to perceive each other are not planned for, or even anticipated.

Instead of finding that their roles complement one another, many adults and children who enter into step-relationships find that their expectations are not being met. Potentially, this is a huge disappointment—or a big surprise. Many disenchanted stepparents and stepchildren have had to revise their expectations and fantasies about one another and adjust to a far different reality than they had anticipated. For example, previously single stepparents often carry with them the fantasy that any children they have with their new mates will create a nuclear family—this is *not* possible!

From the beginning, adults in combined families have unequal ties to at least one child. Remarried parents have blood or legal ties to their children while stepparents and stepchildren have only marital ties to bind them. All the love in the world will not change the fact that a new stepparent can never become an equal participant in the preexisting parent–child relationship. Nuclear and combined families are very different.

DIVIDED LOYALTIES

How can the roles of stepparents and stepchildren complement one another when children carry their loyalties to their outside parents right along with them into combined families? The answer is they cannot—not as we have come to know their roles in combined families. In a demonstration of their loyalties, many children react negatively when stepparents try to assume roles in their combined families that their outside biological parents held in their original families. The severity of children's reactions depends on their individual expectations and the degree of outside and inside interference in stepparent–stepchild relationships.

With their outside parents clearly in mind, the presence of stepparents can cause dilemmas for children.

The Voices of Loyalty

1. Mixed feelings: reactions to the presence of stepparents in their lives.
2. Echoes: loyalties belong with outside parents.
3. Warnings: stepparents cannot replace outside parents.
4. Cautions: to care for a stepparent is to betray an outside parent.
5. Urgings of choice: either love your outside parent or love your stepparent; you cannot have it both ways.

INSIDERS AND OUTSIDERS

When stepparents arrive on the scene, outsiders, with ties to the children, tend to feel threatened; old relationships are perceived to be at risk. The mere existence of a stepparent is sufficient to threaten most outside parents and grandparents. Former spouses fear stepparents because they are rivals for the role these spouses once held in their children's original families. Outside grandparents fear stepparents because they may be denied access to their grandchildren, and stepgrandparents might take their places. Remarried parents fear stepparents because they know these adults do not have the same feelings toward their children that their children's outside parents have. Most of all, stepchildren fear stepparents because these are unknown people who appear after the fact—after the children were born, and after they already have parents.

Outside Interference

When outside parents tell their children that to love their stepparents is to be disloyal to them (their outside parents), children become confused. When children have conflicts about whom to love, they are likely to feel guilty. Children may feel guilt over letting a stepparent get close and even more guilt over ever caring about the stepparent at all. The confusion the child feels often comes out as anger or hostility toward the stepparent, but this does not mean that the child does not like, or even love, the stepparent. It means there is confusion over divided loyalties.

If children are forced to make a choice about to whom they should remain loyal, outside parents will normally win. Here, children can and do make comparisons. Evidence suggests that children's loyalties remain with their outside parents, even if they like their stepparents.[3]

Inside Interference

Inside interference occurs when there is mischievous, deliberate action or inaction by a family member. Most frequently, inside interference in relationships between the remarried parent, stepparent, and stepchildren comes from conflicts generated by members of newly established combined families. Unrealistic expectations usually play a major role in these conflicts.

Stepparents often anticipate that by joining combined families they will experience the joy of adding sons or daughters to their lives. Remarried parents are notorious for leading or guiding new stepparents into making these false assumptions. If, instead of finding loving daughters and sons, stepparents encounter hostile stepchildren, how can outsiders understand the disappointment these new stepparents may feel?

In the early stages of combined family life, stepparents are unlikely to say or do anything about the covert actions or targeted comments of hostile stepchildren, largely because the assailants are the children of their new mates. Wanting to appear warm, loving, and in control when relating to their stepchildren, stepparents usually try to subdue their reactions. Over time, this suppression of their feelings turns to anger and resentment toward those stepchildren who have rejected them. At some point animosity peaks, and stepparents must confront their feelings—or explode. This is where the stepparent mobilizes the remarried parent.[4]

It is difficult for stepparents to determine what rejection by their stepchildren means. Are the children resisting their overtures of friendship because they genuinely dislike these stepparents, or are they fighting off feelings of being attracted to them, physically or emotionally? Stepchildren seem to defend themselves fiercely against any feelings of tenderness and caring toward those stepparents who are being good, kind, and loving toward them. Frequently this rejection represents attempts by these children to remain loyal to their absent biological parents. Sometimes it is just the children's way of testing whether their remarried parents still love them.

Frustrations can go in all directions in combined families: Stepchildren can be so frustrated by their stepparents, they try to turn their remarried parents away from them. Remarried parents can be so frustrated by their new spouses' inability to become "real" parents to their children, they can turn their backs on the very real pain both stepparents and stepchildren are experiencing in their encounters with one another. Remarried parents can opt to let the adults and children fight it out with one another, and resign themselves to perpetual conflict, or they can side with either their children or their new spouses. Any of these alternatives can create major power problems in combined families.

POWER . . . CONFLICT

Triangles can be the outgrowth of internal struggles stepparents and stepchildren endure in order to win or keep remarried parents' love and affection. Triangles help stepparents and stepchildren to maintain their separate relationships with remarried parents, while their own relationships with each other remain hostile or cut off.

The Distribution of Power in Combined Families

Many different power imbalances occur in combined families. Whether they occur in simple or complex combined families, power imbalances destabilize these families.

Too Strong a Couple Bond. The strength of a couple's connection with each other can cause children to feel powerless and abandoned, either isolating them or leading them to band together for their mutual protection and support. As the generations divide against each other, the combined family becomes even less cohesive than when it began.[5]

> Brent was very close to his two sons before he met Lisa. Lisa and her three daughters had been alone for several years, and they were a tight-knit family when Lisa started dating Brent. The couple fell madly in love with each other.
>
> When they were at last able to join their families together, all of the children found themselves feeling completely left out of Brent and Lisa's relationship and very much on their own. In retaliation for being "closed out," the children banded together in an effort to break up their parents' union. They almost succeeded.

Too Strong a Parent–Child Bond. In this scenario, the reverse of the one above, the parent–child bond is too strong, and the potential for a domino effect exists. The stepparent feels left out, which normally leads to a poor stepparent–stepchild relationship. Poor stepparent–stepchild relationships can negatively impact the couple bond,[6] which then threatens the very foundation of the combined family.

Division Along Biological Lines. In a complex combined family in which the household has divided along old family lines, two powerful parent–child coalitions remain. This situation causes the couple bond and the bonds between stepsiblings to become severely damaged. With virtually no cohesiveness left, the family faces the prospect of splitting right down the middle—dividing along old biological family lines.[7]

Old Spouse/New Spouse. Here remarried parents form coalitions with their former spouses which then threaten the positions of their new spouses in combined families. In these instances, stepparents can displace their anger with remarried parents onto their children, thereby creating poor stepparent–stepchild relationships. In short, excessively strong former spouse coalitions can hurt current spouse relationships.[8]

Wherever they occur, the formation of triangles within combined families signals distress. No one is exempt from involvement in a triangle. Whenever triangles appear, however, they must be dismantled (see Chapter 9) to expose the unresolved conflicts perpetuating them.

BOUNDARY PROBLEMS

To make combined families work, remarried parents have to loosen their tight bonds—the special closeness they have developed with their children as single parents. Once remarried, these parents have to find ways to retrieve some of the energy they had invested in their children while living in their old one-parent families. By retracting some of this energy, remarried parents can use their newly reclaimed emotional reserves to reinforce their bonds formed with their new mates. This is necessary because reinforced couple bonds more readily withstand the pull of remarried parents' prior attachments to their children.

Children cannot be expected to take lightly their remarried parents' "pulling away" from them. Such actions will likely be met with alarm. These children may fear that their new stepparents will gain enough influence to detach their remarried parents from them completely. However, this is not the only situation in which children fear parental detachment.

Detachment is also an issue for nonresidential children because they may perceive their outside remarried parents as having established their own families—without them. This is especially true for children who have nonresidential stepparents, and believe they are hostile to them. Even when there is not the perception of hostile nonresidential stepparents, both outside parents and nonresidential children may feel uneasy about their situation. Outside remarried parents may feel guilty because they do not live full-time with their biological children, while these same children may resent any stepsiblings who do live full-time with their biological parents. Foremost among the fears of many nonresidential children is that their stepsiblings will replace them, or at least rob them of their proper places in the affections of their remarried parents.

From another perspective, nonresidential children and their outside parents pose an external threat to new combined families. In complex combined families both adults are remarried parents as well as stepparents. The children of one remarried parent may feel threatened by the other remarried parent's attachments to nonresidential children. Also, members of newly established combined families can feel "at the mercy" of outside parents who arbitrarily dictate when nonresidential children can and cannot live in their combined family households.

An unpredictable outside parent can upset whatever balance a newly established combined family may achieve during the absence of nonresidential children. In such cases, nonresidential children are often held responsible for their residential parent's whims. This can seriously interfere with these children's being accepted by combined family members who regularly reside in the household.

Monty's former wife, Jeanette, started making trouble from the time he and Ann-Marie were wed. Jeanette never could be trusted to send the children with clothes, but worse yet, Monty and Ann-Marie were never sure if the children would arrive at all. Monty and Ann-Marie knew that their many spoiled vacations were the work of Jeanette, but Ann-Marie's children felt that Monty's children were at fault. Eventually, Monty and Ann-Marie began taking only her children with them because there was no way of predicting whether Monty's children would ever be sent for a scheduled vacation.

CLOSENESS AND DISTANCE

Remarried parents often see themselves as being caught between demands from a variety of sources: their new spouses, former spouses, and children. Stepparents and stepchildren see themselves as being pushed and pulled by contradictory forces. Undoubtedly, as combined families are first formed, there are probably more things repelling stepparents and stepchildren than pulling them together, such as competition for remarried parents' love and attention.

To gain a better perspective on some of the dynamics underlying stepparent–stepchild relationships, imagine a continuum that has attracting forces at one pole and repelling forces at the other. Using this continuum, we can identify a wide range of expression and emotion in stepparent–stepchild relationships. Some examples are:

- "You never listen to me," to "Why can't you hear what I am saying?"
- "I don't like you," to "I don't want to like you."
- "You don't care about me," to "Do you care about me?" or, "Why don't you care about me?"
- "You're weird," to "I'm weird."
- "I would hate to grow up anything like you," to "Why couldn't I have been your child so I could be like you?"
- "Let me alone," to "Please don't leave me all alone!"
- "You don't mean anything to me," to "I didn't realize how much you mean to me."

When one is a member of a combined family, one must remain cognizant of the fact that the words and tone of voice used between strangers do not always have the same meanings as they do when used between people who have experience in communicating with one another.

Remarried parents who love their new spouses as well as their children can feel torn apart when those children and spouses are at odds with one another. A child using distancing words may want closeness and not know how to ask for it, but another child who is using the same words may not want closeness at all. Although parents may understand what their children mean by their questions or statements, no one can ever be sure how things will be interpreted between stepparents and stepchildren; these individuals do not have the shared history that allows them to decipher each other's messages correctly.

Helping their children and their new spouses to feel connected requires a good deal of remarried parents' time and attention. Children need private time with their remarried parents, just as couples need time to be together. Opportunities must also be provided for stepparents and stepchildren to develop their own relationships with one another. A delicate balance is required to meet the needs of all of the different individuals and subgroups in combined families.

Taking a Honeymoon

Because of a shortage of money, time, baby-sitting services, etc., couples in combined families do not often get to take legitimate, "vacation-type" honeymoons. But the lack of an old-fashioned honeymoon does not preclude the couple from taking the time to be together. To children who observe their remarried parents acting in overtly sexual ways toward persons other than their outside parents, "in-house" honeymoons can be very distressing.

Teen-agers, in particular, have problems with their parents' being involved in sexual relationships. Adolescents are likely to repeat courtship patterns they have observed in their combined family households when they themselves start dating. Their witnessing of "household honeymoons" may even impel teenagers to start dating earlier because of overexposure to their parents' overt sexuality.

All this does not mean that the adults heading a combined family household cannot have a sexual relationship or show their love for one another. What it does mean, however, is that the couple's actions may be very painful for children to watch. When children are going to be present from the time the couple say their "I do's," the adults need to plan for their being there. The couple needs to prepare in advance for just how they are going to handle their sexual relationship once they consolidate their union, and everyone is living under the same roof.

Extreme care must be taken to avoid inciting children to have even greater sexual fantasies than they might already have. The risk of sexual relationships between stepsiblings, or between step-parents and stepchildren, is always present. The statistics on incest between stepparents and nonbiological children are frighteningly high. Incest between stepfathers and their stepdaughters is over six times more likely than between biological fathers and their daughters.[9] Provocative behaviors, such as those often displayed by couples forced to take their honeymoons with children present, can pose a significant risk to the whole family.

Even young children of either sex must be guarded from sexual abuse. Couples acting out their newfound love can trigger all kinds of unexpected consequences in their combined families. These consequences can be, and too often are, disastrous.

To say that lovemaking should take place behind closed doors is obvious. Therefore, before remarrying, parents have to let their children know that when they go into their bedrooms with their new spouses, their bedroom doors will be closed. It is important to let the children know that these actions are not meant to exclude them—they are a way for parents to enjoy private time with their new spouses.

FINDING COMPLEMENTARITY

When the honeymoon is over, both figuratively and in reality, remarried parents must begin to deal with the differences in feelings between themselves and their new mates toward their children. These differences are to be expected—and accepted. The fantasy that some parents hold—"Love me, love my children"—is not practical or realistic. A remarried parent may love her or his new mate, but that does not mean that the new mate will love the remarried parent's children, or that the children will love their new stepparent.

Nonparent/Nonchildren

The premise of "The Stepparent" chapter was that the only reasonable role for a stepparent in a combined family is that of nonparent. If what we are hoping to achieve is role complementarity, what then would be the role of the stepchild in relation to the stepparent? Answer: the role of the stepchild becomes nonchild to nonparent. Now, what would happen if stepparents and stepchildren were nonparents and nonchildren to one another?

As nonparents, stepparents would not expect to be parents of stepchildren. As nonchildren, stepchildren would not expect to be children of their stepparents. Then, accordingly, remarried parents would not expect their new mates to be parents to their children. These are basic understandings, accords that would radically alter traditional expectations and perceptions.

Just knowing the appropriate relationship between stepparents and stepchildren would benefit all combined family members. For example, remarried mothers and fathers would know, in advance, that they could not substitute stepparents for outside parents. Meanwhile, outside parents would be less fearful of losing touch with their nonresidential children, because they would know that they are expected to continue their parental roles.

Without question, it would be desirable to relieve stepparents and stepchildren of the burden of behaving as if they were parents and children to one another. In making stepparents and stepchildren nonparents and nonchildren to each other, each stepparent–stepchild grouping would be granted the time, space, and freedom to sculpt its own authentic and rewarding relationship.

> Ron was only 3 when his parents, Marcy and Joel, divorced and made him the subject of a long and bitter custody battle which no one won: Ron was sent to live in a boarding school instead of being allowed to live with either parent.

When Ron was 6, his mother, Marcy, married Trevor. The court allowed Ron to live with this new couple. Eventually Ron developed a very close relationship with his kind and loving stepfather, but Ron never confused Trevor's love with his father's love for him.

Sensing the closeness developing between his son and Trevor, Ron's father felt threatened. Eventually Joel found it so painful to see his little boy living with his former wife and her new husband, he gave up trying to maintain a relationship with his son. Deep in his heart Joel felt that now that his son had a new father, Ron was lost to him forever.

The focus of responsibility for the care and nurturing of their offspring belongs with biological parents, yet many nonresidential parents disappear from their children's lives in the mistaken belief that the addition of stepparents to their children's lives effectively replaces them. Many nonresidential parents are totally unaware that their children need them in their lives. Threatened by the presence of stepparents in the primary households in which their children live, many nonresidential parents effectively abandon their children. But they must be put on notice that they cannot be replaced. In order for their children to continue to have two parents, outside parents have to remain part of their children's lives.

REVISED EXPECTATIONS

Finding common goals in combined family life is easier when remarried parents, stepparents, and stepchildren know what they are getting into. For example, it is crucial that stepparents know from the start that they cannot walk into combined families as parents. Stepchildren also will be relieved to realize that they need not consider stepparents as parents because society already recognizes that they have parents.

Acknowledging some of the realities of their former and current lives gives stepparents and stepchildren a chance to start out in well-defined relationships as nonparents and nonchildren to one another. Then, these individuals can pursue meaningful relationships based on their common goal of making their new families work—for the benefit of all.

FOURTEEN

Former Spouses

Irene and Jeff had been divorced two years when Jeff started dating Cindy. Cindy could not understand why Irene called Jeff to fix things at the house and to baby-sit when she had to go out. Jeff did not want all this contact with Irene, but he felt he was doing things to make his children's lives better. Jeff became less available to Irene as he became more involved with Cindy. Eventually he stopped baby-sitting and doing things around the house. Irene felt Jeff was going back on his word to co-parent their children. Their relationship, which had been quite amicable, started to deteriorate, and when Jeff married Cindy, Irene was irate. Irene felt betrayed, and she set out to make things as uncomfortable as possible for the new couple—through the children.

If we look for the source of the combined family, we find its roots embedded in the original union between the remarried parent and her or his former spouse. Once this original couple have either procreated or adopted a child, the adults whose union produced the child are bound by the bonds of blood or the strongest ties the law can provide to be forevermore involved with that child. It does not matter if the woman and man have divorced or never married, or if they have ended their union after adopting a child or before their mutual child was born; it does not even matter if one spouse is deceased and the other is still living—as long as their mutual child lives, parents remain connected to that child, and by logical extension, to each other. Children are the links that forever bind their biological or adoptive parents to each other; they are the "till death do us part" part of their parents' marriage vows.

While other vows can be dissolved or annulled, the child cannot. The child *is*, and in so being, no matter how many times the couple divorces and/or remarries—either each other or new partners—the child remains the "living proof" of his or her parents' prior relationship.

Once their unions have ended, parents are free to continue their individual relationships with their children. However, because children's parents no longer live with each other, children must live with one or the other of their parents in one-parent families. This "separate, but equal" status of divorced parents is destabilized when one or the other of the adults remarries. As remarried parents initiate changes in the lives of their children, conflicts with their former spouses may well escalate.

FORMER SPOUSES AND COMBINED FAMILIES

Former spouses play peculiar roles in combined families. Because remarried parents and their former spouses share equal ties to their mutual children, there is no sure way to seal off combined family boundaries to exclude them. Unanticipated interference in combined family functioning by remarried parents' former spouses can throw couples off balance, creating a sense of urgency and heightening tensions between them. In fact, former spouses need not be living to intrude on combined family life. Children carry their fantasies about or memories of their deceased parents with them as they become members of combined families:

> Jennifer was 9 when her father married Patricia. Jennifer and her dad had lived together since her mother died, when she was 7. From the time she met Pat, Jennifer never lost an opportunity to tell Pat that things could not be moved in the house. They were to remain exactly as they were when her mommy died, and things were to be done only in the way she and her daddy had agreed upon. It was not long before Pat began to feel there was no room for her in this household.

A parent who chooses to marry again cannot substitute a new stepparent for a missing biological parent. Whether the absent parent is deceased, the head of a one-parent family, or a member of a different combined family, the "outside" parent occupied a unique place in the family into which the children were born. Although the new stepparent in a combined family may function in a role which closely resembles the role of the missing parent in the children's original family, the new stepparent cannot assume the absent parent's role in the new family unit. That role is not vacant.

Attempting to displace or replace the children's outside parent with a stepparent is much like trying to complete a jigsaw puzzle using a piece from a different puzzle. No matter how closely that piece resembles the original puzzle piece in size and shape, it is not the missing piece, and its substitution does not recreate the original puzzle.

If we look closely at the situation inside a combined family, the addition of a new spouse/stepparent to the children's preexisting one-parent family brings up a number of sensitive issues. The children's outside parent and inside stepparent are not only (usually) of the same sex, but each of them either has been or currently is the spouse of the children's (remarried) parent. To the children, this has to be terribly confusing. To the new stepparent, the knowledge that her or his stepchildren have a parent, living or deceased, outside the boundaries of the combined family can be very unsettling.

Direct comparisons of the stepparent's role performance to the outside parent's role performance more often than not leave the stepparent in a "one-down" position. After all, the stepparent is not a parent to the remarried parent's children, but their outside parent is. At the same time, the children's outside parent is not a member of the combined family, so it is easy for him or her to feel threatened by the mere thought that some stranger is being allowed to live in the same household with his or her children.

Because outside parents have every right to remain concerned about their children's well-being, and because these adults remain insiders to their children—no matter where, or with whom, their children happen to be living—outside parents can be both powerful and influential. For example, if outside parents do not approve of what they think is going on inside their children's combined families, they can cause courts, schools, social agencies, etc., to become involved in combined family affairs.

> When Mickey's stepfather slapped him, Mickey's father slapped a restraining order on his son's stepfather.

MAINTAINING BOUNDARIES BETWEEN CURRENT AND FORMER SPOUSES

Because the boundaries surrounding combined families are looser than those surrounding nuclear families, there is often a good deal of confusion about personal boundaries separating former spouses. While it is important for two formerly married adults to establish a parenting coalition[1] in behalf of their mutual children, it is imperative that these same adults effect an *emotional divorce*, so each can go on with his or her own life.

Emotional Divorce

What prompts so many formerly married couples to stay involved with one another is their mutual failure to achieve an emotional divorce. To achieve a true emotional divorce, both adults have to work through the loss of the individual hopes and dreams that led them to marry in the first place. When a couple's previous marital ties are properly ended, the energy that was tied up in their old relationship becomes available for each of the adults to use in developing new relationships.

The legal end to a union does not always signal a true end to the ties that sometimes continue to bind former spouses to one another long after their marriages have ended. Those former spouses who, many years later, still keep hauling each other back to court on one pretext or another are good examples of couples who have failed to achieve an emotional divorce; they just cannot seem to "get done" with each other. Apparently there is some truth to the adage "Hate binds as tightly as love."

Many times, the former spouse who is able to go on to form a new relationship with a new partner finds that ties to her or his old partner have not been broken—merely stretched. Relationships that are too close between former spouses can seriously threaten the ability of either or both of these adults to form new attachments. Because of their lingering attachments to their old spouses, some remarried parents are unable to make unequivocal commitments to their new marriage partners. When this happens, new couple bonds are likely to be very unstable. When remarried parents fail to separate emotionally from their old spouses, there is every reason for new spouses to feel left out and angry; old ties are being allowed to intrude on new ones:

> Virginia and her husband, Jordan, ended their marriage when Virginia discovered Jordan had been having an affair with his secretary, Andrea, whom he later married.
>
> At the time of their divorce, Virginia and Jordan were the parents of two young children. Because both of them wanted to remain completely involved in the raising of their children, they chose to cooperate in co-parenting across the boundaries of the dual households in which they now lived: Virginia, alone with the two children, and Jordan, with his new wife.
>
> After some time, the old couple began discussing the issues that had separated them initially. Eventually, Jordan began communicating some of the difficulties he was experiencing in his present marriage to Andrea. By this time, Jordan and Andrea had added a child of their own to their union, and Jordan was obviously upset that Andrea was now devoting more of her attention to the baby than she was to him.
>
> Feeling his current wife's shift in attention—away from him and toward their mutual child—Jordan began to shift his focus away from his current spouse and family and back to his former spouse and original family. The more Jordan revealed about the difficult aspects of his relationship with Andrea, the more Virginia felt the power of her old feelings for Jordan surging over her.
>
> One evening—she was ashamed to admit to herself, let alone anyone else—Virginia allowed herself to be swept away in a tidal wave of old feelings. Virginia was now "the other woman" in the Andrea–Jordan–Virginia triangle. Virginia and Jordan were lovers again.

When former spouses have not completely separated emotionally, the danger to a new spouse is that she or he will be left out
of any parenting coalition that exists between the remarried parent
and his or her former spouse. Had Andrea always been an integral
part of the parenting coalition between Jordan and Virginia, the
chances of an affair taking place between Jordan and his former
spouse would have been greatly diminished.

Couples in Complex Combined Families

Dealing with one outside parent is enough to make combined
family life confusing, yet it can seem simplistic when compared to
life in a complex combined family. In complex families, couples
find themselves dealing with two sets of former spouses outside
their new families, as well as various combinations of siblings,
stepsiblings, and half siblings living inside their combined family
households.

> Two years after they began dating, Marjorie and Roger de-
> cided to join their families together. Marjorie had purchased a
> house for herself and her three children after her divorce. Both
> Roger and Marjorie knew that when Roger moved in, it was not
> going to be easy to have his three children coming in and out of
> her children's territory two weekends a month, but they figured
> the children would be able to work it out for themselves.
> While Marjorie's three children lived with the couple the
> majority of the time, they usually spent two weekends a month
> living with their dad, Clyde. Therefore, sometimes the couple
> had three children, sometimes six, and very occasionally, Roger
> and Marjorie would have a weekend all to themselves.
> The couples' one weekend alone was treasured whenever it
> occurred, but that was not often because either one or the other of
> their former spouses usually found a way to interfere—by not
> living up to previously agreed-upon arrangements. For example,
> Clyde sometimes opted not to take the children on his scheduled
> weekends, which left Marjorie and Roger suddenly "saddled"
> with three children they had not expected that weekend. If Roger
> complained, Marjorie would explain that she was powerless to
> make Clyde take the children, so she had no choice but to keep

them at home. This situation was not unique because Roger's former spouse, Carol, repeatedly dumped the children on Roger and Marjorie for unscheduled weekends, as well as occasional weekdays.

Marjorie was often furious when Roger took his children extra times during the month. She hated the fact that Carol could just call up on any pretense and make Roger come out to pick up the kids. Marjorie repeatedly told Roger how much his actions burdened her—by expanding the number of children in their household and giving her extra meals to prepare and additional children to care for. But Roger's response, although sympathetic, was always to say that he wanted to see his children more than scheduled, and any extra chance he had to see them he considered a bonus.

Although theirs was a couple problem, Marjorie and Roger insisted that it was their spouses, and not themselves, who caused problems between them in their interpersonal relationships, and in their combined family lives.

As couples in complex combined families strive to cope with all the internal and external pressures exerted on them, they must take great care to maintain the integrity of their unions. If they do not, the antics of old spouses can seriously divert couples' attention from their priorities—their new families, and each other. In the face of forces that threaten to drive a wedge between them, couples must work to strengthen their couple bonds.

Over the course of their years of living together, Marjorie and Roger had many reasons to seek counseling. Although it may have been expressed in different ways, all of the children seemed to have difficulties with the never-ending conflict between their remarried and outside parents.

At various times, one or another of the children seemed to get caught in the middle of the conflict between their original parents. Some children seemed angry at their parents for not resolving their conflicts, while others managed to roll with the punches.

Problems with their children's adjustments to their ever-changing home environments, coupled with the attempts of both former spouses to manipulate their home life, caused Roger and

Marjorie to separate on more than one occasion over the course of their children's growing-up years. Marjorie and Roger would wind up living under separate roofs—sometimes for a year or two, sometimes only briefly.

Regardless of the force that drove them apart, their commitment to each other was ultimately the force that would drive them back together. Roger and Marjorie learned that even if they wound up living in separate households, they had to keep the integrity of their union intact.

Eventually, Marjorie and Roger realized that taking time to strengthen their couple bond was the only way they would be able to "make it." Tucking themselves into their own private eggshell was their salvation from the negative impact of their former spouses on their current relationship, and the havoc of living in a house that was constantly being filled and emptied of children.

While participating with their former spouses in joint efforts to make their children's lives as good as they can be, remarried parents have to increase the distance between themselves and their former spouses by limiting the scope of their relationships to the area of parenting. With their lives as couples clearly over, both remarried parents and their former spouses have to become more detached within the parental sphere.[2]

Finally Roger and Marjorie determined that the only way Roger could get any distance from Carol's never-ending intrusions on their lives would be to limit the scope of Roger's interactions with Carol to the area of co-parenting their mutual children. No longer did Roger listen to Carol's tales of woe, or her needs to get away from the children. He made his co-parenting arrangements with her, and if she chose not to honor or meet them, the children were the ones to suffer.

Remarried parents have to make it very clear to their former spouses that any grossly inappropriate actions by any individual, themselves included, seriously threaten the best interests of their mutual children. As for Roger and Marjorie:

Roger informed Carol of his new position. She protested, but seeing that her antics with Roger were no longer effective, she settled down and began trying to make a life for herself.[3]

RELATIONSHIPS BETWEEN FORMER
AND CURRENT SPOUSES

In examining the roles of former and current spouses in relation to remarried parents and their children, we have to take a close look at how any two people who look as if they are occupants of the same role might legitimately expect to feel about one another. *Rivals* might be one of the words used to describe them; *competitors* might be another. However, if we examined their relative positions, we see that stepparents in combined families hold roles that *resemble* those held by outside parents in children's original families; this resemblance has been the cause of much unrest in the hearts and souls of outside parents and stepparents alike.

If we take a look at how outside parents may be viewing what is going on inside the combined families in which their children live, we understand that there is often good reason for them to fear being displaced or even replaced. Even though stepparents may have no desire to usurp outside parents' positions, remarried parents can contribute to tensions between their current and former spouses. For example, remarried parents may insist that their new spouses refer to their stepchildren as "their children," or demand that their children refer to their stepparents as "moms" or "dads."

Outside mothers and fathers can be terribly threatened by remarried parents' requiring their children to call their stepparents by *their* names. Under these circumstances, is it so unreasonable for these adults to worry about losing their children's love—as well as their legitimate identities as their children's parents?

Remarried parents who insist that their children call their new spouses " Dad" or "Mom" immediately put their children into loyalty binds. Whether or not children have living outside parents, even very young children know that they have, or have had, "dads" or "moms" in those roles their remarried parents are now asking them to assign to their stepparents. To children, as well as to their outside parents, stepparents can easily begin to look like usurpers of outside parents' legitimate titles and their fundamental family roles.

The outside parent is not alone in feeling threatened by what goes on inside the combined family. The stepparent too often experiences a tremendous sense of frustration and loss when he or she has been left outside the gate by the remarried parent—the same one the children are leaning on to prevent the stepparent from getting into their old one-parent family.

Removing Threats to the Relationship

Chapter 10, on "The Stepparent" detailed the many reasons why stepparents cannot occupy parents' roles, finally arriving at the conclusion that stepparents can only be nonparents to their stepchildren. Based on this assumption, outside parents and stepparents need not be competitors or rivals for the same role because they do not occupy the same role.

Hopefully, making a clear distinction between parents' roles in children's original families and stepparents' nonparent roles in combined families will be helpful in forging better understanding and greater cooperation between outside parents and inside stepparents. If outside parents could be assured that their roles in their children's lives are not at risk when their former spouses remarry and stepparents are added to their children's lives, just imagine the relief outside parents would feel in finding their positions with their children secure. Under such circumstances, it is conceivable that even very angry outside parents could get to the point where they could view their children's stepparents as people—and want to get to know those adults who are charged with some degree of responsibility toward their children.

PARENTING COALITIONS

Improving Relationships between Current and Former Spouses

When remarried parents do their parts in forging constructive relationships between their current and former spouses, they are also helping to promote the well-being of children who live in both households. *Cooperation* is the operative word when parents and stepparents seek to do the best for those children who are members of two families. When new spouses are able to demonstrate that they seek to cooperate with outside parents in giving *their* children the very best quality of life possible, both new and old spouses are, so to speak, on the same side of the fence.

Under favorable circumstances, adults who share the responsibility for raising the same children can become not only friendly but, given enough time, they can become friends. They do, in fact, have much in common: Both married the same person, though at different times, and there is a need for them to be involved with each other in making arrangements for the comings and goings of those children who hold dual citizenship in both of their households.

Remarried Parents and Their Former Spouses

Those parents who have established good parenting coalitions with their former spouses prior to remarriage may choose to leave their new spouses outside of any arrangements they have regarding the rearing of their mutual children. When this happens, there is no way these new spouses can feel good about themselves. The messages they receive let them know that there is no room for them in these preexisting parenting coalitions. Here again remarried parents are called upon to become gatekeepers in bringing their new spouses into their parenting coalitions with their old spouses.

While establishing parenting coalitions is in the best interests of their mutual children, there are some formerly married adults who cannot tolerate dealing with each other on any level. Some single and remarried parents wish to blame all that is or has been bad in their lives on their former spouses.

When remarried parents refuse to have anything to do with their former spouses, even if it involves the best interests of their mutual children, the services of a well-intentioned third party can be helpful. Under such circumstances, if current and former spouses are able to work with each other in the best interests of the children they are both raising, they can, in effect, become allies. There are other situations, however, in which, instead of working out any of the problems that exist between them, remarried parents and their current and former spouses become involved in triangles—which serve the best interests of no one.

Triangles

Since they often portray their former spouses as such ogres that no one in their right mind would ever think of going near them, one can only begin to wonder how remarried parents could ever have done such foolhardy things as to marry these individuals in the first place. Former wives have become almost as infamous in their roles as "former spouses" as current wives are in their roles as "stepmothers." If coins were minted with stepmothers on one side and former wives on the other, it would probably be a toss-up as to who would appear the "wickedest of them all." A chapter on former spouses must deal with just those sorts of triangles in which remarried parents, stepparents, and former spouses all become tangled up with one another:

> A short time after they moved back to the state where his former spouse and children lived, Mike and his new wife, Erica, became the recipients of a special kind of wedding present: an angry, acting-out, 14-year-old boy. This boy, Vic, was Mike's son, but it seemed to the couple that this was Mike's former wife's revenge on him for having remarried.
>
> Mike loved Erica dearly, but he also loved his son, and he wanted the boy—even though Vic was literally dumped on the new couple's doorstep. It was all Mike could do to dampen the fires between his son and the boy's mother, his son and his new wife, and his new spouse and his old spouse. Mike often felt like he was dancing on hot coals in his efforts to work out compromises between the various warring parties.

Sometimes the way to break the deadlock between the original couple is for the remarried parent's current and former spouses to establish a dialogue with each other. Their talking to each other would take their interaction out of the triangle and put it where it belongs—in one-on-one communication between two adults who are involved in the raising of the same children.

Theoretically, current and former spouses need have no relationship with each other; however, when children are involved, it is virtually impossible for remarried parents to keep their relationships with their current and former spouses separate. When stepparents are included as integral parts of parenting coalitions, former and current spouses can dismiss some of their fantasies about each other and get down to work. As a matter of fact, if good working relationships can be implemented between all the parties concerned in children's upbringing, children's fears of further loss can be considerably diminished.

In seeing to it that the best interests of the children are well served, all the adults involved in raising them will eventually be able to sit back, watch their grandchildren play, and remember back to those times when all of this seemed not only improbable, but totally impossible!

FIFTEEN

Discipline

During a program taping, a television host once asked this author, "When does a stepparent gain the right to discipline a stepchild?" She replied, "Most experts feel that it takes between 18 months and two years." The host then cited a hypothetical example wherein little Elihu steals a car within 18 months of his natural parent's remarriage. He stated that given the fact that the author said most experts feel it takes between 18 months and two years for a stepparent to earn the right to discipline, the new stepparent might say, "Nope, that's all right; steal the car; I can't talk to you about that right now because I'm trying to establish rapport." The audience laughed at the notion. The author's question back to the host was as to whether the stepparent would have a right to discipline if Elihu stole the car the day after the wedding. His response was that he would have to think about that.[1]

The subject of *discipline*[2] seems to be first and foremost in the minds of most remarried parents and their new spouses/stepparents; therefore, it has been separated from Chapter 16, "The Combined Family Household," and given the spotlight in this chapter.

One never knows when a child is going to misbehave. It is a mistake to assume that children will always pick a convenient time to test relationships and restrictions. Therefore, we must look more closely at the problem of discipline to analyze what options and remedies are available to remarried parents and their new marital partners.

THE RIGHT TO DISCIPLINE A CHILD/STEPCHILD

Experts vary in their opinions about how long it takes for a stepparent to earn the right to discipline a stepchild, but all would likely agree that on the day after the wedding, the stepparent does not yet have that right. The right to discipline comes slowly, over time. The stepparent has to earn the child's respect in order to discipline effectively, and most experts agree that it takes at least 18 to 24 months for the stepparent to earn sufficient respect to be able to discipline a stepchild from his or her own authority.[3]

This does not imply that stepparents have no control over what goes on in their combined family households; on the contrary, enforcing household rules is one of the most important functions remarried parents and their new spouses can perform. But until stepparents earn their stepchildren's respect in their own right, remarried parents must use the base of authority they already have established with their children and find a way to extend that base to support their new spouses.

A major way to overcome stepparents' frustration over not being able to discipline their stepchildren is for both of the adults heading a combined family household to *set limits*, jointly. Limits serve as boundaries, like the walls in a room. They can be bounced against, but they will remain standing. It is these same kinds of boundaries, or limits, that children need while they are growing up.

When children do not understand that there are limits, the whole family, whatever its makeup, runs into trouble. This trouble is best avoided by joint action on the part of the couple heading the (combined or nuclear) family household. These adults need to sit down together to establish limits for each child in their household—even if the child is going to be living there only one or two days a month.

Obviously, the adults heading a combined family cannot make rules controlling every type of mischief a child can create but, between them, they should be able to hammer out between four and six *enforceable rules* for each child. The consequences for any infraction of a rule must also be established at this time.

The rules must be clear, concise, and completely understandable to everyone affected by them. They must not be ambiguous. If the behavior the remarried parent and stepparent want to control is excessive talking on the telephone, for example, the child must understand what the rule says: i.e., what constitutes proper use of the telephone (the privilege), and what happens if the rule is not followed (the consequence). An example of an ambiguous rule would be: Sharon cannot make any phone calls after 9 p.m. When the remarried parent and stepparent are dismayed to find Sharon on the phone at 10 p.m., she informs them that she did not make the phone call—a friend called her. To clear up the ambiguity, the new rule might read: No use of the phone after 9 p.m., except to call the police or fire department. (If the parents just say "except in case of an emergency," every and any thing could become an emergency, including checking a homework assignment with a classmate.)

The rules that are selected by the adults should control each child's behavior in the areas in which the remarried parent and stepparent feel the child most needs direction or correction. The adults must also make sure that the rules are enforceable.

Enforceable rules limit a child's behavior; however, these rules also tend to tax the adults heading the household in that they have to be around to enforce the consequences of breaking the rules. For example: If a child is told that he or she is grounded for staying out too late, the remarried parent and/or the stepparent are usually the ones who will have to stay home to enforce the punishment; i.e., they have to make sure someone is around for the entire time period during which the child is grounded. The result is that in order to modify the child's behavior, the adults must also be willing to modify their own behavior. Unfortunately, this is a process that poses considerable inconvenience to the remarried parent and stepparent alike.

Because the adults heading a combined family do not want to be jailed by the sentences they impose, they should look carefully at what kinds of consequences they set. It is helpful to note that since consequences can always be escalated, adults should start with more lenient punishments (e.g., grounding for a day instead of a week). If the maximum consequences are meted out for every offense, there is no way to increase punishments. This means that the threat of adding more stringent consequences cannot be used as a deterrent. The adults leave themselves no room for increasing the consequences if every infraction of the rules merits a severe penalty. Furthermore, when children are punished for everything they do, the remarried parent and stepparent are also punished, since they have to enforce the necessary consequences. To avoid this problem, adults heading a combined family household should list and enforce only the most important rules for each child; this will enhance their chances of establishing limits for the children, and at the same time it will prevent self-imprisonment.

The reason that four to six rules are ideal for each child is because it is the amount the remarried parent and stepparent usually are willing and able to enforce. Needless to say, these rules must control the major problem areas. This means that some things have to be overlooked by the adults for the sake of their own sanity as well as that of the child.

The rules, which can apply to any form of behavior, should be listed for each child—with the consequences for an infraction of each rule listed alongside. With such a list the children can see what behaviors are required of each member of the household. The rules indicate which privileges are being given or restricted (e.g., being allowed to use the family car with the consequence of having the privilege removed for the misuse of the car). One of the best places for such a list is on the kitchen refrigerator where everyone can see it.

It should be made explicit to the child that *either* the remarried parent or stepparent can note when a rule has been broken and can apply the consequences for that infraction without consulting her or his mate. This gives the remarried parent and stepparent equal authority to enforce the rules, which in effect sidesteps the issue of whether or not the stepparent has earned the respect necessary to discipline the stepchild.

If a child does something for which the adults heading the household have no rule but disapprove of strongly, then the child should be given a warning. This means that the remarried parent and stepparent will establish a rule if this particular behavior is repeated. The same concept is involved in a formal warning issued by a traffic policeman: An officer, in certain situations, may give a warning instead of a ticket to a driver who breaks a law inadvertently. When the warning is issued, it is duly noted on the ticket that if the driver is stopped for the same or a similar offense, the punishment will be equal to two traffic tickets: one stemming from the warning (the first offense), and the other from the second infraction. Similarly, a child can be formally warned about intolerable behavior.

A warning, in effect, tells the child which behaviors the remarried parent and stepparent prefer. The child then knows that if this undesirable behavior recurs in the future, there will be a rule limiting it and an appropriate consequence imposed.

Adults can be sure the children will begin testing the rules, just as soon as they understand them. Children test rules to find out whether or not the adults heading the household are serious about setting limits on their behavior. The remarried parent and stepparent must be firm about the enforcement of the rules so the children get a clear understanding of which behaviors these adults find unacceptable. Once the children are assured that the adults heading the combined family household will enforce the rules, they will begin to obey them, or try to change the rules they find objectionable.

Once a set of rules has been established by the remarried parent and stepparent, these rules need to be discussed at a family conference. This is the place where the rules are initially described to the children, and it is also the place where they can be brought up for discussion. If children feel that a particular rule is unreasonable and/or unfair, they can raise their objections at family conferences. They can let the adults know when they feel they have outgrown a particular rule (e.g., an early bedtime hour), or have reached a different developmental level (e.g., when a child starts dating or driving). If the adults heading the household feel that there are sufficient grounds for modification, they can consider a rule change. The remarried parent and stepparent make the rules and they have the power to change them; however, it is important for children to have an input in this decision-making process.

However strongly the children feel the need for a change of rules, the adults should take the time to have a thorough discussion before deciding the best course of action. Though the remarried parent and stepparent should be quick to remedy a rule that turns out to be grossly improper, they should not feel pressured into changing the rules hastily, since they have the power to change the rules at any time. The rules are the guidelines that the adults heading the combined family household establish for members of their new family unit; thus everyone's safety and well-being are dependent upon how well the remarried parent and stepparent implement the rules.

Besides providing a forum for rule changes, family conferences are an excellent way of allowing children to exercise their rights to participate in family discussions. Children's personal involvement in the direction the combined family takes can be one of the major benefits these forums provide. Through family conferences, all combined family members can gain an opportunity to become more familiar with one another and to begin working toward common goals. As combined family members come to know and understand one another better, it becomes easier for them to establish new family goals, traditions, and, most important, an identity as a combined family. All of this will help them to become a more cohesive and integrated family unit.

Along with facilitating the process of integrating the children into their combined family, it is the adults' responsibility to prepare children to integrate into our society. The children need to understand that the rules are there for their own benefit, as well as that of the combined family; these rules will help to equip them to become responsible citizens. Rules teach children what they need to know about society, and about living in a family. They also prepare children for an orderly transition into society. Remarried parents can help their children with this transition by creating an environment in which their children can grow up to become balanced, functional, and responsible members of our society; as remarried parents' mates, stepparents can do their part by participating in this process until they themselves have been recognized by the children as valued members of their combined family households.

With these goals in mind, remarried parents and stepparents can look forward to the rule-making process as one of the cornerstones on which to base their combined families. If this process is conscientiously executed and maintained in each new family unit, the resulting effect on a combined family household can be dramatic. Tensions can lessen, and a sense of well-being can spread to all combined family members. In the end, it is good to remember that harmony is worth the effort that maintaining discipline in the household will cost.

Helpful Points to Remember

- Set limits.
- Post rules.
- Either the remarried parent or stepparent can enforce rules.
- Warn for behavior that is unacceptable but not controlled through existing rules.
- Evaluate possible revisions to rules; don't be hasty.
- Family conferences build personal involvement with combined family direction.
- Integrate combined family practices.
- Be cognizant of building a combined family identity.
- Create an environment conducive to children's growth as responsible members of society.
- Harmony is worth the effort that disciplining the household will cost.

SIXTEEN

The Combined Family Household

Olivia was a widow with three children when she married Bret. Although Bret was younger than Olivia by several years, he had been married twice before and had three children: two girls, ages 14 and 12, from his first marriage, and a son, 6, from his second marriage. Olivia's 16-year-old son, Ethan, lived with the couple on a full-time basis, but her 19-year-old daughter was away at college and only came home on breaks and vacation, while her 22-year-old daughter was married and out of the house.

Bret's daughters lived with their mother the first half of each month and with Bret and Olivia the last half, as per a shared custody agreement. Bret's son lived with the newlyweds every other weekend. With the children rotating into and out of their households on a steady basis, Olivia and Bret were constantly traveling in different directions to pick up and/or deliver Bret's children—molding their time to meet the needs of the children. When the couple did find some time together, they usually were too tired to enjoy it.

While everyone and everything in their combined family seemed to be going around in circles, Olivia's son, Ethan, maintained a unique position. He was the only child living in the household *all* of the time. Ethan frequently complained that he never knew who was going to be living in the house, or when. Finally, a schedule was posted on a bulletin board so everyone

who belonged to the combined family household could tell who
was going to be living in the house—and when.

Adding a new person to a preexisting parent/child family or
incorporating two one-parent families into a single combined family throws a new and different light onto the prism through which
combined family members view their individual relations with one
another. If the addition of just one new person to a preexisting
family creates change, the joining of two preexisting one-parent
families (or members of more than two different families) into a
single combined family can cause major alterations in the way
individual family members think about "family."

In forming a combined family, we cannot open a can, add
water, turn up the heat, and then wait a few minutes before asking,
"Is it soup (i.e., a family) yet?" Indeed, if this mixture is "soup,"
everyone is surely in it, as various people—representing varying
viewpoints and with varied life experiences—are put to the test of
"blending and becoming"[1] a "family." While the couple whose
union has created the combined family may want to create a homo-
geneous blend out of the mixture of people they have assembled
together under one roof, there may be some among their number
who have no desire to make or even allow such a thing to happen.

Attempting to put together a group of people with differing
lifestyles and divided loyalties can create massive problems for
those adults who forge their unions in the hopes that their efforts
will better the lives of all concerned:

> Ralph and his four sons were living in their own version of a
> "bachelor pad" when Ralph met and then married Letty. Letty
> was a beautiful, talented, and powerful woman, who had abso-
> lutely no desire to interfere with Ralph's relationship with his
> sons.
> Ralph and Letty did have a significant problem, however.
> Letty lived and worked in a different city than did Ralph and his
> boys. For a while after they married, Ralph and Letty lived a jet-
> setting life that never cramped anyone else's style; however, it
> eventually began to take its toll on the couple.
> When Ralph and Letty could no longer cope with being
> apart, the couple faced a dreadful dilemma: Letty could not possi-
> bly move her job to a new location, but perhaps, with very careful

planning, Ralph could. Finally, Ralph made what was for him a very painful choice: he decided to pick up his stakes and move.

When Ralph announced his plans to his sons, he gave them the option of coming with him or making alternate plans. Ralph's sons were faced with difficult choices: they could move across the country to start life anew with their dad and a new stepmother, or they could go back to living with their mother. Their other choices were to move in with friends or strike out on their own. None of these choices were viewed with great favor by Ralph's sons.

Ralph's sons were happy that their father was happy with Letty, as long as it did not affect them. Their attitude toward Letty did, however, begin to change once the boys began to think about having to move into her territory. They found it hard to keep from blaming her for their dad's move—and for the disruption of their lives.

The whole experience of adding new people to a family is bound to disorganize the way everyone in the new combined family looks at everyone else. Individuals are likely to become confused about what is expected of them, as each person faces the disruption of his or her "intimate world."[2] If a couple has not established in advance what they expect of each other in areas such as determining priorities, setting policy, taking action, and resolving conflicts, vast chasms can develop between the expectations of these adults and the reality they encounter as joint heads of a combined family household.

DISTRIBUTION OF POWER

Conflicting needs and expectations on the part of family members make it necessary for the couple heading a combined family to come to a consensus regarding a sensitive issue: the distribution of power inside the household.

In their initial attempts to find some basis upon which to build a consensus, the adults need to discuss matters that are important to each of them individually as well as to both of them as a couple. The first order of business is for each of these adults to draw up a list of personal priorities, ranked according to their importance. Using these lists as their base, the couple then needs to draw up a joint list of priorities. In the process of merging their two lists into one, a new order of priorities will emerge. Together the couple will have determined the main issues confronting them. The first item on their list is the one both adults consider to be most in need of their attention; it becomes their top priority.

To illustrate: If a couple determines that finding a place to live is the most important thing they have to do, this topic needs to head their list. Using a new sheet of paper and heading it, "Finding a place to live," the couple needs to draw up a new list, containing all the solutions both adults can think of that might be of help in resolving this issue. When the couple runs out of ideas, both adults have to evaluate the options they have listed. Those solutions that both agree will not work can be eliminated immediately, while those that both agree might work merit more careful consideration.

Because we know that finding a place to live is this couple's primary problem, it does not take a great leap of imagination to recognize that resolving this issue is not likely to be easy for them: one adult's first choice of a place to live could very well be the other adult's last choice. Yet it is the couple's responsibility to resolve their dilemma. Herein lies a major stumbling block that has tripped up many a couple on their way to the altar: In order to reach any kind of agreement, the couple has to resolve their differences of opinion on the subject.

> Clarence and Lynne loved each other deeply, and they wanted to get married, but they could not decide what to do about where to live. Clarence lived about an hour's drive from Lynne's house, and often the couple chose to meet halfway so neither would have to travel the full distance between households.
>
> When it came to the question of marriage, the couple found they had a problem that was even bigger than the physical distance that separated them. Lynne did not want to take her children out of their school system or the neighborhood in which they grew up, and Clarence could not see moving into Lynne's neighborhood—thereby causing his children to have to travel an hour each way if they wanted to see him.
>
> Unfortunately, this turned out to be a problem the couple could not resolve. There was not enough flexibility in either adult's long-range plans to bridge the distance between them.

Couples who seek to form combined families can become embroiled in a wide variety of thorny issues. One issue that appears somewhere near the top of every couple's list is *money*.

Money—how to deal with it, how to allocate it, and what to do when there is not enough of it—continues to be one of the major problems confronting couples during the planning stages of combined family development. Part of this problem stems from the fact that new couples are generally unfamiliar with each other's ways of handling money. Another part of this problem may have its roots in the fact that one or both adults may not be totally in control of their resources. Any number of money-related issues are likely to confront couples heading combined families. To these couples, money is no game; it is serious business.

Questions regarding the distribution of wealth range from, Should there be one pot where all monies that come into the combined family are commingled? to, Should the adults maintain separate but equal rights to all incoming funds? What happens when the money is handled separately but unequally? When there are large imbalances in the personal resources of the two adults heading the household, how do these adults determine what proportion of whose wealth is to be used in running their combined family household? Who makes the decision, and whose opinion prevails?

Sometimes money-related issues between couples are not of their own making. When there are large discrepancies between incoming and outgoing funds, couples can face some very real problems on both economic and emotional levels. For many couples, alimony or maintenance and child support going out vie with those same items coming in. Therefore, in planning their household budgets, many couples are forced to deal with uncertainty about how much money they will have available to them; funds owed them may or may not arrive on time—or they may not arrive at all.

> Linda Sue had spent eight topsy-turvy years with her first husband, Zeke, when she finally decided to take her two children, and her chances, and end her marriage to a man who had never made a living for his family.
> Linda Sue had only been single a short time when she met Jeff, and after a whirlwind romance, the couple were married. Jeff had never stopped to consider the consequences of taking on two

children whose father rarely if ever sent child support—either on time, or at all.

When, after a few months, it became apparent to Jeff that Zeke was a deadbeat, Jeff assumed full support of Linda Sue's children. What Jeff did not share with Linda Sue was how much he resented the burden of supporting her children and how angry he was that Zeke did not contribute anything to his children's support. As Jeff's resentment grew, so did major rifts in his relationships with his wife and stepchildren.

There are often discrepancies between the flow of money into and out of combined family households. These discrepancies become magnified when outside parents default on child support payments. What happens inside combined families when outside parents default—and inside stepparents refuse to take up the slack? Conversely, how are remarried parents to feel when their new spouses assume the entire burden of supporting their children? Relieved? Guilty? Indebted? Sometimes the amount of support a stepparent contributes toward the upkeep of a stepchild creates a shift in the balance of power inside the combined family. Combined families are not the only ones in which money equates to power; i.e., the more you have of one, the more you have of the other.

When the issue is not an abundance but a scarcity of money, stepparents may be forced to deal with their own feelings of resentment when they are asked or expected to contribute to the support of their spouses' children. Stepparents can feel terribly angry and hurt when they are forced to delay, or even forego, having children of their own because of the amount of money being siphoned off to support another household. Unless money matters are discussed in advance, couples may be astonished to learn they hold contrary opinions regarding the allocation of scarce resources.

Attitudes toward money that were established in former relationships often color what happens between couples in subsequent relationships. Obviously, the best way for couples to avert catastrophe further on down the line is for them to put their financial arrangements in order prior to joining forces.

Prenuptial Agreements

Signing a prenuptial agreement prior to marrying leaves no doubt in either adult's mind about entitlements. Prenuptial agreements can later be nullified if the couple so desires, but while they remain in effect, these agreements serve to establish clear provisions as to who is entitled to what.

Inheritance

Unless inheritance is taken into consideration in advance, it can be one of those issues that tears a combined family to pieces. If money is an issue in any family, then in a combined family the subject of inheritance may loom over a couple's relationship like an argument waiting to happen. Inheritance causes adults to come face to face with such issues as: Who has a right to expect what from the remarried parent? From the outside biological parent? From grandparents? Does entitlement come only as the result of birth, or can it be acquired? What is fair? Are the rights of new spouses above or below the rights of old children? And as an even more complex twist on combined family dynamics, Are the children of either spouse entitled to inherit from the other spouse? Some of these questions have no answers as yet, and some never will.

Power and Control

Where power begins and ends in one combined family may differ decidedly from where it begins and ends in another. However, all adults in all combined families need to realize that they themselves have the power to control only that which goes on in their own households.

How a couple handles the distribution of power inside their family appears to be a good indicator of combined family functioning in general. For example, if a couple cannot agree on how money is to be handled or how their combined family is to be run, some rather fearsome power struggles can ensue. If the couple cannot resolve these issues, how then are they going to manage to resolve those myriads of other unanticipated events that are bound to create problems over time?

IN SEARCH OF A CONSENSUS

Failure to reach a consensus cripples couples' efforts to create any kind of stability within their families. Thus, a couple's lack of agreement about the rearing of children can conceivably stymie their efforts to provide a warm and loving environment for those children who live with them. Such a lack of agreement can also keep the couple from making reasonable rules to govern children's behavior. In a combined family, this is a recipe for disaster. A new recipe must be concocted—one that allows the couple to be creative in their efforts to reach a consensus, and happy with the results of their efforts. But how can they achieve this?

Let us examine some of the ways in which couples can expect to be challenged in their efforts to reach a consensus, and what their responses to these challenges might be.

Child Rearing

When the adults in a nuclear family have disagreements over child-rearing practices, they have the benefit of society's belief that both of them hold the best interests of their children foremost in their hearts and minds. However, when the adults forming a combined family have sharp differences of opinion as to how the children are to be reared, the whole area of child rearing can become a battleground between them. Unless their plans for resolving such conflicts have been determined in advance, it can be difficult for the couple heading a combined family to handle many of the situations that are likely to confront them on a daily basis.

Because the whole subject of child rearing can produce major conflict in combined families, the primary source of this conflict— i.e., *discipline*—has been given a chapter of its own (see Chapter 15). However, discipline is only one part of the picture when it comes to rearing children in combined families. The other part of the picture is not only outside the combined family's jurisdiction, it is outside the combined family itself.

Outside each combined family, there is at least one other parent who has a vested interest in the care and rearing of at least one child inside the combined family. As long as both parents are living and involved in the upbringing of their mutual children, no solid boundary can be drawn around either parent's household.

On several occasions, Darlene noticed bruises on her 4-year-old son's body after he returned home from spending the weekend with his father and stepmother. When Darlene finally called the child welfare agency to report suspected child abuse on the part of her former husband and/or his wife, it was as a result of having to pick up her son from the hospital after he had sustained a brain concussion from what his father claimed was "a bad fall."

While remarried parents and their new spouses maintain power and control over what goes on inside their combined families, there are many ways outside parents can intrude on combined family functioning. An outside parent can call on the services of an outside agency, either legitimately, as above, or for the sole purpose of harassing the couple heading the combined family. Outside parents can also choose to call at inconvenient times, make unreasonable demands, or "forget to give back" all that their children brought with them, so children will be missing homework, clothing, or anything else that might cause headaches for the couple inside the combined family household—and for their children as well.

Couples inside combined families do have some ability to preclude children's outside parents from wreaking havoc inside their households. Such things as court orders and telephone answering devices—used to screen out unwanted calls from "nuisance" callers—can be employed to protect those inside the combined family household from those outsiders whose only desire is to make trouble. Of course, a much better solution is for former spouses to work out their feelings about what went wrong in their past relationships. Then, remarried and outside parents can get on with their own lives, while cooperating in the best interests of their mutual children.

Rule Making

Couples heading combined family households need to keep in mind the fact that the rules that apply inside their households may bear no resemblance at all to the rules their children are expected to follow in the other households in which they live. Neither remarried nor outside parents have the right to impose their rules on each other's households. Thus, children who live in combined families frequently find themselves faced with two entirely different sets of rules, depending on which of their parent's houses they happen to be living in. Children can learn to live with a different set of rules in each parent's household; however, each time they change residences, children need time to shift gears. As they move from one household to the other, children need time to adjust to the differences between the two environments in which they live: i.e., the one they just left, and the one they are just entering.

Membership

No one has the power to control anyone else's feelings about who is a member of another person's family, so here combined family members are on their own. Who is and is not a member of a particular family is one of those questions that becomes a hot topic when combined family members attempt to put labels on who and what they are to one another. However, while membership (i.e., who is in and who is out of a particular family) may be of primary importance in one combined family, resolving conflicts about *territory* may be at the top of another family's list.

Territory

The merger of two one-parent families into a combined family is probably best accomplished on neutral territory, that is, with everyone moving into an "ours" house. When such a move is out of the question, an extremely delicate situation arises. One household must be dismantled, with the children uprooted, while the other household must sustain an invasion, in which all of the children will vie for space that until now has been in the sole possession of the children who have been living there. Unless both groups of children have been properly prepared for this major transition in their lives, chaos can prevail—not only on moving day, but on every day thereafter.

When space is at a premium, and the crowding or bunching together of unrelated children is unavoidable, it is probably best for parents to allow their children to work out their own solutions to such issues as: Who gets what space? Under what conditions?

When? Territory is most definitely a power and control issue, but it is one that parents do not seem to do as good a job in settling for children as children seem to do for themselves. Parents can help their children resolve these issues by providing them with a suitable forum—such as a family conference—where every child (who can) has an opportunity to participate in the decision-making process.

Allowing children to resolve their own conflicts is good experience for them. The decisions they make are of their own doing, and they have to live with the consequences of unwise ones. In providing their children with a forum, parents free themselves from blame for decisions that were not of their making. Still, these adults retain the authority to alter any decisions that prove unworkable.

An additional complication to the issue of territoriality occurs when the adults heading a combined family are confronted with the problem of allocating space for nonresidential children; i.e., those who live in the household episodically—on rare or special occasions. Many conflicts are generated in the process of figuring out who is going to live with whom when it comes time for nonresidential children to move into the territory of those children who live in the household all or most of the time. Here again, a family conference may save the day.

The Allocation of Scarce Resources

While the allocation of space in a combined family is a "concrete" problem, the problems couples face in figuring out how to allocate their own time and energy may be far more difficult for them to resolve. All of the individuals in a new family unit need time: time to be alone, time to be with those they love, time to become acquainted with the strangers in their midst, and time to be with the entire combined family. Questions then arise, such as: Who gets to spend how much time with whom? What is enough time, and what is not enough, or too much? And where on earth are the adults heading a combined family household going to find the energy, let alone the time, to resolve all the issues that confront them?

CONFLICT RESOLUTION

In the process of coming up with an organized plan for their family's future functioning, the adults who form a combined family gain experience in figuring out how to resolve their conflicts. They may choose to resolve their conflicts on the basis of *power and control:* "We're going to do this my way"; *strict problem-solving techniques:* listing the pros and cons of each proposed solution, and then going down the list from the most likely to the least likely solution, to find a workable solution; *negotiation:* "You think it is best to handle the situation this way, and I think it would be better handled this other way, so let's put our ideas together and see if we can come up with some kind of compromise that we both think will work"; or whatever other methods they can find to aid them.

Any methods couples use to resolve their disagreements must provide them with concrete answers. For example: "This is your (my) son, so you are (I am) going to have to handle him," or "The standard we set for the children should be a household standard, regardless of whether the children are yours or mine, or whether they live here some or all of the time."

When couples are at different stages of their life cycles, conflict resolution may be more difficult:

> When Amy married Kent, she was 29, and he was 43. While this was a first marriage for Amy, Kent and his children, Murray, 13, and Dyann, 11, had spent the last three years living together in a one-parent family.
>
> Kent's first marriage to his children's mother, Jodi, came about as a result of Jodi's getting pregnant on the eve of Kent's departure overseas, as a sailor on active duty.
>
> Because the couple had been very young when they married, Jodi felt robbed of her own teen-aged years. When her children were in grammar school, Jodi left them with her parents and "took off" for parts unknown. Jodi's parents were appalled by their daughter's behavior, and they helped Kent greatly with raising the children, as did his parents. Eventually, Kent assumed total responsibility for Murray and Dyann, and they all seemed to manage quite well together as a one-parent family.
>
> When Kent met Amy, only gradually did he introduce her

into his relationship with his children. Actually, Kent kept Amy at such a distance, she never really got to know his children. Likewise, Kent's children never knew when his relationship with Amy moved from friendship to engagement.

When they found out that Kent and Amy planned to marry, Kent's children became irate. Because Amy had always been kept at a distance, Murray and Dyann never felt they would be expected to make room for her in their lives. Their father had not asked them to look at her in any other way than as a friend of his, and they had had enough of their mother's unreliability to make them wary of women. Now they were questioning their father's judgment.

Kent was dismayed at his children's reactions, but he and Amy went ahead and married. Amy did her best to forge connections with the children; however, Murray soon moved in with his grandparents, and Dyann lived in constant fear that her stepmother might want a baby of her own. Dyann clearly indicated to her father that she was totally opposed to his having any more children.

After being married for three years, Kent and Amy finally consulted a therapist; their problem—whether or not to add a child to their union so Amy could have a child of her own. Kent felt he was too old. Amy, however, had real questions about staying in a union in which her original expectations of developing close ties to her stepchildren had been frustrated beyond her wildest expectations. Now she needed to decide whether she really wanted to have a child of her own.

Eventually, Kent's objections to becoming a father at his age seemed to wane in the face of his wife's real unmet need to have a biological child. After several months of discussion, the couple resolved their problem, and Amy got pregnant. As they knew she would be, Dyann was furious about her father's giving in to Amy. She distanced herself from the couple entirely. Kent was sad, yet hopeful that, over time, Dyann would come to accept both the couple's decision, and the baby.

When their daughter, Miri, was born, Amy and Kent were overjoyed. Kent was happy with his decision, and having a child of her own had given Amy what she was missing—the comfort of knowing that she neither was, nor had been, a bad parent. Amy simply had never been allowed to penetrate the boundaries of Kent's old one-parent family.

Kent never knew that it had been his responsibility to bring his new wife into his old parent–child family. Now, however, all of that was behind the couple. With the birth of their mutual child, not only was Miri connected to every other member of the family, but Amy was too.[3]

The entire subject of "how to live together under one roof" is guaranteed to give couples seeking to form, or already living in, combined families a good deal of exercise in whatever methods of conflict resolution they have chosen to use. For example, when a mutual child is added to a combined family, how are the couple to decide what is fair between their mutual child and the remarried parent's child or children? Deciding what is fair between siblings, stepsiblings, and half siblings, as well as between residential and nonresidential children, can consume enormous amounts of a couple's time and energy.

The ways in which couples resolve conflicts are many and varied. All that can be said about conflict resolution is that whatever formula a couple arrive at, that formula is bound to be tested over and over again. Couples have to plan on resolving conflicts "till death do us [them] part"; no couple agrees about everything all the time.

Family Conferences

During the course of combined family life, when issues arise that have great bearing on the direction the family is going to take, decisions need to be arrived at in ways that are satisfactory to everyone in the household. This is where family conferences can be of tremendous benefit—in helping combined family members find satisfactory solutions to what may at first seem to be irreconcilable differences. If family members are successful in resolving their conflicts, they should be quite capable of handling anything else that comes along.

There should be no doubt left in the reader's mind about the author's message in writing this chapter: Combined families are fragile, especially during the early stages of their formation. They start out with no less than three people: a parent, child, and the parent's new spouse. Couples had best plan for unevenness, not only in their family number but in their family ties. Planning strategies as to how power will be distributed within their households should eventually lead couples to find well-balanced and well thought-out ways to resolve their conflicts.

Combined family living will try and test couples' commitments to each other and to the families their unions have forged. Therefore, couples heading combined family households need to plan: plan on being tested; plan to meet these tests; plan!

SEVENTEEN

The Larger Frame

As she entered her counselor's office, Corrine appeared thoughtful—and grim. Derek had had yet another showdown with his former spouse, Brenda, who acted as if his present family did not exist—despite the fact that Derek and Brenda's children alternated weekends between their father's and mother's houses. Corrine thought the whole situation bizarre. How could Brenda have removed herself so far from reality that she could not recognize that what went on in one of the households in which her children lived was bound to have an impact on the other household. Corrine was simply in despair as she said: "Doesn't Brenda understand that she has to expand the frame she sees around her children and herself to include the rest of us?"

EXPANDING THE FAMILY FRAMEWORK

Corrine's thoughtful contemplation had exposed the crux of the combined family's dilemma: Society is still looking at the combined family in a nuclear family frame. However, that frame no longer fits; it is much too small. In a combined family, there are simply too many related people to be crammed into a nuclear family frame. The combined family's expanded kinship network would have people hanging over the edges, climbing up the back, and pushing out of the sides of that frame. So, what size frame is needed to view the combined family properly? To this question, there is no simple answer. The combined family's expanded kinship network breaks the nuclear family mold, so the framework within which each combined family operates has to be individually crafted; the task is enormous. At best, the reader can only be given a glimpse of just how many people can become involved in combined family affairs.

Let us go back to the example of Corrine and Derek's combined family. Corrine had never been married before, but since Derek had, Corrine knew in advance that there was no chance for the two of them to form a traditional family; Derek's children would be living with them every other weekend. Even so, Corrine never anticipated that she would have to have anything to do with Brenda. Brenda was Derek's "old business." Corrine knew that Derek's connection to Brenda would end sometime in the future, so never, at any point, did she seriously entertain any thoughts about Brenda as being part of her expanded family network.

Then, too, while Derek knew something of what he would be exposing Corrine to when he asked her to marry him, he never in the world dreamt that his parents—who had helped him enormously when he was head of a one-parent family—would object to, let alone reject, Corrine. But this too eventually came to pass. To go back a bit in time:

> When their third child was 2, Derek's wife, Brenda, divorced him to enter a relationship with another woman. It took Derek a long time to recover from the blow, and his parents were very supportive of him the entire time he was alone. Whenever his children were in his care, his parents were there to help him with them.

> When Derek met, and eventually married, Corrine, his folks were "cool" toward her, but they were not unkind. Things took a downward spiral, however, when Derek informed his folks that Corrine was pregnant. Instead of looking forward to the prospect of adding another grandchild to their lives, Derek's parents seemed threatened, and they quickly sought to renew their ties to their former daughter-in-law.

> Neither Derek nor Corrine could understand Derek's parents' behavior, and his folks never gave the new couple a reason for their actions. However, when Corrine gave birth to a daughter, Marianne, it became obvious that Derek's parents had de-

cided to favor his old family over the new one. They never came to see the baby. In fact, it took all of the couple's energy just to persuade Derek's folks to come to their new grandchild's christening.

Why, one might wonder, would grandparents reject a beautiful and kind new daughter-in-law in favor of a daughter-in-law who had so callously rejected their son? To this, there is no easy answer, but there are some suppositions that can be made. For example:

> Derek's parents lived in a modest home in Burbank, California, and their first three grandchildren lived nearby, in Glendale. When Derek and Corrine married, they chose to move to Beverly Hills. Derek's parents may have been stunned by their son's "upwardly mobile" move.
>
> It also may be that Derek's parents were uncomfortable in associating with Corrine and her family because Corrine's parents had lived a life of travel and adventure, while Derek's parents had been born and raised in Burbank. Neither had ever felt the need to travel very far from it.
>
> While Derek had started out like his parents, the way his first marriage ended had led him to do a great deal of soul-searching. Derek's parents may not have been able to keep up with their son's developmental "growth spurt."

As we think of how Derek's parents were so helpful to him prior to his remarriage, and then think of their current rejection of both his new wife and child, we can only wonder at what prompted their actions:

> If class difference was not seen to be a problem for Derek's children, who moved easily between their mother's and their father's households, and if these children so obviously adored their new half sister, what else might be a factor in Derek's parents' strenuous rejection of his new family?
>
> Here was one riddle Derek and Corrine could not solve. Was it because Derek's parents were fearful that they would never have access to their first three grandchildren if they accepted Corrine and her child? Was it that they hated Corrine so much that they were willing to lose their only son in order to avoid her?

Whatever was impelling Derek's parents to move along the path they were taking, Derek and Corrine were devastated by their actions.

Here we are focused on Derek's parents' rejection of their son's marriage, wife, and child. Yet, the vignette that started this chapter was not about Derek and Corrine's pain, it was about the inability of Derek's former spouse to see that she and Derek were inextricably linked through their mutual children. Once again we can see just how much Corrine had grown: from a girl who had never before been married into the mature young woman who entered her therapist's office—despairing over her stepchildren's mother's lack of vision.

> Corrine was complaining about Brenda's inability to see that both of the families in which her children lived were part of a larger family system—one that would require Brenda to expand her concept of "family" and to enlarge the frame in which she saw both herself and her children. As much as she might hate to do so, Brenda needed to include the other family in which her children lived as part of her children's lives—and, by extension, as part of her own.
>
> After all, Brenda's children had a half sister, Marianne. Marianne's mother was Corrine, Brenda's children's stepmother. Derek was father to all four children. For Brenda to refuse to acknowledge the family in which her children lived every other weekend was tantamount to denying that her children had any life at all when they were not living with her in their one-parent family.

So, what is this "larger frame" to which the author keeps referring? The larger frame is the greatly expanded frame of reference that we need to use to examine the combined family. By using a larger frame, we can view all the various and sundry connections that link large numbers of people into a vastly expanded kinship network. However, in combined families, there is often no agreement as to who is in the family. For example:

> If, prior to their half sister's birth, we were to have asked Derek and Brenda's children to tell us who was in their family, it is likely that they would have told us that they and their original

parents were the only ones who belonged. They might never have mentioned Corrine or her extended family.

If all of the adults involved in parenting Derek and Brenda's children were asked to draw a picture around those people they considered to be integral parts of their separate family units, Derek might exclude Brenda, his former in-laws, and their extended families; while Brenda might exclude Derek, his new in-laws, and their extended families. Corrine would probably have told us that she was not in a parenting role to Derek's children, but she might have agreed that she had to function in such a role when Derek's children lived with them.

If a therapist were drawing the circle, all the people that we have mentioned in this series of vignettes would have to be included in the picture, as well as any others who had at some time been added to or subtracted from this group of people.

Of course, once Marianne was added to the picture, Corrine became a mother as well as a stepmother. Derek became a father again. Marianne became a half sibling to Derek's other children, and Corrine's parents became grandparents to Marianne, in addition to being stepgrandparents to Derek's other children. All that Brenda's parents would be likely to know about the other family in which their three grandchildren lived was that they now had a half sister, whom they might or might not take an interest in, depending on how their grandchildren felt about the baby.

Meanwhile, Derek's parents now had a fourth grandchild, but for some unknown reason they seemed to be choosing to reject both this grandchild and her parents.

To the family therapist, all of these people, past and present, would have to be considered as part of the combined family picture. Anyone living in or dealing with combined families needs not only larger frames, but detailed maps (called *genograms*) to indicate where various individuals place in these enormously complex kinship networks.

CHANGING COMBINED FAMILY BOUNDARIES

As the intact family ruptures and is replaced by either one or two one-parent families, relationships are disrupted at three distinct generational levels: grandparent, parent, and child. Any new relationship patterns that develop during the one-parent family stage are subject to further modification, for example, when one or both parents remarry. These new relationship patterns are also subject to disruptions, as when a parent divorces for the second time and marries for the third. When intact families multiply by dividing—and then grow by adding or shrink by subtracting—the lives of former, present, and future family members can, are, or will be impacted by the accordion-like rhythms of combined family development.

Because some members of newly formed combined families retain complex ties to previous marriages, any or all of these members may find themselves in a situation in which many new people have been added to their lives. These newcomers, however, do not necessarily fit into any societally recognized pattern. Remarried parents, their former spouses and new spouses, the parents and relatives of these people, and even the offspring of outside parents and their new spouses—all of these people can intrude on combined family life.

When all the extended families of all the various combined family members are added up, the number of possible interactions between these related and unrelated people expands into the millions. Disagreements between combined family members as to who is in and who is out of their family can lead from factionalism to all-out warfare. Be that as it may, as family boundaries change, family relationships change.

For example, when a child's outside grandparent dies, the responsibility for accompanying the child to the funeral might very well fall to the remarried parent—whose ties to the deceased grandparent might have ended years ago. The combined family's problem: Whereas the remarried parent, as the adult accompanying the child, might be able to attend a former in-law's funeral without giving offense to other mourners, it is more than likely that it would be considered totally inappropriate for that parent's new spouse to attend the funeral as well. The new spouse would clearly be an outsider at this event. What distinguishes the position of the remarried parent from that of the new spouse is that the remarried parent is not quite an outsider to people who have, at one time, been his or her relatives. All of these people retain ties to the child whose grandparent has died. (Paul Bohannon uses the term "quasi-kin" to refer to these former in-law relationships.[1])

FAMILY CELEBRATIONS

Finding balance within their new family units is not all that combined family members face as they seek to weave their lives into a new family pattern. Family celebrations often bring combined family members face to face with their own worst fears—disagreements over such questions as: Who is in the family? and Whose celebration is it, anyway?

Holidays

What makes holiday time particularly stressful for combined families is the fact that family members are likely to hold a wide variety of opinions as to "the right way" to celebrate holidays and ritual occasions. When children live in two households, they are sure to encounter different sets of people at different holiday functions. When they get back to a residence they share in common, these children may have many different ideas as to "right" and "wrong" ways to celebrate holidays, as well as about who is and who is not a member of their family. This often leads to heated disagreements between members of the same combined family. This is a point at which grandparents can also get into the act.

Grandparents' Roles

As Emily and John Visher are quick to remind us, "Grandparents can build walls—or bridges."[2] Here are a couple of examples of one type of problem grandparents face during holidays and other family celebrations: Outside grandparents are not directly connected to the combined family; they are the parents of children's outside parents. Their dilemma revolves around whether to give presents to their grandchildren's half siblings or stepsiblings. Stepgrandparents have the same problem with children who are not biologically or legally related to them. Should stepgrandparents give presents to those children from remarried parents' prior unions?

If grandparents choose to give presents to children who are in some way tied to their children or grandchildren, of what value should these presents be? When grandchildren and step-grandchildren live in the same household, should stepgrand-children's presents be of the same value as those presents given to biological grandchildren? What if outside or stepgrandparents only give presents to their biological grandchildren, and completely ignore their grandchildren's half siblings or stepsiblings?

What if couples heading combined families tell their parents or former in-laws that their uneven patterns of gift-giving create serious relationship problems between children who are stepsiblings, half siblings, or even full siblings to one another—and these adults refuse to modify their behavior? How do couples control the tensions that are sparked between children because of their own parents' or former in-laws' actions?

Whereas the examples of "wall-building grandparents" cited above do their share to heighten tensions in combined families, there are, happily enough, many examples of "bridge-building grandparents" as well. Bridge-building grandparents give families cause to celebrate; they are there for the children when times are good, but they are also around to provide love, comfort, and understanding for those children who are frustrated by living with stepsiblings, distressed by the birth of half siblings, angered by seeing one of their parents "head over heels" in love with another adult who is not their parent, and so forth.

Children who are having difficult times adjusting to combined family life can use hugs that come with "no strings attached" or "shared secrets" that are kept, and grandparents are often experts in providing just that little extra added touch of warmth and kindness that can make a profound difference.

Relationships between grandparents and grandchildren need have no bounds where "just plain love" is concerned. Both grandparents and grandchildren are good at giving and receiving love, so the more the merrier. If children have four sets of grandparents, that gives them the potential for eight adults to love them, and for them to love. If they have more (and there can be more than four sets of grandparents involved), children in combined families can find their lives enriched by a wealth of experience that can prove a great source of strength and comfort to them over the course of their own lifetimes.

Combined Family Celebrations

Because combined families have so many different threads woven into them from so many different family patterns, it is extremely difficult to predict what shape any particular family's holiday celebrations will take, what their rituals will become, and what life as it is lived in their family will be like ten years down the road.

The only thing that can really be said about ceremonies, rites of passage, and holidays is that there are no hard and fast rules for combined families. From the time a couple gets together with the children to discuss their wedding ceremony through the time they collaborate on how to celebrate holidays, consideration must be given to what the members of that particular family want or expect to happen. For example, if a child who is a member of the household will not be present for Thanksgiving dinner, how is that child's absence going to be handled? Is this family going to celebrate Thanksgiving on Friday as well as Thursday, or is the child going to be expected to eat two Thanksgiving dinners on the same day? And what about the Fourth of July?

Christmas, on the other hand, is a holiday that families of good spirit are able to split more easily. In these families, one household in which children live celebrates Christmas on Christmas Eve, while the other household's celebration takes place on Christmas Day.

If children are always with their outside parent during school vacations, combined families can plan holiday celebrations in January, September, or any other time of year. In this way the children who have missed celebrating the holidays with members of their combined family will not feel left out.

Too Many People, Too Few Days

While the multitude of people in the combined family's expanded kinship network can create a multitude of problems, their increased numbers can also provide family members with opportunities to participate in even more holiday celebrations than they would normally have in traditional families. When extended family members feel comfortable enough to extend holiday celebrations beyond the actual day or dates of traditional celebration, opportunities abound for children to experience a variety of celebrations in a variety of ways, with a multitude of people—some related, some not!

When combined family members use their abilities to stretch their minds and extend their thinking beyond traditional family boundaries, they are afforded almost limitless opportunities to be creative in framing their own individualized expressions of celebration. On the other hand, an unwillingness to be open to change can give rise to problems.

Family Conferences

Holiday celebrations and other rites of passage can produce conflict and instability in combined family households unless upcoming celebrations are discussed and planned for in advance. Family conferences are ideal for these purposes. Here, it is possible for all new or prospective combined family members to get together to discuss the issues that are likely to confront them in planning celebrations. Family conferences give family members room to negotiate. Each individual can lobby hard for those customs and traditions that he or she considers most vital, while conceding others of lesser importance. The result can be a harmonious package of concessions and compromise that is acceptable to all.

Differences in Values and Beliefs

While it is possible for members of combined families to share similar values and beliefs and to celebrate rituals in similar fashion, this is not at all likely to be the case when transcultural issues are involved. In combined families in which family members celebrate different rites, based on different cultural patterns, there has to be some give and take as to which customs and traditions are incorporated into their new family celebrations and which are left out.

Members of a newly formed combined family may not be willing to get into any serious discussions about their personal belief systems until they get to know and trust one another, yet there may be certain ritual observances some family members feel they must have if they are to feel comfortable. What one family member feels he or she must have in the way of a family ritual may be precisely what other family members feel they cannot live with.

Rituals develop as a normal part of growing up. It is not until after a family disbands—and outside influences are allowed to penetrate each individual family member's thinking—that members of the family are likely to give thought as to how their family traditions developed. Only when their own family rituals are challenged will some combined family members notice that not all families are alike.

Negotiating new family traditions requires a tremendous amount of give and take and good will among and between combined family members. Even then, when a cherished custom is relinquished, the person giving it up feels loss. Everyone can be expected to feel loss in negotiating new ways of celebrating holidays and other occasions. Trial and error takes the place of custom and tradition. When a suggestion is acceptable to all, victory is at hand. Victories are hard won in combined families; however, creating new family traditions are well worth the battles fought to achieve them.

WHOSE CELEBRATION IS IT, ANYWAY?

When it comes to actual rites of passage, such as graduations, confirmations, bar and bat mitzvahs, weddings, etc., questions such as, Whose celebration is it, anyway? and, Who will and will not be invited? are put under a magnifying glass. Here is where the whole issue of who is or is not in the family shows up in living color.

Whether or not a person is considered part of the family figures prominently in whether he or she gets invited to a family celebration. When it is a holiday celebration that is under discussion, presumably all those who are deemed to be part of the family need to be included in figuring out how the holiday is to be celebrated. However, if it is a particular person's rite of passage that is to be celebrated, who gets to make the decision about who is in that individual's family? Who does the inviting to any formal or informal celebrations of the occasion? Who gets invited to the actual event, and who gets excluded?

A graduation, for example, is a one-time event. There may be only four tickets available to accommodate two parents, two stepparents, two siblings, four stepsiblings, and a wide assortment of grandparents. When there is no agreement as to who is to be invited to a particular rite of passage, sometimes those the child considers significant are invited, and other times the adults make the decision.

There are also times when one side of a child's family refuses to be present at an occasion when the other side is going to be there too. Oftentimes, the adults paying for a celebration refuse to allow outside relatives to attend. Under such circumstances, it is not unusual for children's parents to attend a particular rite of passage separately, with both later hosting separate parties to celebrate the same occasion.

When parents have created a succesful parenting coalition, they will find ways to make happy occasions happy. Unfortunately, the reverse is also true:

> Valerie's father had always remained involved and loving toward her and her brother, but he had always used money as a tool of power and control in the co-parenting of his children. Now, when she was grown and planning her wedding, Valerie hoped her dad would abandon those tactics and participate with her, her future husband, her mother, and her stepfather in the planning of and payment for her wedding celebration.
>
> War broke out almost immediately as Valerie's father indicated how much he was willing to contribute while at the same time dictating who was to be invited with his share of the cost. Frantic, Valerie felt her dad was using his money as leverage to control not only how, but with whom, she was going to be allowed to celebrate what she had hoped would be one of her life's happiest occasions.
>
> In the end, Valerie's dad's tactics so enraged everyone, Valerie's mom and stepfather agreed to pay for the entire fete; her dad and his second family could come, but the invitation list stopped there.
>
> Recognizing her stepfather's genuine desire for her happi-

ness, and his generosity in paying for a wedding that was really beyond his means, Valerie asked him to give her away as a bride. Learning of her decision, Valerie's father chose not to attend the wedding. He was left with his money and his grief at not being present at the marriage of his eldest child.

Luckily, there is great variety available to individuals who choose wisely and well. Notice how different the outcome is when a very tactful young woman arranges to have her father and all three of his wives, two former and one current, present at her wedding—and takes responsibility for making them all comfortable:

> When Julia married Earl, she became stepmother to his 7-year-old daughter, Randi. Randi's mother, Kim, lived nearby, so Randi spent the majority of her childhood growing up in two households. Kim never remarried, but when Randi was 9, Julia and Earl added an "ours" baby, Todd, to their combined family.
>
> Randi's mom, Kim, and her stepmother, Julia, worked hard to coordinate their schedules to make sure that the moves Randi made between her father's and mother's houses were as comfortable as possible for her. As a token of her appreciation for Julia's efforts, Kim made sure to remember Todd's birthday each year.
>
> When Todd was 6, and Randi, 15, Julia and Earl ended their marriage. Randi no longer lived with her stepmother and father, so Julia did not get to see her stepdaughter on any kind of regular basis from that point forward. However, Todd was still Randi's half sibling, and the contact between the children was ongoing when both Randi and Todd lived in their dad's house.
>
> When Randi was 24, she met her future husband, Jeff. When the couple decided to marry, they realized that planning their wedding was going to be a logistical nightmare, especially since Randi's father, Earl, had married again.
>
> Randi had maintained close contacts with all her grandparents and stepgrandparents as she was growing up, so when it came to figuring out who was going to be where on her wedding day, Randi came up with this arrangement: Her mother and stepmother were to be seated together on the right side of the aisle, with their families in the rows behind them. Randi's father was to escort her down the aisle, and then take his seat beside his third wife, Pam, on the left side of the aisle. The seating arrangement Randi had so carefully crafted worked out well.

Julia felt validated. Kim had always been grateful for the care and attention Julia paid to her daughter when Randi lived in Julia's house. Kim seemed happy to share the spotlight on the day of her daughter's wedding with the stepmother who had been so loving and kind to her child. Earl and Pam also appreciated Randi's thoughtfulness in respecting Pam's feelings as well as Earl's position: his current and two former wives were all present, but they did not get in each other's way. And so it was that all the adults and all the grandparents who had been so important to her as she was growing up were there to share Randi's happiness on her wedding day.[3]

Family Pictures

Actually, one of the best examples of the "larger frame" can usually be found in family pictures themselves. At the wedding of your stepchild, are you included in any pictures in his or her wedding album? At your niece's wedding—where your children and your immediate family are present—are you, your children, and your second husband recognized as a family when your sister asks your brother's family to gather for a family picture? Or are you ignored because she does not recognize that your combined family is a family? If you are not asked, do you point out the discrepancies?

The problem with the larger frame is that most people in our society do not even realize that they have seen their own extended family ties *contract* through divorce and expand through remarriage. Members of a combined family are just as guilty of this offense as are any other members of our society. If your third cousin, Winifred, marries a man with eight children, some of whom live in the household, some of whom are married, and some of whom are divorced, how concerned are you? Do you even consider Winifred's husband to be a relative of yours? How about his children? His grandchildren? Such loose and unrecognized linkages among people in the combined family's expanded kinship network are endless. Apparently, this is one of the reasons why society does not even want to begin to recognize combined families. Where would one draw the line?

Yet the whole experience of combined family members'

stretching their minds while expanding their family kinship networks can be very positive, very creative, and very much a source of comfort and happiness for all involved—if they choose to view their family life in this way. All that is needed to start the process is a larger frame of reference. The rest will follow.

EIGHTEEN

Stages of Development

As the five couples in a combined families stepparenting group looked back on their earlier years, they all agreed: No one could ever have told them how hard it was going to be. Was it worth it? The answers were long in coming: no one person or couple said yes right off the bat. The consensus was, it must have been, otherwise they all would not have been at the five-year reunion of their original stepparenting group.

Did these five "successful" couples have the same experiences during that five-year period? Of course not. But perhaps these families underwent similar broad patterns of adjustment to resolve their unique family problems.

If combined families' common problem areas are described—as they have been in this book—and then placed in chronological order, a continuum, or social yardstick, can be constructed. Such a device allows family members to measure their progress (or lack of it) and prepare themselves for whatever challenges lie ahead.

Not all combined families will experience each and every developmental stage along the continuum, nor will all of them progress at the same rate. However, merely having a yardstick against which to measure their progress can be of tremendous benefit to all combined families—those that are feeling positive and wondering what developmental stage they are in as well as those that are feeling overwhelmed and wondering whether they are traveling backwards or forwards.

Those couples who expend the time and energy needed to make themselves aware of potential combined family problems may be able to skip a stage or two in this process—especially in the early stages of their development. However, just because some families skip a stage does not mean that the problems associated with that stage do not exist. Sometimes an unanticipated stress or event can cause even the most forward-looking families to slip back down the developmental ladder—to rework or complete some tasks associated with an earlier stage.

While members of a combined family need to know how to map their family's development, creating the yardstick by which combined families are to be measured represents no small undertaking. It takes years of thinking about how families come together to calculate the millions of baby steps necessary to bring combined family members to the point where their house feels like a home and the people who live in it feel like a family.

Jack and Carolyn Moynihan Bradt[1] define the developmental process combined family members have to go through on their way to establishing their newfound identities as:

1. go back!
2. making room
3. struggles of realignment
4. recommitment
5. rebalancing relationships—acceptance
6. relinquishing feelings of deprivation and burden
7. growth toward integration
8. moving on

Using a quite different format, Patricia Papernow describes what she calls the "Stepfamily Cycle" as occurring in three stages over a period of four to seven years (or longer). Her "developmental framework" includes seven tiers, or stages: "Fantasy," "Immersion," and "Awareness" comprise the "Early Stages" of development. "Mobilization" and "Action" are the focus of the "Middle Stages," and "Contact" and "Resolution" make up the "Later Stages."[2]

This model works well with the shifting alliances that appear to be part and parcel of combined family development. Until membership in the combined family has been decided, family boundaries cannot be drawn, and there is likely to be little collective agreement as to who is in or out of the family. Without such agreement, combined families have trouble defining themselves—to themselves, and to others.

In her recently released book *Becoming a Stepfamily: Patterns of Development in Remarried Families*,[3] Patricia Papernow has refined her conceptual framework to the point where she has produced a developmental yardstick that members of a combined family can use to measure their progress toward becoming a "family."

THE EARLY STAGES

As Papernow projects the stepfamily passing through Early, Middle, and Later Stages of development, we see that every stage has subdivisions, and each subdivision includes a variety of tasks that are associated with it. The tasks associated with each stage have been given descriptive labels; the main task of the combined family during the Early Stages is "Getting Started without Getting Stuck." The Early Stages are further clarified by Papernow's breaking them apart and letting us know that in "Stage One: Fantasy," for example, everyone in the family carries an "Invisible Burden."[4]

Visions of everyone living "happily ever after" in instant families filled with instant love are stuffed into the baggage most couples carry with them into their unions. In couples' fantasies of combined family life, everyone in the new family is an insider. What happens then when all of these people move in together, and stepparents find that they are outsiders in their spouses' old one-parent families?

Fantasy. When stepparents' fantasies, such as "I love my new spouse, so, of course, I'll love her or his children," break down in the face of their realizations that their stepchildren's loyalties remain with their biological parents, stepparents are more likely to experience feelings of disappointment, frustration, anger, and/or despair—rather than love. What has happened to cause this change? Reality has entered the picture, and the pink dust lying on the floor may be all that is left of stepparents' rose-colored glasses.

As Papernow states clearly, "The key to getting started with the work of the Early Stages lies in relinquishing enough of the fantasies and 'shoulds' . . . to engage in the real work needed."[5]

Many of the myths that are discussed in Chapter 2 of this book are mentioned by Papernow as being carried in to the Fantasy Stage of combined family development by adults who hope

- to love and be loved;
- to make up for children's previous family ruptures by providing a better quality of family life than the children had before—especially if their outside parents are viewed as being deficient in some way;
- to prove themselves better parents than the ones who are missing;
- to make their new marriage partners' lives easier;
- to make up for all the bad experiences of the past by being perfect mates—the ones who should have been in the original wedding pictures; and, to add frosting to their fantasied wedding cakes,
- to have "just us"[6] present in their new marriages.

As one might expect, children's fears and fantasies assume a far different shape than those of adults. Many a child in a combined family has as his or her primary goal a burning desire to put his or her original family back together again; if this entails getting rid of an unwanted stepparent, so be it. However, children also fear that their losses will be compounded if they lose their new families. On the positive side, children can hope to get "more" as the result of having added new people to their lives.[7]

In summarizing Fantasy, Papernow talks about discrepancies in the relative positions of adults, who may relish the thought of instant love in instant families, and children, most of whom cling to fantasies of putting their original families back together again by reuniting their parents. In the face of children and adults' bringing very different fantasies to combined family life, "these fantasies seem an invisible burden upon both adults and children."[8]

Immersion. In Papernow's "Stage Two: Immersion," the primary challenge confronting combined family members seems to be "Sinking versus Swimming."[9] As reality replaces fantasy, combined family members may find themselves viewing a variety of problems from a number of different perspectives—each their own. For combined family members immersed in their own problems, listening to others, or even wanting to hear what they have to say, seems particularly difficult at this stage.

Combined family members lack a common historical base and a generalized knowledge of one another. This means they are also missing a "family" perspective to facilitate communication between them. Without a commonly held point of view, combined family members are left with only their own interpretations of events. Individual interpretations are, of course, subject to debate. This debate, however, does not take place in Immersion, during which time family members are struggling to swim, not sink in their confusion. If asked, most family members are not even able to pinpoint exactly what is troubling them, and, if individual family members could put words to their feelings, most would fear their new family unit had not yet gelled sufficiently to provide a safe context in which to express those feelings.

In Immersion, combined family members sense that "something's wrong here," but they cannot quite sort out what it is. The feeling that "it must be me" is the interpretation stepparents are likely to make, but stepparents' pain in experiencing self-blame is often compounded by remarried parents and children's agreement with stepparents' assessments of themselves.[10]

In the Early Stages of combined family formation, remarried parents are in central roles; they are most decidedly insiders in their new families. However, it is precisely because they are insiders that remarried parents may be totally unaware of how much their new spouses feel like outsiders in these same families. Remarried parents may have no basis for empathy with their new spouses' outsider positions. For example, when remarried parents are interrupted by their children, most parents experience the interruption as close personal contact, or spending quality time with their children. On the other hand, when it is stepparents' close personal time with their new mates that is being interrupted, stepparents may feel great pain. The fear of being looked upon as childish if they admit to the pain keeps most stepparents silent during this period; they are the ones who are supposed to act grown up—no matter how threatened and insecure they feel.

Aggravating stepparents' pain in finding themselves outsiders in their own families is the fact that not only are their intimate relationships with their new spouses interrupted by their stepchildren's actions, but they themselves are excluded from intimacies that take place between remarried parents and their children. Stepparents are hard pressed to make their marriage fantasies come true in the presence of closer, stronger parent–child bonds.

Stepparents are at the forefront when it comes to encountering resistance to their entering their spouses' old one-parent families. While remarried parents continue to experience closeness with their children, even as they attempt to fulfill their gatekeeping functions, stepparents all too often are given the very clear message: "We're glad you're here, but don't come in."[11] This scenario goes from bad to worse when remarried parents fail to meet their gatekeeping responsibilities; stepparents are particularly vulnerable to feeling friendless and left out.

Without the support of remarried parents, stepparents can find themselves in the grip of "powerful negative feelings: jealousy, resentment, inadequacy, and just plain loneliness."[12] When stepparents make overt attempts to feel better by reaching out to their stepchildren, they are likely to encounter hostility and overt rejection. Unprepared for an all-out assault on their rights to hold membership in one-parent families, stymied stepparents all too quickly learn the meaning of being outsiders in their own families.

In their central, insider roles, remarried parents may have no basis for empathy with their new spouses' outsider positions. Therefore, remarried parents may counter any negative expressions of feeling on the part of stepparents toward their children with "disbelief, protectiveness . . . and sometimes criticism."[13]

Struggling to cope with their own feelings of inadequacy and pain at not being able to join remarried parents' old biological families, stepparents may be unable to comprehend the pain behind their new husbands' or wives' apparent insensitivity to their feelings. But how can remarried parents hear their new mates? What will happen to their own remarriage fantasies if they do? Could these remarried parents have been mistaken in their desires to create better lives for themselves and their children with supportive new mates who could make up for all the losses suffered in their own and their children's lives? When all they wanted was to make things better, have they inadvertently made things worse?

Remarried parents may never have anticipated just how overwhelmed they could become in the grip of the contradictory demands on their time, energy, and loyalties—exerted by none other than their former and current spouses and their children.[14] Even if stepparents could frame their thoughts clearly at this point, which most cannot, how could they make themselves heard over the din sounding inside most remarried parents' heads?

At this stage of their combined families' development, remarried and stepparents alike may find themselves at a loss to understand children's reactions to living in combined families. They may have no basis for understanding children's feelings of loss. To children, entering a combined family may feel like just another loss in a string of losses "over which they have no control."[15] Whether or not children want to become members of combined families, they automatically do so when one or both of their parents remarry. Children do not ask for their original families to end, nor do they ask for stepparents to intrude on their relationships with their single parents. Nonetheless, both happen.

Little do most stepparents realize the loyalty conflicts children experience in watching their remarried parents embrace *them* (outsiders) as consorts. When stepparents attempt to recruit their stepchildren into brand-new family systems that exclude children's outside parents, the children may feel they have no alternative but to reject their stepparents' overtures.

Children who live in combined families have many pulls on their allegiances. Loyal to both their remarried and outside parents, there is likely to be little room for stepparents in children's lives during the Immersion phase of the Stepfamily Cycle. Remarried parents' unsympathetic responses to their new spouses' outside positions leave stepparents alone and unsupported during this period.

When Madge and Patrick were married, Madge did not set aside any space for Patrick's son, Kevin, to call his own. The couple lived in very tight quarters, and Kevin only lived with them alternate weekends. Patrick did not object to these arrangements until one afternoon, when Madge was out, Kevin could contain his feelings no more. He started telling his father how left out it made him feel not to even have a niche that he could call his own at his dad's house.

Patrick vowed to himself that he would make amends to Kevin for his wife's lack of sensitivity to his son's needs. Patrick forgot completely that all household arrangements had been made jointly. When Madge returned home, she knew something had happened during her absence. Instead of telling Madge of Kevin's frustration and unmet needs, Patrick chose to team up with his son in vilifying his wife. Madge felt overpowered and abandoned.

Prior to entering a local stepparenting group, Madge believed her only alternative was to leave. However, with the help of fellow stepparents who coached Madge on how to talk to her husband about her pain, Madge was able to tell Patrick how left out she felt when he and his son acted as if she did not exist. As he listened to Madge tell of her feelings, Patrick realized that without his support, Madge had no position at all in their new family.

Worrying about their own processes of adapting to new mates in new marriages—all the while living in a new form of family—both remarried and stepparents can find themselves astonished and distraught over children's reactions to combined family formation. Nonetheless, it may suit the adults to discount children's feelings of distress; they may not be ready to pay attention to what the children are saying, let alone interpret their "underlying concerns."[16]

The children themselves may be at a loss to explain their feelings. Some are overpowered by them, while others find themselves stuck in the doldrums. As a remedy for some of the confusion children experience at this point in the combined family's developmental cycle, Papernow suggests "bibliotherapy"—to help normalize children's feelings by generalizing them to all children going through the difficult process of sorting out the differences between biological and step-relationships. One specific recommendation Papernow makes is that readers see Larry Ganong and Marilyn Coleman's *Bibliotherapy with Stepchildren* (Springfield, Illinois: Charles C. Thomas, 1988).[17]

While children are bound to experience intense loyalty conflicts, longing for their outside parents and the comfort of their old families, their expressing their angry feelings toward their stepparents in both overt and covert ways makes "Immersion" a far more uncomfortable stage for stepparents and stepchildren than it is for remarried parents. Papernow suggests that the developmental task inherent in this period is to bear "the discomfort long enough to accurately name feelings and to hear other family members' experiences." Failure to negotiate this task is likely to result in family members' sinking into "shame" or "blame."[18]

Awareness. As the chaotic period of Immersion begins to fade, combined families find themselves in "Stage Three" of the Stepfamily Cycle, which Papernow refers to as "Awareness: Mapping the Territory."[19] Here, at last, members of the combined family begin to develop a sense of what is happening in their lives and how it impacts their family as a whole. In this stage, family members begin to consider problem areas with the hope that they will be understood and addressed.

Papernow indicates that Awareness holds both individual and joint tasks for combined family members. Individually, each person has to map her or his own terrain and talk about personal needs currently not being met by other family members; and jointly, family members have to bridge the gaps they have in their basic knowledge of one another to get a clearer picture of what each family member is "feeling and needing."[20]

By the time they have reached Awareness, combined family members are beginning to piece together what is happening in their lives; they get a sense of where all of them are going as a family. It is also in this stage that family members begin to understand and label the sources of their distress. For example, a stepparent may begin to label a child's interruption of the couple's private time as a problem.

"As soon as we close our bedroom door, I wait for the knock," says Alana to her stepparenting compatriots. "Sure enough, not two minutes go by before Tommy comes knocking at the bedroom door to ask his daddy some trumped up question— to which his father responds in full, of course!"

Alana has identified a problem area and is beginning to put her feelings into perspective. As the family approaches the Middle Stages of combined family development, the stepparent can finally label the source of her or his painful feelings—without feeling shame or assigning blame. As family members start brushing off the confusion of Immersion, and become inquisitive about the experiences of others pertaining to a particular situation, or to combined family life in general, they begin to ask questions of themselves and others.

The new mate/stepparent, who likely has been blaming him or herself for whatever has gone wrong in the combined family, finally makes the determination that he or she does not bear sole responsibility for everything wrong in the new family. It takes a great deal of support and understanding for a new stepparent to go from thinking "This whole situation is rotten, and I'm to blame" to "Something is rotten in . . . Denmark."[21]

The remarried parent is also becoming more aware that fantasized relationships between new spouse and old children are not coming to pass. Being in the middle starts to cause the remarried parent some stress. The often incompatible demands of protecting his or her children and satisfying a new spouse start to wear the remarried parent down. Additional stress may be forthcoming from the remarried parent's former spouse.

When the remarried parent and her or his former spouse have not completed their mutual task of separating their lives from one another, their failure to achieve an emotional divorce places a heavy burden on the remarried parent's new union. The new spouse may be pressuring the remarried parent to get done with his former relationship and get on with the new marriage. For various reasons, such as fear of the loss of financial support for or access to the children, the remarried parent may be reluctant to sever all ties with her or his former spouse. The new spouse may see the remarried parent's unwillingness to "finish" with the former spouse as a lack of commitment.

Children too must start recognizing where they are and labeling how they feel. They do better when they receive help in the areas of "naming their losses and gains," talking about their pain in being both an insider (to their remarried parent) and outsider (to their stepparent) in their family, "identifying what will change and what will stay the same," and naming what they need from their new family.[22]

To put it quite simply, unless combined family members know who they are and what kind of family they are living in, they cannot change anything. In working to enhance their "mutual understanding," members of a combined family are laying "the foundation for joint decision making in the Middle Stages."[23]

As combined families proceed from the Early to the Middle Stages of development, they begin to gain some awareness of what needs to be changed in order to make first one individual and then another feel comfortable with what is going on in the new family. If children are going to be added to a combined family, the likelihood is that a mutual child will be born during the Early or Middle stages of combined family development.

Adding A Mutual Child

Anne Bernstein, author of *Yours, Mine, and Ours* (New York: Charles Scribner's Sons, 1989), suggests that there are likely to be different reactions on the part of preexisting children to the birth of a half sibling into the new family within the first two years of combined family development. Children in the 6- to 9-year-old range are likely to experience the birth of the new baby as "very difficult." (Bernstein suggests that 6- to 9-year-olds get very angry with toddlers.) Children between 2 and 5 manifest "varied" reactions to the birth of a mutual child, while 10- to 13-year-olds find the baby's birth "difficult," but better than do children of most other ages. Children 14 and up are likely to experience the baby's birth as "difficult."[24]

For Bernstein's purposes, the middle stages of combined family development start from three to five years after the new family unit has come into existence. (In Papernow's paradigm, there is no "year" marker that differentiates the Early and Middle Stages of combined family development. Combined families get to the Middle Stages when they get there.)

Bernstein suggests that the birth of a mutual child three to fives years down the road in a remarriage is "fine, but infrequent" with 2- to 5-year-olds, "varied" with 6- to 9-year-olds, and "better" with children 10 and older.

In "established" remarried families, those that have been together four to seven years, Bernstein suggests that the birth of a mutual child is "optimal, but rare" for 2- to 5-year-olds, "better" for 6- to 9-year-olds, and "fine" for children 10 and older. She adds that the mutual child's birth is "most difficult for 'only' children," but it is hard on the "only and the youngest" when the children are separated in age from the new baby by five years or less. The mutual child is most concerned with the relationship with the next oldest child above him or herself.[25]

Papernow indicates that the birth of a mutual child "prior to completion of the Action Stage . . . is more likely to increase the split between insiders and outsiders."[26]

THE MIDDLE STAGES

Papernow suggests that as combined families enter "The Middle Stages: Restructuring the Family," members of previous one-parent families tend to keep their biological focus. Generally, there is insufficient middle ground established "to hold the couple together when they differ about step issues." Stepparents and step-children are also unlikely to sustain any kind of solid interpersonal relationships in the presence of remarried parents.[27]

Mobilization. In "Stage Four: Mobilization," the primary challenge confronting combined families seems to lie in "Exposing the Gaps."[28] It is in this stage, Papernow tells us, that there comes a time when stepparents can take no more. They take a stand. Stepparents start telling their spouses and stepchildren just how they feel and what they need; they reveal their own perceptions of how things are in their combined families. To put it simply: these step-parents have had it, and they are not going to take it anymore.

Stepparents are not alone in wanting to extricate themselves from uncomfortable positions. Remarried parents too seem to be feeling the need for some relief from their insider positions at this time, and children also let it be known that they want to have their say about what is going on in their families. If the combined family problem heretofore has been that family members have not been able to have their needs met, the shift that starts to take place in Mobilization moves them in the direction of rallying "around their unmet needs."[29]

Once individual differences, likes, and dislikes start to be expressed by those who have felt the most dissatisfied and left out in the family, communication becomes possible, but this early communication may be hard to hear, and harder to accept. Those who make trouble by airing their grievances are the agents of change in a combined family. Their refusal to put up with the status quo eventually leads other family members to see that some changes will have to be made in the way their family functions.

During these tempestuous times, it is important to remember that the particular issue being argued about is almost immaterial. The real struggle is for the outsider to have his or her needs met. When the outsider is the stepparent, the old one-parent family is threatened. To those on the inside, the stepparent's demands for change can rock the very foundation of the parent–child structure. Whether the change is in a bedtime ritual or putting the lock on a bedroom door, the real issue for the one rocking the foundation of the combined family is to have his or her needs for intimacy and comfort met.

For those who are causing the disturbance, no longer is it an issue of the "odd man" being out. Instead, the issue becomes: "If you don't let me in, I'm getting out." There is real pain involved in an outsider's finally reaching this point. The problem for combined family members becomes, How do we resolve the issue that is causing the pain without creating more pain for those who have heretofore been insiders?

When the issues are aired, everyone in the combined family may find changing the situation difficult. There is no right or wrong way to find a reasonable solution; what must be kept in mind is that a solution can be found if only the couple and all members of the combined family keep working on it.

In summarizing Mobilization, Papernow indicates that the challenges facing couples in this stage are substantive. Unless the couple bond is strong enough to endure the pressures that "intense struggle[s] over differences" are likely to put on the couple's relationship, the entire combined family is at risk of splintering or "slipping permanently back into the unspoken disequilibrium of the Early Stages."[30]

The task of the stepparent is twofold: "to identify a few changes that matter" and to keep up her or his efforts to be heard "while maintaining respect and empathy for the biological subsystem's needs for some stability."[31]

The remarried parent again is called upon to function as a mediator: to give voice to the needs of the children and former spouse "while supporting and empathizing with the stepparent's need for change." For their part, children are more vociferous in stating "their needs to ease their loyalty binds."[32]

The challenges that confront combined families in Mobilization do not make their movement through this period easy for anyone. In her discussion of the Middle Stages, Papernow writes: "Conflict is aired in Mobilization and resolved during Action."[33]

Action. As combined families enter the second half of the Middle Stages, Papernow tells us, they will find themselves in "Stage Five: Action." Here, combined family members are challenged to find a way of "Going into Business Together."[34] They have to find a way to create a new family structure that works to meet the demands of their combined family. In this stage, the bonds of prior family ties start to give way to the imperatives of the combined family.

As the combined family begins to reorganize around new family priorities, the remarried parent finds that she or he has to back off and let the stepparent and stepchildren resolve their own interpersonal issues. The stepchildren have to start coming to terms with the fact that the old rules of the biological family no longer work.

As the couple continues to work together to resolve their differences, they find that going into business together allows them to build a more intimate relationship. They also come to appreciate the full meaning of becoming the executive heads of their combined family household, as they work with each other and the rest of the family to find solutions that work—ones that take into consideration the needs of all family members. The scales of justice get a heavy workout during this phase of combined family development.

During this period, combined family members find they can now use their new skills of understanding and expression to resolve old problems, such as who takes out the garbage, and together they can create new techniques to help them resolve specialized combined family problems, such as how to celebrate holidays, birthdays, anniversaries, and other rites of passage. All these require the creation of new family traditions. Family members also have "to find some ways to accept and live with the differences they cannot, or choose not to, resolve."[35]

Another area of conflict that approaches some degree of resolution in Action is the separation of the combined family from the old family "without depriving the children of a relationship with their other biological parent." Papernow suggests creating "a boundary with a hole in it" to allow "open channels of communication between ex-spouses about children" while also putting "distance between ex-spouses on other issues." The purpose of creating such a boundary is to establish the stepparent as "the insider in the new marriage."[36]

By the end of the Middle Stages, the couple bond should be well established, and stepparent–stepchildren relationships should be able to stand on their own merit, without the remarried parent's intervention on one side or the other. For all intents and purposes, the uphill portion of the battle to create a combined family is won; the Later Stages are downhill from this point.[37]

THE LATER STAGES

As the goal of the Later Stages is "Solidifying the Stepfamily,"[38] Papernow describes the challenge found in "Stage Six:

Contact" as the search for "Intimacy and Authenticity in Step Relationships." She suggests that "the subtitle for this phase of the
Stepfamily Cycle might be, 'Now that we are alone together, who
are we anyway?' "[39]

Contact. Papernow says that it is in the Contact Stage, which
takes place after all the major restructuring efforts of the Mobilization and Action stages have been set into motion, that a workable
stepparent role can finally be described. The "Qualities of a Workable Stepparent Role"[40] include:

1. Not usurping (or competing with) the role of the outside
   parent.
2. A sanctioning of the stepparent's role in the combined family, especially by the remarried parent.
3. An appreciation for the "special qualities this stepparent
   brings to this family."[41] The qualities which are at this point
   deemed special may have been the very ones which created
   animosity and tension in the Early Stages. To appreciate
   them, some family members had to change their orienta-
   tion as to what was and what was not a valuable contribution to combined family functioning.
4. A generational boundary between stepchild and stepparent, with the stepparent "remaining noncompetitive
   with the absent biological parent."[42]
5. The role must maintain the right amount of closeness and
   distance to be " 'mutually suitable' for stepparent and stepchild"[43] as well as for the couple.
6. The stepparent is placed in the position of "an 'intimate
   outsider' "[44] to his or her stepchildren.

Relationships may never be uniform within the combined family. Not every stepparent–stepchild relationship allows for intimacy between the pair. Easy stepparent–stepchild relationship can
only be worked out on an individual basis. Having made "contact"
does not mean the stepchild and stepparent will like one another
or choose to get along; choosing not to relate is also a relationship.
What defining the "mature stepparent role" provides is a slot a
new stepparent can aim for while in the process of making the shift
from the ultimate outsider to an intimate outsider.

The process of moving through the Stepfamily Cycle to the Contact Stage allows shifts in interpersonal relationships to take place. The stepparent is now a definite insider in relation to the remarried parent, and each adult has empathy with the other's position in the family. The remarried parent no longer has to remain the ultimate insider. She or he can relax while the stepparent and stepchild work at their own relationship. Papernow says that at this point, "The family at last has its honeymoon," and the fact that it's earned "makes this period all the more precious."[45]

Resolution. By the time combined families reach "Stage Seven: Resolution," they find their remaining challenge is "Holding On and Letting Go."[46] Family members have at last developed the sense of being a family. New rules and regulations have been put into effect which clearly indicate this family's way of handling things. Unfinished fights left over from the Early Stages are resolved. Stepparent and stepchildren are more likely to have meaningful discussions with one another, and the couple have consolidated their relationship to the point where they are a real comfort to each other, no matter what the issue.

If it is first in Contact that the stepparent's role is described, Papernow says that it is in Resolution that "the very differences that caused great discomfort and conflict in previous stages of the stepfamily often form the foundation of the stepparent's perceived role in the family."[47] A stepmother who is free and expressive in an army captain's household, for example, may come to be known as the one who helped family members to let down their hair and relax.

When relationships between stepparents and stepchildren work, these relationships usually feel stable and trustworthy to both parties. Of course, there are some stepparent–stepchild relationships that never gel. What is important is that the relationship between the couple works well; all the rest can be managed.

By the time combined families reach Resolution, step-relationships have lost their sting and found their strength. No longer are family members afraid to consider them part of their family's foundation.

Stepparents seem to have grown used to occupying their very special places within the framework of combined families. They may be looked upon by their stepchildren as intimate enough to be confided in, but distant enough for the children to be able to bring up subjects they do not feel comfortable in discussing with their remarried parents, i.e., sex, drugs, etc. This hard-won, privileged exchange can be very rewarding for both stepparents and stepchildren alike.

Papernow indicates that although combined families appear to function "less cohesively and more 'chaotically' than first-time families,"[48] that does not mean that they are not functioning well. Nuclear families do not have to deal with outsiders penetrating their families' boundaries or children who rotate in and out of the household as if it were a revolving door. "Different" is the operative word when comparing nuclear and combined families.

Problems still crop up after combined families have reached Resolution. Some of them may temporarily unbalance the equilibrium combined family members have achieved. Stepparents and outside parents may be present at the same children's graduation or wedding ceremonies. College money may not be available for a stepchild. The couple in the combined family may plan to have a mutual child, and not all family members may look upon its arrival as a "blessed event." All of these issues can throw kinks into an otherwise smoothly functioning combined family. Nevertheless, when trust has been established between members of the combined family, they rely on one another to find solutions together, no matter how stressful the problems may be.

As part of their continuing developmental task in Resolution, family members are challenged "to 'hold on' to the depth and nourishment of mature stepfamily relationships while revisiting unresolved grief about 'once removed' step status and the necessity of sharing children with ex-spouses."[49]

Combined families that make it to Resolution can feel justifiably proud of themselves because they have succeeded in building "'bonds without blood,' bonds that are incredibly rich and strong because they have to be created on purpose."[50] Combined families that make it to this stage may find that some life cycle events throw their families back into the struggles of earlier stages of development. However, having gone around once, these families can trust themselves to make it back to the Resolution Stage, where they can once again congratulate themselves.

One might wonder how long it takes to complete the Step-family Cycle. Patricia Papernow addresses this question in a table located in an appendix of her book, *Becoming A Stepfamily*.[51] She indicates it will take "fast-paced" families one to two years to complete the Early Stages; "average" families will need two to three years; and "slow/stuck" families may require four or more years. "Fast-paced" families are likely to complete the Middle Stages in one to two years, while "average" families need two to three years and "slow/stuck" families two to three or more years. "Fast-paced" families are likely to take one to two more years to complete the Later Stages, for a cycle completion total of four years. "Average" families need another one to two years, for a total of seven years. And "slow/stuck" families need another one to two years to complete the cycle, which brings their total to at least nine years.

NINETEEN

Establishing an Identity

From time to time, over a number of years, this author has come to know a man who not only lives in a combined family, but has been willing to share the process of that family's building its own identity. His family also has been willing to share a part of that process in the hope that it will offer encouragement to others who live in combined families and are finding it difficult. According to Bob and Linda and their family, it has all been worth the effort—and it shows!

Figuring out who *we* are to *us* has to be one of the most difficult challenges that members of a combined family face. The issue is joined from the moment the couple says "I do."

As they start out, combined families do not have an integrated system of family values, beliefs, and behaviors that family members hold in common. Instead, these families are hybrids—woven together from the separate strands of each member's previous life experiences, interlaced with those that are new. As the process of reweaving these family stories progresses, we see that each combined family is unique. No two are alike. They are one-of-a-kind families displaying designers' labels, and the designers are the members themselves.

Given combined families' unique beginnings, the challenge to those of us who strive to understand and aid them is to build a conceptual model tailored to fit the complex reality of combined family life. Combined families cannot be crammed into nuclear family molds, nor can they be tied to the nuclear family's "aging, fading norm."[1] New norms have to be tailor-made to fit combined families' needs. These alterations are sure to be painful to those family members who liked the fit and feel of their old families better. However, others may be inspired to create new styles, shapes, textures, and weaves that will allow their new family units to stretch and grow beyond most family members' wildest imaginings.

> When Linda Sorkin met Bob Eisenberg, she was widowed, and he was divorced. Both had three children. The couple hit it off immediately and were married six months after their first date. Bob brought his son Mitchell to live with Linda's three children, Jon, Josh, and Elana. Bob's two oldest children, Laura and David, were away at college, and they lived with their mother during school breaks.

Undoubtedly, the personality of a one-parent family is bound to encounter challenge and change when merged with just one member of another family unit. When two one-parent families are joined, the character of each family unit—its customs, values, traditions, beliefs, opinions; everything that defines it as a "family"— is challenged by the other family's structure.

Of course, it is unrealistic to expect members of a combined family to homogenize their individual life experiences into a well-integrated and smoothly functioning family overnight. When there are differences between what individual family members expect and what they get as the result of merging their separate family cultures into one unit, time is needed for them to adjust. "Families in this early period of reorganization do not have time-worn strategies for working together, there is no sense of stability, and there are no rules for comfortable closeness or for reasonable distance."[2]

In looking for a kinship structure they can call their own, combined family members need to draw upon the vast riches of one another's histories, to collect everyone's contribution in a single crucible, and to distill that which appeals to the majority. The result: the combined family's own unique definition of itself.

> Linda recalls she had unreasonably high expectations of combined family life. "It sounds like a cliché, but I had always wanted six children just like 'The Brady Bunch,' and here we were with four boys and two girls. I saw us taking long family

vacations and enjoying holidays by the fireplace, but that just wasn't the case. We were not family back then, but we were slowly beginning to emerge as a family. The beginning stages seemed a little bit difficult to overcome—until the trust came."

The process of establishing a combined family identity unfolds slowly, over time. Family identity is not constructed piece by piece, but rather day by day. The more time the entire family spends together, the more that family members are likely to come to understand and trust one another—and the more history they will share. "By the end of the first day, their common past has begun,"[3] but family members may not recognize this very obvious fact for years.

Of course, the whole idea behind establishing an identity as a combined family is to integrate the combined family's two original family cultures, not to negate one in favor of the other. However, this seemingly simple procedure means that each combined family member has to deal with the experience of betraying her or his original family.[4]

"Many people fear dealing with the experience of betrayal . . . [yet] if they get beyond their initial resistance to facing the past, the process can develop a momentum of its own . . . in the act of sorting through old memories the family . . . [begins] to excavate its own common heritage."[5] When members of an old one-parent family fill the rest of the combined family in on the history of an old family joke, they provide new sources of information about themselves for others to build on. Learning about one another's pasts helps make family members' present actions more understandable; this "works to build a common language and a common version of history."[6]

DEVELOPMENTAL TASKS OF COMBINED FAMILIES

As family therapist Virginia Goldner notes:

> In a sense, all remarried families are faced with an impossible developmental challenge. They must accomplish the task of forming a family. At the same time, they must function like a family further along in the family life cycle. In other words, they

must operate as if they had developed the complex inner structure of a family who has been together at least as long as the age of the oldest child while actually possessing only the rudimentary structure of a family just starting out. In short they must function at two stages of the life cycle at once.[7]

Forming a combined family is like beginning all over again from the middle. Only some members of a combined family may have lived together before as members of the same two- or one-parent families. When formerly single women immediately become stepmothers to teen-agers, or children lose their family positions or find themselves living with children who share their same first names, their ages, or both—disequilibrium is not only expectable, it is predictable.

By its very nature, forming a combined family is disorienting and disorganizing. Everyone and everything is out of the order it has previously been in, and there is no established order for anything to fall back into. Goldner continues to be insightful on this subject:

> The disruptive effects of these arbitrary rearrangements in a family's internal structure are further amplified when the new family members try to read one another. They cannot lean on the effortless familiarity that comes from time and physical proximity. Just sharing a household with an emotionally distant father, for example, provides easy access to all kinds of humble and intimate details about the man's character and habits that are invisible to the outside world. . . . Families absorb this sort of data about one another by osmosis. The data lose something in the translation.[8]

Over the years, Emily and John Visher have defined eight tasks that members of a combined family need to accomplish, presumably along the way to establishing their identity as a combined family.[9]

1. *"Dealing with Losses and Changes"* (Ref. 10)

As their separate families are joined to create a combined family, individual family members are confronted with their own personal sense of loss and change. Those who have joined the combined family from a one-parent family often face an identity crisis as they watch the fabric of their former family unit start to fray. A similar sense of disruption faces every other combined family member as well. Everyone entering a combined family has to learn to adjust to the disorientation and insecurity that cloud the initial stages of combined family life. For the couple that has been looking at becoming a combined family as a gain, the fact that everyone entering a combined family experiences loss often comes as a surprise.

> As Linda recalls, "I guess the first time I realized it was going to be so hard was when I realized my children and I had to give up our family vacations. When my first husband was alive, we all used to go away on elaborate vacations every year, and I kept up the tradition after he died. But after I married Bob, who tends to be a workaholic, I realized that my kids and I just couldn't go traipsing off on a safari. I figured if we were going to become a family, it had to be all of us that went—or none of us at all."

2. *"Negotiating Different Developmental Needs"* (Ref. 11)

Each family member needs to recognize and accept the fact that other family members may be at different developmental stages.

> Although there were many potential hazards to their combined family's success, Linda and Bob realized they had one thing in their favor: Both they and their children were for the most part at the same developmental stages. In fact, Bob's son Mitchell and Linda's son Josh quickly became best friends and helped support each other through the trauma of their teen-age years.
>
> As Bob tells it, "They were both going through that horrible stage of development where they seemed determined to 'do their own thing.' Both of them were totally opposed to good parental influence. They hung out together constantly and were awful influences on each other but, in a way, it was easier to handle the two of them together.
>
> "Under other circumstances, I might have been really hard on my stepson for such behavior, but given the situation, how could I be? My son was right along side of him, breaking every rule in the book."
>
> Linda remembers the boys as being "two peas in a pod."

3. *"Establishing New Traditions"* (Ref. 12)

Members of preexisting one-parent families, and those who join with them to form combined families, all bring their own unique sets of customs, attitudes, and beliefs to the new family units their mergers form. The task of newly formed combined families is to establish sets of values and traditions that will define who they are and what they mean to one another. A new family order can be established by borrowing from old family patterns and by creating new ones. "By its very nature, building new alliances makes old divisions less rigid."[13]

In the process of establishing new family patterns, family members must realize that competing family rituals are not right or wrong, they are just different. Coming up with family rituals that are "just right" for members of a particular combined family can be as simple as resolving the dilemma that confronted Goldilocks when she entered the dwelling of the three bears: Try all the options, and then select the ones that fit best.

The tenuous stability that can be achieved in selecting daily rituals can be disrupted in the pressure-cooker atmosphere surrounding holidays and celebrations. "As discussed by Reiss (1980), family ceremonies embody a version of family history. Their reenactment plays a critical role in forming family identity and a sense of stability."[14] For example, any combined family's ceremony simultaneously contains the "narratives of former families, their troubled times, the one-parent families, and the time of change in the new family."[15] Thus, when combined families do begin to create their own unique blend of past and present experiences, these are bound to be reflected in their family ceremonies.

Because a vast variety of inconsequential conflicts can trip up combined family development, it is important that members focus on only those events that are most important to them as a family unit. The process of establishing priorities necessitates that the combined family hold regular family conferences to establish a new set of rules, regulations, and consequences by which the household will be governed. The parent and stepparent also need to ensure that everyone is given a say in the establishment of the household rules. Children who have had a share in decision making in their one-parent households can more readily accept a process in which they can participate than one which is adult-dominated. "Since exclusion from other subsystems is already an important issue for stepfamily members, exclusion from decision-making can be a barrier to accepting the new system."[16]

> With six teen-agers and only two adults, the couple had to find some mechanism for maintaining stability within their new family unit. They turned to family council meetings, an old technique Linda and her former husband had used in raising their children. Attendance was mandatory, so all family members, even those who lived outside the household, were required to be there.
>
> Jon remembers that a major issue at family council meetings was that of allowances. He says, "We were given modest allowances, only if we deserved them."
>
> According to Linda, "They [the meetings] were not autocratic, and in a way they were more democratic because everybody was equal. There was no 'parental stuff.' If I had something to say, it was just another opinion.
>
> "At our meetings, we were working on being a family and on being caring, and responsible, and loving to each other."
>
> Linda goes on to say that the children used the meetings to bring up things that might be worrying them about one another's behavior. "They didn't tattle on each other; they told the story at the family meeting because they wanted to help [whoever it was]. They knew if they brought it [the behavior] up at the family meeting, it would be discussed, and there would be something positive that would come from it.
>
> "It wasn't about the kids against us. If there was negativity with the kids, it wasn't like we were going to come down on it; they came down on each other. That was the most powerful thing. That was the best! And they weren't being tattletales. And that is the most successful thing about the whole thing."

4. "Developing a Solid Couple Bond" (Ref. 17)

Remarried parents are sure to feel the strain of being pulled between their old children and their new spouses. In the beginning, the parent may remain steadfastly loyal to the needs of the children, who have endured such tremendous loss and change. This parent needs to offer his or her children constant reassurance that they are loved and valued no matter what shape the family constellation takes. Nevertheless, these ties must eventually be loosened to the point that, over time, the couple bond becomes primary. Because it is on the strength of the couple's relationship that the combined family stands or falls, the bond between the couple must be strengthened to the point that all who depend on it *can* depend on it.

> The whole story of Linda and Bob's love affair with each other and all their children elucidates this theme. How they respect, honor, support, and appreciate one another becomes self-evident as one reads a portion of the story of their lives as the couple heading a combined family.

5. *"Forming New Relationships"* (Ref. 18)

The combined family is only as strong as the relationships that comprise it. It is crucial, therefore, that all members of the new family make an effort to understand one another. Remarried parents need to make room for stepparents and stepchildren to interact with one another directly. During this process, remarried parents cannot expect that stepparents and stepchildren will immediately like, much less love, one another; their only requirement is that they learn to deal with one another.

> As Bob and Linda discuss Bob's entrance into her old one-parent system, Linda says, "When Bob stepped into the family, the most important thing was for the kids not to think that he was replacing their father, so he had to be really careful. Bob was aware of this, so, because he could not be [my children's] father, he just functioned in a parenting role.
>
> "It's about parenting. By doing that, whoever he was parenting, whether it was my kids or his kids, it was on another level. When Bob spoke, or when he got involved, it was important. It wasn't this constant chatter of 'You should do this, you should do that, or why don't you.' Whenever he parented, the children accepted what he said. They all had a mutual respect for each other."

Bob adds, "They had a respect for my judgment, I would say. And, if I had a view that was contrary to theirs, I think that they weighed it and listened to it."

"This pretty much happened immediately," chimes in Linda. "They were so happy that I was happy." Bob continues, "They had a feeling that I was a stable person. A kid can tell that intuitively, especially a teen-ager. They know when someone is stepping in the picture. It doesn't take anybody more than five minutes to figure somebody else out."

"They tested me; it's not like they didn't," Bob says. Linda adds, "Your kids tested you more than mine." Bob laughs and says, "They're still testing me; they are!"

The ability of stepparents, stepchildren, and stepsiblings to relate and resolve conflicts in mutually satisfactory ways serves the best interests of the combined family unit as a whole. Their success at establishing and building upon mutual relationships inevitably spurs combined family integration.

6. "Creating a 'Parenting Coalition'" (Ref. 19)

The remarried parent needs to establish a parenting coalition with the outside parent to resolve issues of child care and custody—for the sake of the children. It is essential that the remarried parent treat the outside parent as a "parenting partner" and not as a "spouse." The remarried parent's ability to distinguish this difference and live within its constraints strengthens this person's relationship with his or her current spouse and reinforces the boundaries between the two households in which his or her children live.

Linda stresses that "as far as loyalties, we'll never infringe on Bob's former wife's traditional celebrations. If she has her children over on Christmas Eve, we would never even bother asking them; so we try to work it out."

Bob says, "We know that with my kids, their loyalties are to their mother. If their mother has an occasion, or wants them for any reason, that is where they are at."

"So," Linda continues, "with holidays, I don't always know how it will be. But whatever it is, we'll say when we are doing it [planning to celebrate], and it's up to them [the children]."

Linda goes on to say, "Years ago, I told Bob that he needed to say [to his children], 'I expect you to come, and I want you to come,'—like not say, 'if you can,'—[that he should] make demands on them. But now my feeling is that they are older, and if they don't come, it's really okay. You know, at this point in their lives, it's all right to say, 'We're having this, it'd be nice if you could come'; whereas, before, you really needed to take a stand: 'I want you to be there.'"

In establishing a combined family boundary, the remarried parent needs to ensure that the lines of communication are open between the households in which the children live. Parents need to avoid power struggles. Failing that, they need to resist enlisting the children in their power struggles.

7. "Accepting Continual Shifts in Household Composition" (Ref. 20)

Children who live part-time in the combined family household need to be granted the time and space to adjust to their changing environment each and every time they have to leave or reenter the household. To ease children's transitions, remarried parents and stepparents need to provide them with personal space within their household, and they need to respect the children's privacy while they are living with them. While it is essential to establish a combined family boundary, it is also necessary that the boundary around their household be sufficiently permeable to permit the comings and goings of children between the two households in which they live.

When Bob married Linda, it proved very important to Mitchell that he have a bedroom of his own. Consequently, a room downstairs was partitioned off for him, and although it was small, Mitchell was happy to have it. It was *his* space.

Whenever any of the children in the household were having troubles with one another regarding the use of personal property or personal space, the problem was left for those involved to resolve themselves. Linda cites one example. "My kids never exchanged clothes, and Bob's always did, so that was real interesting." Bob adds, "Well, they worked it out between them."

8. "Risking Involvement despite Little Societal Support" (Ref. 21)

Combined family members may resist being drawn into the combined family for a number of reasons. They may feel that in order to be close to their new families, they have to abandon their former families—and, more specifically, their nonresidential parents. Or, they simply may resist replacing old patterns and rules with new, uncertain ones. Oftentimes, however, these members resist establishing new family relationships on the assumption that this family unit, too, will fail them. As Mary Whiteside states: "Success can be a double-edged sword. Any changes, even those with undeniable positive results, may bring up feelings of loss and conflicting loyalties. Growing feelings of attachment and affection carry with them fears of rejection once again."[22]

The survival of the combined family depends on the ability of its members to recognize differences, resolve conflicts, and live with the ambiguities of combined family life while participating in the slow process of combined family integration. But, even more crucial, the success of the combined family depends on the willingness of its members to risk (yet again) getting involved and possibly getting hurt.

> While Linda was unsuccessful in persuading Bob to leave his business for a couple weeks' vacation, she did manage to convince him to buy a summer home. Bob says he bought the cottage only to please Linda but, as Linda says, "In time, even he came to view the family's weekend holidays there as a special time for everyone—and the most affordable time because we were all together, and we were home.'
>
> During their getaways, Linda and Bob worked on getting to know their children and stepchildren better. Both remember one weekend in particular as a turning point for the combined family as a whole. As Linda recalls, "Bob, Josh, and Mitchell went off for a 'warrior' weekend—one of those weekends where guys get together to talk about the male experience and about how to express themselves more meaningfully. Well, when the three of them came home, I knew something had changed."
>
> Bob comments, "The experience created a common bond between the three of us."

Linda continues, "I was happy that they'd found each other on this level; however, I did feel left out because it was so special—and just because they shared, because it was men's stuff."

Bob enters the conversation again, saying to Linda, "It was a male bonding. It was a bonding that males have together that you don't share with females, necessarily, and so you did feel left out."

Linda agrees. "They had something special that I could never be involved with as a woman."

Some things about the family this couple formed has to be very noticeable by now. They are a family.

Bob adds, toward the end of the interview, "I know that all of our children feel they have a family with us, that they are part of our family. When they get together they do feel like a family. They do have a history together."

Now the couple is facing the fact that they no longer know what is going on between their children, because they only find things out after the fact, like "Josh got David a job" or "David went to dinner at Jon's house with his girlfriend." And is that not what most parents work so hard to achieve: self-sufficiency and independence on the part of their children?

Some final notes on this incredibly successful combined family. The author asked the couple whether it was all right to identify the family by name:

Linda said yes, with the same proviso as Bob, who said, "Yeah, if it's okay with the children, in regard to what we said about them, I would like to use our real names. It is our family's history, and an autobiography. I like the idea that if you want to hear our story you can pick up a copy of Taube's book at Kroch and Brentano's [a local book store]. Yeah, that would be kind of neat."

TWENTY

What to Do When Help Is Needed

Everyone in the Evans/Dorn family made excuses for not scheduling combined family conferences. The Dorn children always had homework or something else of importance to do whenever the couple suggested a family meeting, and Ralph and Stacy Evans both worked, so time was at a premium. Finally their family was in such trouble that they went to a family counselor. At their very expensive two-hour session, it was pointed out that all the counselor was doing was demonstrating to them how to hold a combined family meeting. From then on, family conferences were set for Monday night at 8 p.m., and everyone was expected to attend.

WHAT YOU CAN DO TO HELP YOURSELF

Throughout this book, the author has suggested that the practice of holding family conferences (discussed as "family council meetings" in Chapter 19) can be of tremendous value in getting combined family members working together, even prior to combined family formation. Wherever and whenever disagreements between family members arise, family conferences can prove useful tools in helping to resolve these disputes. When it comes to family policy, however, family conferences are a crucial vehicle for discussing and implementing family rules, and there is no substitute for them in setting family goals.

Just getting combined family members to sit down together is important. Unless these individuals take time to communicate with one another, members of a combined family can live in the same household for years without ever really getting to know and understand one another.

Sometimes combined families encounter difficulties that the adults feel unequipped to handle on their own. When such is the case, there are a number of other options available.

Support Groups

At this time, self-help groups are available for almost any kind of problem; however, running support groups for people who live in combined families requires a certain amount of expertise. The Combined Family Association of America has been successful in running five- or ten-week support groups for stepparents in the Chicago area. The Stepfamily Association of America has groups all over the country. Both organizations have trained leaders who provide group members with a start; some of these groups then continue on for years afterwards as self-help groups.

Support groups for children who live in combined families are also an option, but care should be taken to find out the qualifications of the leaders of these groups. Children cannot be lumped together just because they are part of a combined family. Preteens and older adolescents do not face the same developmental issues as younger children.

As regards children who live in combined families, the most probable place for support groups to be formed is inside their schools. With trained counselors, children can safely meet with their peers to discuss issues that are of particular significance to their age group. Not all children who live in combined families live there all the time. Children who live in one-parent families live with different dynamics than those who live in combined families, and those who live in two combined family households face different issues than those who alternate their time between a combined and a one-parent family. Group leaders not only need to be familiar with differences in each of these family's dynamics, but they must also have a basic understanding of the issues that confront children at different ages and stages of development. Whether support groups for children are run inside or outside the school system, responsible adults must be sure that those who are commissioned to lead these groups are fully qualified to do so.

When No Support Is Available

When there are no support groups nearby, start looking around for other people who are in situations similar to yours. Then see whether you can get together with a couple or a few other couples to form some kind of self-help or support group on your own. Your local mental health agency may be of help in getting you started. They may even be able to provide you with a trained leader for a minimal fee.

Classes

Look for adult education courses for remarried and stepparents; these are usually taught in the evening in high schools or community colleges. These may prove of benefit to couples who feel they learn best in a classroom environment.

Reading Material

Although this has been true for only the last few years, there is now a considerable body of reading material available for those who are either living in, or about to become members of, combined families. Here again the Stepfamily Association of America can be helpful in directing interested parties to reading material that might be of particular significance to them. Currently the number for the organization's *Catalog of Resources* is (402) 477-7837. The present address is 215 Centennial Mall South, Suite 212, Lincoln, Nebraska 68508.

Other Resources

If you are having problems that do not respond to any of the above measures, family therapy might be your combined family's best resource. If you, as an individual or couple, feel that either you or some or all of the members of your combined family are in desperate need of help, most communities have lists of resources available to the public at the local level. If not, your state's Marriage and Family Therapy Association should be able to provide you with a list of marriage and family counselors in your area. Otherwise, the American Association for Marriage and Family Therapy (AAMFT) is located at 1100 17th Street NW, 10th Floor, Washington, D.C. 20036-4601. The phone number is (202) 452-0109. Clinical members of the AAMFT are required to undergo a great deal of training. Hopefully, their membership lists will offer you a selection of marriage and family therapists located in your vicinity.

Clinical social workers are also available to do work with individuals, families, couples, and groups. The American Board of Examiners in Clinical Social Work publishes a *Diplomate Directory* which provides the reader with "an alphabetical listing of Board Certified Diplomates in Clinical Social Work within each city and state." It lists the modalities and dimensions of each individual's practice as well as the age group served; it also provides the reader with the focus of each therapist's practice.[1] The American Board of Examiners in Clinical Social Work offices are located at 8484 Georgia Avenue, Suite 700, Silver Spring, Maryland 20910.

The National Association of Social Workers publishes a *Register of Clinical Social Workers*, which provides the reader with "a complete listing of clinicians alphabetically within city and state, and an alphabetical listing of all registrants."[2] This register provides readers with the name, address, year and place of graduation, recent work experience, register number, area of specialization, and unit of intervention (i.e., type of practice) for each registrant.[3] Clinical social workers can be found in all 50 states, Puerto Rico, and the Virgin Islands, and there is also an International Chapter in Europe. The *Register of Clinical Social Workers* can be ordered from Publication Sales, National Association of Social Workers, P.O. Box 92180, Washington, D.C. 20090-2180.

The information provided in this chapter is current as of the date of publication of this book. Certainly there is enough here to provide a start for those living in combined families and finding it hard. Help is available. When you live in a combined family, you do not need any excuse in asking for it.

Family therapy is a very good choice for combined families who are "in trouble." Therapy does not have to be long-term, and it does not necessarily have to be in-depth. Often, therapy for combined families can be looked upon more as a family course in "How to . . . " than anything else. Sometimes therapy consists of showing individual combined family members how to live together as a group; sometimes it deals with relationships between former spouses and figuring out how new spouses can be brought into old parenting coalitions.

If "a picture is worth a thousand words," drawing a genogram —a family map—can do wonders in showing members of a combined family where they are "stuck"—whether in triangles, on seesaws, or outside the combined family itself.

CONCLUSION

This book's entire structure has been devoted to explaining just one phenomenon: how combined families work. Were it the author's intention to address only those who lived in combined families, or only those who treat their problems, this book probably would not have ventured along so many varied and alternative paths to get the reader to this conclusion.

The extensive reach of this work has been undertaken to attract as wide an audience as possible. But not satisfied with just attracting readers, the author has also attempted to reach across the breadth of readers and to offer each one deep insights into as many of the intricacies of combined family life as one writer can communicate to one reader the span of one book.

The task has been daunting, and the journey has taken years. All through the seven years it has taken to write this book, the author has heard that our nation's families are undergoing severe strain, that our schools are not educating our children, and that there is violence in our streets. Though this work is plainly too difficult for children to read, it will benefit those who have to deal with the upsets children suffer due to changes in their family structures—on a smaller scale, their parents, relatives, teachers, and peers; in the bigger picture, their schools, communities, and society at large.

To the author's way of thinking, the supposition that these subjects are unrelated is naive. The family is the basic unit of our society, and it is changing. In fact, it is changing so fast, most of us cannot keep up with its pace. Fifty percent of intact families rupture—most of them within the first seven years. Approximately sixty percent of combined families dissolve—most within the first four years.

Let us stop talking about nuclear families and start talking about the families that are expected to be in the majority in the twenty-first century: combined families. They are hard to live in and difficult to maintain because we give the adults heading them too little information about what is expected of them in their roles as remarried and stepparents, and too little guidance as to how to make their new family units function well. We also give the adults heading combined families far too little societal support.

As if our lack of preparation for the adults is not bad enough, most children enter combined families totally unprepared for what awaits them. After having been members of at least one and perhaps two or more previous family units, children find themselves in living situations that even their parents may not fully comprehend.

Given our current state of knowledge, it seems fair to say that combined families remain basically unexplored. Well, dear reader, it is time to take the blinders off and look at who is living in our house, or next door, or down the street. We can all be fairly well assured that it is not Ozzie and Harriet Nelson. They went out with the fifties.

While all of this light is being focused on the subject, the author wants to communicate something else to her readers. While a great deal of effort goes into forming and maintaining combined families, those efforts can be rewarding and fulfilling for all who are prepared to persevere in their endeavors to create families that stay together because most, if not all, of their members want it that way.

Despite the negative stereotypes and public apathy that await combined families today, family members' efforts—what they are learning and what they can teach the rest of us—offer our society some much-needed lessons in coping, caring, and creating cohesive family units. We need to know what these families can teach us. We need to learn from their successes as well as their failures. Redivorce statistics do not tell us how to make combined families work. The Eisenbergs and Sorkins of Chapter 19 tell us how to make combined families work.

We need more of these families to come forward and tell us their secrets of success, starting from the ground up. Sure, they will be telling us where their efforts went astray in the process, and sure, not every member of every single combined family can expect to feel happy all the time. Who can? But we are still beginners in defining combined family dynamics, and everything that successful combined families can contribute to help us teach what future combined family members will need to know is enabling. Current combined family members are the people who will establish the prototypes that other combined families—further down the line—will be able to build on, so that more and more combined families will not only "make it," but they will "make it" with an inescapable *joie de vivre*.

As for the author's efforts: This book is based not only on my own experiences, but on the experiences of literally hundreds of others as well. I wish to thank the dozens of people who have granted me permission to tell you of their experiences inside combined families. I hope this book will guide those of you in combined families to successful stepparenting, to successful remarried parenting, and to the raising of happier and healthier children who grow up successfully in combined families.

As for my reasons for writing this book: I have always wanted to be a philanthropist, but continue to lack the means. So what does a philanthropist without money have to contribute to society? Hopefully, the answer speaks for itself.

TWENTY-ONE

Introduction to the Famtu

The material in this chapter explains how the author would change our present English words to create an entirely new vocabulary—thereby eliminating the negative connotations the prefix *step* has gained.

> *Famtu(s):* A famtu is formed when someone with a child establishes a household with someone who has no legal or biological ties to that child. The new family combines blood-related, legally related (as in adoption), and marriage-related persons. The term *famtu* replaces *stepfamily, blended family, combined family, reconstituted family, remarried family,* and *merged family.*

The word *famtu* is created from the abbreviation for family, i.e., "fam," to which the suffix "tu" has been added. A double meaning is intended by utilizing the French *tu*. The pronunciation of *tu* is the same as the English pronunciation of the word *too*, which means "also."

The French *tu* is a personal pronoun which connotes closeness or familiarity with the person toward whom it is addressed. By using the double meaning of the English *too* (i.e., "also"), along with the French *tu* (i.e., "connoting closeness or familiarity"), a famtu can be defined as a family which is (also) close, although not necessarily blood-related or legally related.

A third meaning for famtu comes more from the homophonic nature of *tu* which causes it to sound like the number "two." Since famtus are built on a preexisting one-parent family unit, a famtu is, at the very least, the second type of family structure in which these individuals will live; for them a famtu is family number two (or three, four, or more).

The following are the only two exceptions to adding the "tu":

Formate(s): Former marriage partner(s), i.e., former spouse(s). Replaces current usage of the term "ex" in referring to a person's former husband or wife.

Remparent(s): Remarried parent(s). A single parent who has remarried. A child's mother or father who has remarried.

All the rest of the words that follow use the soft "tu" ending which connotes kinship resulting from "affinal" or marriage-related ties. Words can be formed by dropping the last syllable of existing relationship terms and adding "tu"; thus, brother becomes *brotu* when implying kinship, but not (necessarily)[1] blood or legal ties.

Famtu(s): Family (families) in which there is at least one step-parent–stepchild relationship.

Matu(s): Stepmother(s).

Patu(s): Stepfather(s).

Dautu(s): Stepdaughter(s).

Sontu(s): Stepson(s).

Partu(s): Stepparents(s).

Chiltu(s): Stepchild or stepchildren. This also means one's spouse's child or children by a formate.

Sibtu(s): Stepsibling(s). One's stepparent's child or children.

Brotu(s): Stepbrother(s).

Sistu(s): Stepsister(s).

Half-sibling(s): Remains the same.

Bromatu(s): A male half sibling born to a child's father and his wife. A brother by one's father's wife.

Sismatu(s): A female half sibling born to a child's father and his wife. A sister by one's father's wife.

Bropatu(s): A male half sibling born to a child's mother and her husband. A brother by one's mother's husband.

Sispatu(s): A female half sibling born to a child's mother and her husband. A sister by one's mother's husband.

Grandtu(s): Co-grandparent(s). Any and all stepgrandparents.

Grandpartu(s): Stepgrandparent(s).

Grandmatu(s): Stepgrandmother(s).

Grandpatu(s): Stepgrandfather(s).

Grandchiltu(s): Stepgrandchild or stepgrandchildren.

Granddautu(s): Stepgranddaughter(s).

Grandsontu(s): Stepgrandson(s).

Auntu(s): Step-aunt(s). A child's stepparent's sister(s).

Unctu(s): Step-uncle(s). A child's stepparent's brother(s).

Niectu(s): Step-niece(s). A sibtu's daughter(s).

Nephtu(s): Step-nephew(s). A sibtu's son(s).

Coustu(s): Step-cousin(s). Sibtu's children.

References

CHAPTER ONE

1. *Webster's Third New International Dictionary*, s.v. "step."
2. E. B. Visher and J. S. Visher, *Stepfamily Workshop Manual* (1980), p. A2.
3. The description of a "cocoon" here is for illustrative purposes only to indicate that the nuclear family is considered self-contained. In real life there are no "cocoons." There are only mothers, fathers, and their children who live together as families.
4. E. Shorter, *The Making of the Modern Family*, as quoted in K. N. Walker and L. Messinger, "Remarriage after Divorce: Dissolution and Reconstruction of Family Boundaries," *Family Process* **18**, 186 (1979).
5. K. N. Walker and L. Messinger, "Remarriage after Divorce: Dissolution and Reconstruction of Family Boundaries," *Family Process* **18**, 186 (1979).
6. See E. Wald, *The Remarried Family: Challenge and Promise* (New York: Family Service Association of America, 1981). Sometimes a combined family has as its base not the couple's legal marriage, but their living together in a committed relationship. Wald defines families that are formed through "live-in" relationships as "socially remarried," p. 2.
7. E. B. Visher and J. S. Visher, *Old Loyalties, New Ties* (New York: Brunner/Mazel, 1988), p. 10.
8. In their book, *The Family Life Cycle: A Framework For Family Therapy* (New York: Gardner Press, 1980), E. Carter and M. McGoldrick talk about the family life cycle as "predictable developmental stages of American middle-class families in the last half of the twentieth century," p. xxi.
9. E. B. Visher and J. S. Visher, *Stepfamily Workshop Manual* (1980), p. A2.
10. E. B. Visher and J. S. Visher, *Old Loyalties, New Ties* (New York: Brunner/Mazel, 1988), p. 10.
11. E. B. Visher and J. S. Visher, *Stepfamily Workshop Manual* (1980), p. A2.
12. G. Dean and D. T. Gurak, "Marital Homogany the Second Time Around," [a study published in the *Journal of Marriage and the Family* **42** (Aug) 559–70, (1978)]

as discussed in J. J. Jacobs and F. Furstenberg, Jr., "Changing Places: Conjugal Careers and Women's Marital Motility," *Social Forces* **64**(3), 714–732 (1986).

13. E. B. Visher and J. S. Visher, *Stepfamily Workshop Manual* (1980), p. A3.

14. Ibid.

15. Although the names of the individuals and the ages and sexes of the children have been altered to protect the families involved, the content of this vignette is based on one combined family's experience during the early years of their remarriage.

16. K. Walker and L. Messinger, "Remarriage after Divorce: Dissolution and Reconstruction of Family Boundaries," *Family Process* **18**, 186 (1979).

17. K. Walker and L. Messinger, "Remarriage after Divorce: Dissolution and Reconstruction of Family Boundaries," Ref. 17, p. 186.

18. E. B. Visher and J. S. Visher, *Stepfamily Workshop Manual* (1980), p. A3.

19. This figure is the one currently being cited by the Stepfamily Association of America.

CHAPTER TWO

1. V. Goldner, "Remarriage Family: Structure, System, Future," in L. Messinger (ed.), *Therapy with Remarriage Families* (Rockville, Maryland: Aspen Publications, 1982), pp. 189–206.

2. "I'm My Own Grandpaw," (Dwight Latham and Moe Jaffe), © 1947 COLGEMS–EMI Music Inc., Copyright renewed 1975 COLGEMS–EMI Music Inc. All Rights Reserved. Used by Permission.

3. P. Glick, "Marriage, Divorce, and Living Arrangements," *Journal of Family Issues* **5**(1), 7–26 (1984).

4. G. Schulman, "Myths That Intrude on the Adaptation of the Stepfamily," *Social Casework*, **49**, 131–139 (1972).

5. E. B. Visher and J. S. Visher, *Stepfamily Workshop Manual* (1980), p. A2.

6. E. B. Visher and J. S. Visher, *Old Loyalties, New Ties*, (New York: Brunner/Mazel, 1988), p. 130.

7. E. B. Visher and J. S. Visher, *Old Loyalties, New Ties*, Ref. 6, p. 128.

8. E. B. Visher and J. S. Visher, *Old Loyalties, New Ties*, Ref. 6, p. 131.

9. P. C. Glick, Adjunct Professor of Sociology, Arizona State University, telephone conversation with author, 6 November 1992.

CHAPTER THREE

1. S. Minuchin, *Families & Family Therapy* (Cambridge, Massachusetts: Harvard University Press, 1974), p. 97.

2. J. Wallerstein and J. B. Kelly, *Surviving the Break-Up: How Children and Parents Cope with Divorce* (New York: Basic Books, 1980), p. 36.

3. J. Wallerstein and J. B. Kelley, *Surviving the Break-Up: How Children and Parents Cope with Divorce*, Ref. 2, p. 36.
4. L. Messinger and K. Walker, "From Marriage Breakdown to Remarriage: Parental Tasks and Therapeutic Guidelines," *American Journal of Orthopsychiatry* **51**, 431 (1981).
5. L. Bumpass, J. Sweet, and T. Castro Martin, "Changing Pattern of Remarriage," *Journal of Marriage and the Family* **52**, 747–756 (August 1990).
6. L. Bumpass, J. Sweet, and T. Castro Martin, "Changing Pattern of Remarriage," Ref. 5, p. 753.
7. L. Bumpass, J. Sweet, and T. Castro Martin, "Changing Pattern of Remarriage," Ref. 5, p. 753.
8. L. Weitzman, *The Divorce Revolution: The Unexpected Social and Economic Consequences for Women and Children in America* (New York: Free Press, 1985), p. 339.
9. C. M. Johnson et al., *Child Poverty in America* (Washington, D. C., Children's Defense Fund, 1991), p. 8.
10. J. Wallerstein and J. B. Kelly, *Surviving the Break-Up: How Children and Parents Cope with Divorce*, Ref. 2, p. 45.
11. J. Wallerstein and J. B. Kelly, *Surviving the Break-Up: How Children and Parents Cope with Divorce*, Ref. 2, p. 36.
12. J. Wallerstein and J. B. Kelly, *Surviving the Break-Up: How Children and Parents Cope with Divorce*, Ref. 2, p. 36.
13. E. Carter from personal notes taken at her workshop in San Francisco, October 1989. Conference sponsored by the American Association for Marriage and Family Therapy.

CHAPTER FOUR

1. A. Lincoln, from a speech delivered at the Illinois House Republican State Convention, Springfield, Illinois, 16 June 1858. *Bartlett's Familiar Quotations*, 15th ed.
2. Although the names of the individuals and the ages and sexes of the children have been altered to protect the families involved, the content of this vignette is based on one couple's rendition of the first few years of their remarriage.
3. Cohabitation as "a form of social remarriage"—is included in this definition. See E. Wald, *The Remarried Family: Challenge and Promise* (New York: Family Service Association of America, 1981), p. 2.

CHAPTER SEVEN

1. T. Wolfe, *You Can't Go Home Again* (New York & London: Harper & Brothers, 1940).
2. V. Goldner, "Remarriage Family: Structure, System, Future," in L. Messinger

(ed.), *Therapy with Remarriage Families* (Rockville, Maryland: Aspen Publications, 1982), p. 195.
3. V. Goldner, "Remarriage Family: Structure, System, Future," Ref. 2, p. 203.
4. V. Goldner, "Remarriage Family: Structure, System, Future," Ref. 2, p. 203.
5. V. Goldner, "Remarriage Family: Structure, System, Future," Ref. 2, p. 194.
6. V. Goldner, "Remarriage Family: Structure, System, Future," Ref. 2, p. 194.

CHAPTER EIGHT

1. P. Boss and J. Greenberg, "Family Boundary Ambiguity: A New Variable in Family Stress Theory," *Family Process* **23**, 535 (1984).
2. P. Boss and J. Greenberg, "Family Boundary Ambiguity: A New Variable in Family Stress Theory," Ref. 1, p. 535.
3. P. Boss and J. Greenberg, "Family Boundary Ambiguity: A New Variable in Family Stress Theory," Ref. 1, p. 535.
4. J. Wallerstein and S. Blakeslee, *Second Chances* (New York: Ticknor & Fields, 1989), p. 245.

CHAPTER NINE

1. Compliments of S. V. Pearlman.
2. "The predictable stages of American middle-class families in the second half of the twentieth century." E. Carter and M. McGoldrick, *The Family Life Cycle: A Framework For Family Therapy* (New York: Gardner Press, 1980), p. xxi.
3. A. Cherlin, "Remarriage as an Incomplete Institution," *American Journal of Sociology* **84**(3) 634–650 (1978).
4. A. Cherlin, "Remarriage as an Incomplete Institution," Ref. 3, p. 634.
5. A. Cherlin, "Remarriage as an Incomplete Institution," Ref. 3, p. 642.
6. E. Carter spoke about the necessity of parents becoming "gatekeepers" during her workshop on "Stepfamilies," presented at the 65th Annual Meeting of the American Orthopsychiatric Association in San Francisco, 1988.
7. From personal notes taken at E. Carter's 1988 workshop.
8. Ibid.
9. *The New American Webster Handy College Dictionary*, 1981, s.v. "mediator."
10. J. K. Keshet, *Love and Power in the Stepfamily* (New York: McGraw-Hill, 1987), p. 7.

CHAPTER TEN

1. J. Bernard, *Remarriage: A Study of Marriage*, 2d ed., (New York: Russell & Russell, 1971), p. 14.
2. Sometimes the law takes a look at the relationship between a stepparent and stepchild in the case of the death of a parent, where there has been a very long-

standing relationship between a stepchild and stepparent. Very occasionally, a stepparent is favored over a biological parent in situations where the remaining biological parent is unwilling, unable, or unfit to assume the burden of raising the child(ren).

3. J. Bernard, *Remarriage: A Study of Remarriage*, Ref. 1, p. 14.
4. I. Fast and A. Cain, "The Stepparent Role; Potential for Disturbances in Family Functioning," *American Journal of Orthopsychiatry* **36**, 485–491 (1966).
5. I. Fast and A. Cain, "The Stepparent Role; Potential for Disturbances in Family Functioning," Ref. 4, p. 485.
6. I. Fast and A. Cain, "The Stepparent Role; Potential for Disturbances in Family Functioning," Ref. 4, p. 489.
7. I. Fast and A. Cain, "The Stepparent Role; Potential for Disturbances in Family Functioning," Ref. 4, p. 488.
8. M. Mead, "Anomalies in American Postdivorce Relationships," in P. Bohannon (ed.), *Divorce and After* (Garden City, New York: Doubleday, 1970), pp. 105–106.
9. D.E.H. Russel, "The Prevalence and Seriousness of Incestuous Abuse: Stepfathers vs. Biological Fathers," *Child Abuse and Neglect* **8**, 15–22 (1984).
9a. I. Fast and A. Cain, "The Stepparent Role; Potential for Disturbances in Family Functioning," Ref. 4, p. 489.
10. M. Mead, "Anomalies in American Postdivorce Relationships," Ref. 8, pp. 105–106.
11. M. Mead, "Anomalies in American Postdivorce Relationships," Ref. 8, pp. 105–106.
12. *Webster's Third New International Dictionary*, s.v. "consort."
13. Biological parents may relinquish their ties to their children, which then leaves room for other adults to become legally involved in these children's lives, through formal adoption. Although there is no way to change children's biological make-up, in the eyes of the law, children who are adopted are considered to be the legitimate offspring of their adoptive parents.
14. I. Fast and A. Cain, "The Stepparent Role; Potential for Disturbances in Family Functioning," Ref. 4, p. 486.
15. Although the names of the individuals and the ages and sexes of the children have been altered to protect the families involved, the content of this vignette is based on one couple's rendition of their first years of remarriage.
16. B. Maddox, *The Half Parent* (New York: Evans, 1975), p. 20.
17. B. Maddox, *The Half Parent*, Ref. 16, p. 22.
18. W. Shakespeare, *Hamlet*, Act III, Scene 1, *The Complete Plays and Poems of William Shakespeare*, The New Cambridge Edition (Cambridge, MA: The Riverside Press, 1942), p. 1066.
19. Copyright © 1987 Hemdale Film Corporation. All Rights Reserved.
20. A. Simon, *Stepchild in the Family* (New York: Odyssey Press, 1964), p. 158.
21. E. B. Visher and J. S. Visher, *Old Loyalties, New Ties*, (New York: Brunner/Mazel, 1988), p. 28.
22. M. Mead, "Anomalies in American Postdivorce Relationships," Ref. 8, p. 110.
23. M. Mead, "Anomalies in American Postdivorce Relationships," Ref. 8, p. 105.

CHAPTER ELEVEN

1. B. Bettelheim, *The Uses of Enchantment: The Meaning and Importance of Fairy Tales,* p. 67, as discussed in M. Radomisli, "Stereotypes, Stepmothers, and Splitting," *The American Journal of Psychoanalysis* **41**(2), 124 (1981).
2. B. Bettelheim, *The Uses of Enchantment: The Meaning and Importance of Fairy Tales,* p. 134, as discussed in M. Radomisli, "Stereotypes, Stepmothers, and Splitting," *The American Journal of Psychoanalysis* **41**(2), 124 (1981).
3. B. Bettelheim, *The Uses of Enchantment: The Meaning and Importance of Fairy Tales,* Ref. 2, p. 136.

CHAPTER TWELVE

1. E. B. Visher and J. S. Visher, *Old Loyalties, New Ties* (New York: Brunner/Mazel, 1988), p. 120.
2. Children who are raised in conflict-riddled intact families are considered at risk. Only these children seem to be truly relieved by the reduction of anxiety they experience when their parents' marriages end.
3. E. B. Visher and J. S. Visher, *Stepfamily Workshop Manual* (1980), A2.
4. J. Wallerstein, "Children of Divorce: The Psychological Tasks of the Child," *American Journal of Orthopsychiatry* **53,** 230–243 (1983).
5. J. Wallerstein, "Children of Divorce: The Psychological Tasks of the Child," Ref. 4, p. 242.
6. J. Wallerstein and S. Blakeslee, *Second Chances* (New York: Ticknor & Fields, 1989), p. 293.
7. J. Wallerstein, "Children of Divorce: The Psychological Tasks of the Child," Ref. 4, p. 233.
8. J. Wallerstein and S. Blakeslee, *Second Chances,* Ref. 7, p. 289.
9. J. Wallerstein and S. Blakeslee, *Second Chances,* Ref. 7, p. 289.
10. J. Wallerstein and S. Blakeslee, *Second Chances,* Ref. 7, p. 289.
11. J. Wallerstein, "Children of Divorce: The Psychological Tasks of the Child, Ref. 4, p. 235.
12. J. Wallerstein and S. Blakeslee, *Second Chances,* Ref. 7, p. 289.
13. J. Wallerstein and S. Blakeslee, *Second Chances,* Ref. 7, p. 290.
14. J. Wallerstein and S. Blakeslee, *Second Chances,* Ref. 7, p. 290.
15. J. Wallerstein and S. Blakeslee, *Second Chances,* Ref. 7, p. 290.
16. J. Wallerstein and S. Blakeslee, *Second Chances,* Ref. 7, p. 290.
17. J. Wallerstein and S. Blakeslee, *Second Chances,* Ref. 7, p. 291.
18. J. Wallerstein and S. Blakeslee, *Second Chances,* Ref. 7, p. 291.
19. J. Wallerstein and S. Blakeslee, *Second Chances,* Ref. 7, p. 291.
20. J. Wallerstein and S. Blakeslee, *Second Chances,* Ref. 7, p. 292.
21. J. Wallerstein and S. Blakeslee, *Second Chances,* Ref. 7, p. 292.
22. J. Wallerstein and S. Blakeslee, *Second Chances,* Ref. 7, p. 292.
23. J. Wallerstein and S. Blakeslee, *Second Chances,* Ref. 7, p. 292.

24. J. Wallerstein and S. Blakeslee, *Second Chances*, Ref. 7, p. 293.
25. J. Wallerstein and S. Blakeslee, *Second Chances*, Ref. 7, p. 293.
26. J. Wallerstein and S. Blakeslee, *Second Chances*, Ref. 7, p. 293.
27. J. Wallerstein and S. Blakeslee, *Second Chances*, Ref. 7, p. 293.
28. J. Wallerstein and S. Blakeslee, *Second Chances*, Ref. 7, p. 294.
29. J. Wallerstein and S. Blakeslee, *Second Chances*, Ref. 7, p. 294.
30. E. B. Visher and J. S. Visher, *Old Loyalties, New Ties*, (New York: Brunner/Mazel 1988), p. 216.
31. *Webster's Third New International Dictionary*, s.v. "psychosomatic . . . 4: evidencing bodily symptoms or bodily and mental symptoms as a result of emotional conflict."
32. J. K. Keshet, "From Separation to Stepfamily. A Subsystem Analysis." *Journal of Family Issues* 1(4), 517–532 (1980).
33. W. R. Beer, "Stepsibling and Half-Sibling Relationships," in W. R. Beer (ed.), *Relative Strangers* (New Jersey, Rowman and Littlefield, 1988), p. 115.
34. W. R. Beer, "Stepsibling and Half-Sibling Relationships," Ref. 33, p. 115.
35. W. R. Beer, "Stepsibling and Half-Sibling Relationships," Ref. 33, p. 116.
36. M. Mead, "Anomalies in American Postdivorce Relationships," in P. Bohannon (ed.), *Divorce and After* (New York: Doubleday, 1970), pp. 105–106.
37. M. Mead, "Anomalies in Postdivorce Relationships," Ref. 36, p. 105–106.
38. W. R. Beer, "Stepsibling and Half-Sibling Relationships," Ref. 33, p. 125.
39. W. R. Beer, "Stepsibling and Half-Sibling Relationships," Ref. 33, p. 128.
40. W. R. Beer, "Stepsibling and Half-Sibling Relationships," Ref. 33, p. 128.
41. M. Coleman, L. Ganong, and R. Gingrich, "Stepfamily Strengths: A Review of Popular Literature," *Family Relations* 34, 587 (1985).
42. M. Coleman, L. Ganong, and R. Gingrich, "Stepfamily Strengths: A Review of Popular Literature," Ref. 41, p. 587.

CHAPTER THIRTEEN

1. These titles include some chapter headings found in E. B. Visher and J. S. Visher, *Old Loyalties, New Ties* (New York: Brunner/Mazel 1988), p. v.
2. E. Carter and M. McGoldrick, *The Family Life Cycle: A Framework For Family Therapy* (New York: Gardner Press, 1980), p. xxi.
3. P. Lutz, "The Stepfamily: An Adolescent Perspective," *Family Relations*, 32, 367–375 (1983).
4. P. Papernow, "The Stepfamily Cycle: An Experiential Model of Stepfamily Development," *Family Relations*, 33, 355–363 (1984).
5. E. B. Visher and J. S. Visher, *Stepfamily Workshop Manual* (1980), p. B2.
6. Ibid.
7. Ibid.
8. Ibid.
9. D. E. H. Russell, "The Prevalence and Seriousness of Incestuous Abuse: Stepfathers vs. Biological Fathers," *Child Abuse and Neglect* 8, 15–22 (1984).

CHAPTER FOURTEEN

1. E. B. Visher and J. S. Visher, *Old Loyalties, New Ties* (New York: Brunner/Mazel 1988), p. 28.
2. J. K. Keshet, *Love and Power in the Stepfamily* (New York: McGraw-Hill, 1987), p. 519.
3. Although the names of the individuals and the ages and sexes of the children have been altered to protect the families involved, the content of this vignette is based on one combined family's experience during the first few years of their remarriage.

CHAPTER FIFTEEN

1. W. Saunders, host, *The WARNER Show*, NBC-TV, taped 19 June 1985.
2. Much of the content of this chapter is based on principles espoused in K. Kaye's book, *Family Rules* (New York: Walker and Co., 1984).
3. E. B. Visher and J. S. Visher, *Stepfamilies: A Guide to Working with Stepparents and Stepchildren* (New York: Brunner/Mazel, 1979).

CHAPTER SIXTEEN

1. See E. Wald, *The Remarried Family: Challenge and Promise* (New York: Family Service Association of America, 1981), p. 186.
2. V. Goldner, "Remarriage Family: Structure, System, Future," in L. Messinger (ed.), *Therapy with Remarriage Families* (Rockville, Maryland: Aspen Publications, 1982), p. 193.
3. Although the names of the individuals and the ages and sexes of the children have been altered to protect the families involved, the content of this vignette is based on one couple's rendition of the first few years of their remarriage.

CHAPTER SEVENTEEN

1. P. Bohannon, "Divorce Chains, Households of Remarriage, and Multiple Divorcers," in P. Bohannon (ed.), *Divorce and After: An Analysis of the Emotional and Social Problems of Divorce* (New York: Doubleday, 1970), pp. 127–139.
2. Emily and John Visher are the author's source for this expression. She has heard them use it many times during their workshops.
3. Randi's stepmother was the source for this heartwarming story.

CHAPTER EIGHTEEN

1. J. O. Bradt and C. M. Bradt, "Resources for Remarried Families," in M. A. Karpel (ed.), *Family Resources* (New York: Guilford Press, 1986), p. 288.
2. P. L. Papernow, "The Stepfamily Cycle: Seven Steps to Familydom," *Stepfamily Bulletin* Fall 1986, p. 1.
3. P. L. Papernow, *Becoming a Stepfamily: Patterns of Development in Remarried Families* (San Francisco: Jossey-Bass, 1993).
4. P. L. Papernow, *Becoming a Stepfamily*, Ref. 3, pp. 70–71.
5. P. L. Papernow, *Becoming a Stepfamily*, Ref. 3, p. 70.
6. P. L. Papernow, *Becoming a Stepfamily*, Ref. 3, p. 78.
7. P. L. Papernow, *Becoming a Stepfamily*, Ref. 3, p. 83.
8. P. L. Papernow, *Becoming a Stepfamily*, Ref. 3, p. 83.
9. P. L. Papernow, *Becoming a Stepfamily*, Ref. 3, p. 84.
10. P. L. Papernow, *Becoming a Stepfamily*, Ref. 3, p. 85.
11. P. L. Papernow, *Becoming a Stepfamily*, Ref. 3, p. 87.
12. P. L. Papernow, "The Stepfamily Cycle: Seven Steps to Familydom," Ref. 2, p. 12.
13. P. L. Papernow, *Becoming a Stepfamily*, Ref. 3, p. 117.
14. P. L. Papernow, *Becoming a Stepfamily*, Ref. 3, p. 101.
15. P. L. Papernow, "The Stepfamily Cycle: Seven Steps to Familydom," Ref. 2, p. 15.
16. P. L. Papernow, *Becoming a Stepfamily*, Ref. 3, p. 117.
17. P. L. Papernow, *Becoming a Stepfamily*, Ref. 3, p. 110.
18. P. L. Papernow, *Becoming a Stepfamily*, Ref. 3, p. 382.
19. P. L. Papernow, *Becoming a Stepfamily*, Ref. 3, p. 118.
20. P. L. Papernow, *Becoming a Stepfamily*, Ref. 3, p. 119.
21. W. Shakespeare, *Hamlet* (New Cambridge Edition, 1942), Act I, Scene iv, p. 1055.
22. P. L. Papernow, *Becoming a Stepfamily*, Ref. 3, p. 140.
23. P. L. Papernow, *Becoming a Stepfamily*, Ref. 3, p. 382.
24. A. Bernstein, from personal notes taken at 1989 American Orthopsychiatric Association Conference.
25. A. Bernstein, Ref. 24.
26. P. L. Papernow, *Becoming a Stepfamily*, Ref. 3, p. 383.
27. P. L. Papernow, *Becoming a Stepfamily*, Ref. 3, pp. 152–153.
28. P. L. Papernow, *Becoming a Stepfamily*, Ref. 3, p. 156.
29. P. L. Papernow, *Becoming a Stepfamily*, Ref. 3, p. 157.
30. P. L. Papernow, *Becoming a Stepfamily*, Ref. 3, p. 170–171.
31. P. L. Papernow, *Becoming a Stepfamily*, Ref. 3, p. 171.
32. P. L. Papernow, *Becoming a Stepfamily*, Ref. 3, p. 171.
33. P. L. Papernow, *Becoming a Stepfamily*, Ref. 3, p. 383.
34. P. L. Papernow, *Becoming a Stepfamily*, Ref. 3, p. 171.
35. P. L. Papernow, *Becoming a Stepfamily*, Ref. 3, p. 186.
36. P. L. Papernow, *Becoming a Stepfamily*, Ref. 3, p. 191.
37. P. L. Papernow, *Becoming a Stepfamily*, Ref. 3, p. 195.

38. P. L. Papernow, *Becoming a Stepfamily*, Ref. 3, p. 197.
39. P. L. Papernow, *Becoming a Stepfamily*, Ref. 3, p. 198.
40. P. L. Papernow, *Becoming a Stepfamily*, Ref. 3, p. 207.
41. P. L. Papernow, "The Stepfamily Cycle: The Final Steps to Familydom," *Stepfamily Bulletin* Winter 1986, p. 8.
42. P. L. Papernow, *Becoming a Stepfamily*, Ref. 3, p. 208.
43. P. L. Papernow, *Becoming a Stepfamily*, Ref. 3, p. 208.
44. P. L. Papernow, *Becoming a Stepfamily*, Ref. 3, p. 208.
45. P. L. Papernow, *Becoming a Stepfamily*, Ref. 3, p. 212.
46. P. L. Papernow, *Becoming a Stepfamily*, Ref. 3, p. 212.
47. P. L. Papernow, "The Stepfamily Cycle: The Final Steps to Familydom," Ref. 41, p. 8.
48. P. L. Papernow, *Becoming a Stepfamily*, Ref. 3, p. 228.
49. P. L. Papernow, *Becoming a Stepfamily*, Ref. 3, p. 386.
50. P. L. Papernow, "The Stepfamily Cycle: The Final Steps to Familydom," Ref. 41, p. 15.
51. P. L. Papernow, *Becoming a Stepfamily*, Ref. 3, p. 387.

CHAPTER NINETEEN

1. V. Goldner, "Remarriage Family: Structure, System, Future," in L. Messinger (ed.), *Therapy with Remarriage Families* (Rockville, Maryland: Aspen Publications, 1982), p. 189.
2. M. F. Whiteside, "The Role of Explicit Rule-making in the Early Stages of Remarriage," in Alan Gurman (ed.), *Questions and Answers in the Practice of Family Therapy*, (New York, Brunner/Mazel, 1981), vol. II, p. 214.
3. V. Goldner, "Remarriage Family: Structure, System, Future," Ref. 1, p. 195.
4. V. Goldner, "Remarriage Family: Structure, System, Future," Ref. 1, p. 203.
5. V. Goldner, "Remarriage Family: Structure, System, Future," Ref. 1, p. 203.
6. M. F. Whiteside, "The Role of Explicit Rule-making in the Early Stages of Remarriage," Ref. 2, p. 217.
7. V. Goldner, "Remarriage Family: Structure, System, Future," Ref. 1, p. 196.
8. V. Goldner, "Remarriage Family: Structure, System, Future," Ref. 1, p. 197.
9. E. B. Visher and J. S. Visher, *Old Loyalties, New Ties* (New York: Brunner/Mazel 1988), p. 235.
10. E. B. Visher and J. S. Visher, *Old Loyalties, New Ties* (New York: Brunner/Mazel 1988), p. 235.
11. E. B. Visher and J. S. Visher, *Old Loyalties, New Ties* (New York: Brunner/Mazel 1988), p. 235.
12. E. B. Visher and J. S. Visher, *Old Loyalties, New Ties* (New York: Brunner/Mazel 1988), p. 235.
13. M. F. Whiteside, "The Role of Explicit Rule-making in the Early Stages of Remarriage," Ref. 2, p. 216.

14. M. F. Whiteside, "The Role of Explicit Rule-making in the Early Stages of Remarriage," Ref. 2, p. 217.
15. M. F. Whiteside, "The Role of Explicit Rule-making in the Early Stages of Remarriage," Ref. 2, p. 217.
16. Jamie K. Keshet, "From Separation to Stepfamily. A Subsystem Analysis," *Journal of Family Issues* 1(4), 530, (1980).
17. E. B. Visher and J. S. Visher, *Old Loyalties, New Ties* (New York: Brunner/Mazel 1988), p. 235.
18. E. B. Visher and J. S. Visher, *Old Loyalties, New Ties* (New York: Brunner/Mazel 1988), p. 235.
19. E. B. Visher and J. S. Visher, *Old Loyalties, New Ties* (New York: Brunner/Mazel 1988), p. 235.
20. E. B. Visher and J. S. Visher, *Old Loyalties, New Ties* (New York: Brunner/Mazel 1988), p. 235.
21. E. B. Visher and J. S. Visher, *Old Loyalties, New Ties* (New York: Brunner/Mazel 1988), p. 235.
22. M. F. Whiteside, "The Role of Explicit Rule-making in the Early Stages of Remarriage," Ref. 2, p. 217.

CHAPTER TWENTY

1. American Board of Examiners in Clinical Social Work, *1991 Diplomate Directory*. The information resides in a computer data base. Library of Congress Catalog Card Number: 82-643082.
2. National Association of Social Workers, *1991 Register of Clinical Social Workers*. The information in this Register has been computerized. Library of Congress Catalog Card Number: 75-42777.
3. National Association of Social Workers, *1991 Register of Clinical Social Workers*, Ref. 2.

CHAPTER TWENTY-ONE

1. Sometimes a famtu is formed as the result of a parent's marriage to a person who does have a blood tie to the child, i.e., a woman becomes a *partu* to her deceased sister's child. This partu and *chiltu* are blood related, but their new family tie is an affinal or marriage-related one. In such a situation, if the marriage between father and aunt were to end, the child and aunt would still remain related to each other as a result of their blood tie.

Selected Bibliography

Anderson, J., and G. White, "An Empirical Investigation of Interaction and Relationship Patterns in Functional and Dysfunctional Nuclear Families and Stepfamilies," *Family Process* **25** (1986).

Becker, G., E. Landes, and R. Michael, "An Economic Analysis of Marital Instability," *Journal of Political Economy* **85** (1977).

Beer, W., *Relative Strangers* (Rowman and Littlefield, New Jersey, 1988).

Bernard, J., *Remarriage: A Study of Marriage*, 2d ed., Russell & Russell, New York, 1971).

Bernstein, A. C., "Unraveling the Tangles: Children's Understanding of Stepfamily Kinship," in Beer, W. R., *Relative Strangers* (Rowman and Littlefield, New Jersey, 1988).

Bernstein, A. C., *Yours, Mine, and Ours: How Families Change When Remarried Parents Have a Child Together*, Charles Scribner's Sons, New York, 1989).

Bohannan, P., *Divorce and After* (Doubleday, New York: 1970).

Booth, A., D. Brinkerhoff, and L. White, "The Impact of Parental Divorce on Courtship," *Journal of Marriage and the Family* **46** (1984).

Boss, P., and J. Greenberg, "Family Boundary Ambiguity: A New Variable in Family Stress Theory," *Family Process* **23** (1984).

Bowerman, C., and D. Irish, "Some Relationships of Stepchildren to Their Parents," *Marriage and Family Living* **24** (1962).

Bradt, J., and C. M. Bradt, "Resources for Remarried Families," in Karpel, M. S., (ed.), *Family Resources* (Guilford Press, New York, 1986).

Brand, E., and K. Bowen-Woodward, "Family Relationships and Children's Psychological Adjustment in Stepmother and Stepfather Families," in Hetherington, E. M. and J. D. Arasteh (eds.), *Impact of Divorce, Single Parenting, and Stepparenting on Children.* (Lawrence Erlbaum Associates, Publishers, Hillsdale, New Jersey, 1988).

Brand, E. and E. G. Clingempeel, "Interdependencies of Marital and Stepparent–

Stepchild Relationships and Children's Psychological Adjustment," *Family Relations* **36** 1987).

Brown, C. B., R.-J. Green, and J. Druckman, "A Comparison of Stepfamilies With and Without Child-focused Problems," *American Journal of Orthopsychiatry* **60**(4) (1990).

Bryan, L. R., M. Coleman, L. H. Ganong, and S. H. Bryan, "Person Perception: Family Structure as a Cue for Stereotyping," *Journal of Marriage and the Family* **48** (1986).

Bryan, S., L. Ganong, M. Coleman, and L. Bryan, "Counselors' Perceptions of Stepparents and Stepchildren," *Journal of Counseling Psychology* **32** (1985).

Bumpass, L., "Some Characteristics of Children's Second Families," *American Journal of Sociology* **90** (1984).

Bumpass, L., and R. Rindfuss, "Children's Experience of Marital Disruption," *American Journal of Sociology* **85**(1) (1979).

Bumpass, L., J. Sweet, and T. Castro Martin, "Changing Patterns of Remarriage," *Journal of Marriage and the Family* **52** (August 1990).

Burchinal, L. G., "Characteristics of Adolescents from Unbroken, Broken, and Reconstituted Families," *Journal of Marriage and the Family* **26** (1964).

Carter, E., and M. McGoldrick, *The Family Life Cycle: A Framework for Family Therapy*, (Gardner Press, New York, 1980).

Cherlin, A., "Remarriage as an Incomplete Institution," *American Journal of Sociology* **84**(3) (1978).

Cherlin, A., and J. McCarthy, "Remarried Couple Household: Data from the June 1980 Current Population Survey," *Journal of Marriage and the Family* **47** (1985).

Clingempeel, W. G., and E. Brand, "Quasi-kin Relationships, Structural Complexity, and Marital Quality in Stepfamilies: A Replication, Extension, and Clinical Implications," *Family Relations* **34** (1985).

Clingempeel, W. G., E. Brand, and R. Ievoli, "Stepparent–Stepchild Relationships in Stepmother and Stepfather Families: A Multimethod Study," *Family Relations* **33** (1984).

Clingempeel, W. G., E. Brand, and S. Segal, "A Multi-level, Multi-variable Developmental Perspective for Future Research on Stepfamilies," in Pasley, K., and M. Ihinger-Tallman (eds.), *Remarriage and Stepparenting: Current Research and Theory* (Guilford Press, New York, 1987).

Clingempeel, W. G., and S. Segal, "Stepparent–Stepchild Relationships and the Psychological Adjustment of Children in Stepmother and Stepfather Families," *Child Development* **57** (1986).

Coleman, M., and L. Ganong, "Marital Conflict in Stepfamilies: Effects on Children," *Youth and Society* **19**(2) (1988).

Coleman, M., and L. Ganong, "Remarriage and Stepfamily Research in the 1980s: Increased Interest in an Old Family Form," *Journal of Marriage and the Family* **52** (November 1990).

Coleman, M., and L. Ganong, "Stepfamily Strengths: A Review of the Popular Literature," *Family Relations* **34** (1985).

Coleman, M., L. Ganong, and R. Gingrich, "Effect of Family Structure on Family Attitudes and Expectations," *Family Relations* **33** (1984).

Crosbie-Burnett, M., "The Centrality of the Step Relationship: A Challenge to Family Theory and Practice," *Family Relations* **33** (1984).

Crosbie-Burnett, M., and J. Giles-Sims, "Adolescent Power in Stepfamilies: A Test of Normative-Resource Theory," *Journal of Marriage and the Family* **51** (November 1989).

Crosbie-Burnett, M., and A. Skyles, "Stepchildren in School and Colleges: Recommendations for Educational Policy Changes," *Family Relations* **38**(1) (1989).

Dawson, D. A., "Family Structure and Children's Health and Well-being: Data from the 1988 National Health Interview Survey on Child Health," National Institute on Alcohol Abuse and Alcoholism, *Journal of Marriage and the Family* **53** (August 1991).

Draughon, M., "Step-mother's Model of Identification in Relation to Mourning in the Child," *Psychological Reports* **36** (1975).

Fast, I., and A. Cain, "The Stepparent Role: Potential for Disturbances in Family Functioning," *American Journal of Psychiatry* **36** (1966).

Finkelhor, D., and L. Baron, "Risk Factors for Child Sexual Abuse," *Journal of Interpersonal Violence* **1**(1) (1986).

Furstenberg, F. F., Jr., "Child Care after Divorce and Remarriage," in Hetherington, E. M., and J. D. Arasteh (eds.), *Impact of Divorce, Single Parenting, and Stepparenting on Children* (Lawrence Erlbaum Associates, Publishers, Hillsdale, New Jersey, 1988).

Furstenburg, F. F., and C. W. Nord, "Parenting Apart: Patterns of Childrearing after Marital Disruption," *Journal of Marriage and the Family* **47** (1985).

Furstenburg, F. F., C. W. Nord, J. L. Peterson, and N. Zill, "The Life Course of Children of Divorce: Marital Disruption and Parental Contact," *American Sociological Review* **48** (1983).

Furstenburg, F. F., and G. B. Spanier, *Recycling the Family* (Sage Publications, Beverly Hills, California, 1984).

Ganong, L. H., and M. Coleman, "The Effects of Remarriage on Children: A Review of the Literature," *Family Relations* **33** (1984).

Ganong, L. H., and M. Coleman, "Preparing for Remarriage: Anticipating the Issues, Seeking Solutions," *Family Relations* **38** (1989).

Ganong, L. H., and M. Coleman, "Stepfamily Self-help Books: Brief Annotations and Ratings," *Family Relations* **38** (1989).

Ganong, L. H., and M. Coleman, "Stepparent: A Pejorative Term?" *Psychological Reports* **52** (1983).

Gardener, R. A., "Intergenerational Sexual Tension in Second Marriages," *Medical Aspects of Human Sexuality* (August 1979).

Giles-Sims, J., "Social Exchange in Remarried Families," in Pasley, K., and M. Ihinger-Tallman (eds.), *Remarriage and Stepparenting: Current Research and Theory* (Guilford Press, New York, 1987).

Giles-Sims, J., "The Stepparent Role: Expectations, Behavior, Sanctions," *Journal of Family Issues* **5**(1) (1984).

296   Bibliography

Giles-Sims, J., and M. Crosbie-Burnett, "Adolescent Power in Stepfather Families: A Test of Normative-Resource Theory," *Journal of Marriage and the Family* 51 (November 1989).
Giles-Sims, J., and D. Finkelhor, "Child Abuse in Stepfamilies," *Family Relations* 33 (1984).
Glick, P. C., "Marriage, Divorce, and Living Arrangements," *Journal of Family Issues* 5(1) (1984).
Glick, P. C., "Remarried Families, Stepfamilies, and Stepchildren: A Brief Demographic Profile," *Family Relations* 38(1) (1989).
Glick, P., and S.-L. Lin, "Recent Changes in Divorce and Remarriage," *Journal of Marriage and the Family* 48 (1986).
Goldner, V., "Remarriage Family: Structure, System, Future," in Hansen, J. C., and L. Messinger (eds.), *Therapy with Remarriage Families* (Aspen Publications, Rockville, Maryland, 1982).
Greif, J. B., "Fathers, Children, and Joint Custody," *American Journal of Orthopsychiatry* 49(2) (1979).
Grief, J. B., "The Father–Child Relationship Subsequent to Divorce," in Hansen, J. C. and L. Lessinger (eds.), *Therapy with Remarriage Families* (Aspen Publications, Rockville, Maryland, 1982).
Gross, P., "Defining Post-Divorce Remarriage Families: A Typology Based on the Subjective Perceptions of Children," *Journal of Divorce* 10 (1987).
Guidubaldi, J., J. D. Perry, and B. K. Natasi, "Adjustment and Intervention for Children of Divorce," in Hetherington, E. M., and J. D. Arasteh (eds.), *Impact of Divorce, Single Parenting, and Stepparenting on Children*. (Lawrence Erlbaum Associates, Publishers, Hillsdale, New Jersey, 1988).
Guisinger, S., P. A. Cowan, and D. Schuldberg, "Changing Parent and Spouse Relationships in the First Years of Remarriage of Divorced Fathers," *Journal of Marriage and the Family* 51 (May 1989).
Henry, C., and C. Ceglian, "Stepgrandmothers and Grandmothers of Stepfamilies: Role Behaviors, Role Meanings, and Grandmothering Styles," *Eric Microfiche* 86 (1989).
Hess, R., and K. Camara, "Post-Divorce Family Relationships as Mediating Factors in the Consequences of Divorce for Children," *Journal of Social Issues* 35 (1979).
Hetherington, E. M., "Coping with Family Transitions: Winners, Losers, and Survivors," *Child Development* 60 (1989).
Hetherington, E. M., "Divorce: A Child's Perspective," *American Psychologist* 34 (1979).
Hetherington, E. M., "Family Relations Six Years after Divorce," in Pasley, K., and M. Ihinger-Tallman (eds.), *Remarriage and Stepparenting: Current Research and Theory* (Guilford Press, New York, 1987).
Hetherington, E. M., "The Role of Individual Differences Family Relationships in Children's Coping with Divorce and Remarriage," in Cowan, P. A., and E. M. Hetherington (eds.), *Family Traditions* (Lawrence Erlbaum Associates, Publishers, Hillsdale, New Jersey, 1991).
Hetherington, E. M., M. Cox, and R. Cox, "Divorced Fathers," *The Family Coordinator* 25(4) (1976).

Hetherington, E. M., M. Cox, and R. Cox, "Long-term Effects of Divorce and Remarriage on the Adjustment of Children," *The Journal of the American Academy of Child Psychiatry* **24**(5) (1985).
Ihinger-Tallman, M., "Sibling and Stepsibling Bonding in Stepfamilies," in Pasley, K., and M. Ihinger-Tallman (eds.), *Remarriage and Stepparenting: Current Research and Theory* (Guilford Press, New York, 1987).
Isaacs, M., "Facilitating Family Restructuring and Relinkage," In Hansen, J. C., and L. Messinger (eds.), *Therapy with Remarriage Families* (Aspen Publications, Rockville, Maryland, 1982).
Jacobs, J. "The Effect of Divorce on Fathers: An Overview of the Literature," *American Journal of Psychiatry* **139** (1987).
Jacobs, J. J., and F. F. Furstenberg, "Changing Places: Conjugal Careers and Women's Marital Motility," *Social Forces* **64**(3) (1986).
Jacobson, D. S., "Stepfamilies, Myths & Realities," *Social Work* **24**(3) (1979).
Jacobson, D. S., "Family Type, Visiting Patterns, and Children's Behavior in the Stepfamily: A Linked Family System," in Pasley, K., and Ihinger-Tallman (eds.), *Remarriage and Stepparenting: Current Research and Theory* (Guilford Press, New York, 1987).
Johnson, C. L., "In-Law Relationships in the American Kinship System," *American Ethnologist* 1990.
Kaye, K., *Family Rules* (Walker and Co., New York, 1984).
Keshet, J. K., "Cognitive Remodeling of the Family: How Remarried People View Stepfamilies," *American Orthopsychiatric Association* **60**(2) (1990).
Keshet, J. K., "From Separation to Stepfamily. A Subsystem Analysis," *Journal of Family Issues* **1**(4) (1980).
Keshet, J. K., *Love and Power in the Stepfamily* (McGraw-Hill, Inc., New York, 1987).
Keshet, J. K., "The Remarried Couple: Stresses and Successes," in Beer, W. R., (ed.), *Relative Strangers* (Rowman and Littlefield, New Jersey, 1988).
Knaub, P. K., S. L. Hanna, and N. Stinnett, "Strengths of Remarried Families," *Journal of Divorce* **7** (1984).
Landau, M., "Therapy with Families in Cultural Transition," in McGoldrick, M., J. K. Pearce, and J. Giordano (eds.), *Ethnicity and Family Therapy* (Guilford Press, New York, 1982).
Lutz, P., "The Stepfamily: An Adolescent Perspective," *Family Relations* **32** (1983).
McGoldrick, M., and E. A. Carter, "Forming a Remarried Family," in Carter, E. A., and M. McGoldrick (eds.), *The Family Life Cycle: A Framework for Family Therapy* (Gardner Press, New York, 1980).
McGoldrick, M., and R. Gerson, *Genograms in Family Assessment* (W. W. Norton & Co., Garden City, New York, 1985).
Mead, M., "Anomalies in American Postdivorce Relationships," in Bohannon, P. (ed.), *Divorce and After* (Doubleday, Garden City, New York, 1970).
Messinger, L., "Remarriage between Divorced People with Children from Previous Marriages: A Proposal for Preparation for Remarriage," *Journal of Marriage and Family Counseling* **2** (1976).
Messinger, L., and K. Walker, "From Marriage Breakdown to Remarriage: Parental

Tasks and Therapeutic Guidelines," *American Journal of Orthopsychiatry* **51**(3) (1981).

Messinger, L., Walker, K., Freeman, S. (1977). Preparation for Remarriage following divorce: The use of group techniques. *American Journal of Orthopsychiatry,* **48**(2) 263–272.

Mills, D. M., "A Model for Stepfamily Development," *Family Relations* **33** (1984).

Mills, D. M., "Stepfamilies in Context," in Beer, W. R. (ed.), *Relative Strangers* (Rowman and Littlefield, New Jersey, 1988).

Mitchell, B. A., A. V. Wister, and T. K. Burch, "The Family Environment and Leaving the Parental Home," *Journal of Marriage and the Family* **51** (August 1989).

Norton, A., and P. Glick, "One-Parent Families: A Social and Economic Profile," *Family Relations* **35** (1986).

Nye, I., "Emerging and Declining Family Roles," *Journal of Marriage and the Family* **36** (1974).

Orleans, M., B. J. Palisi, and D. Caddell, "Marriage Adjustment and Satisfaction of Stepfathers: Their Feelings and Perceptions of Decision Making and Step-children Relations," *Family Relations* **38** (1989).

Papernow, P., "The Stepfamily Cycle: An Experiential Model of Stepfamily Development," *Family Relations* **33** (1984).

Papernow, P., "The Stepfamily Cycle: Seven Steps to Familydom," *The Stepfamily Bulletin* (Fall 1986).

Papernow, P., "The Stepfamily Cycle: The Final Steps to Familydom," *The Stepfamily Bulletin* (Winter 1986).

Papernow, P. L., "Stepparent Role Development: From Outsider to Intimate," in Beer, W. R. (ed.), *Relative Strangers* (Rowman and Littlefield, New Jersey, 1988).

Papernow, P. L., *Becoming A Stepfamily: Patterns of Development in Remarried Families* (Jossey-Bass Publishers, San Francisco, 1993).

Parker, H., and S. Parker, "Father Daughter Sexual Abuse," *American Journal of Orthopsychiatry* **56** (1986).

Pasley, K., and C. L. Healow, "Adolescent Self-Esteem: A Focus on Children in Stepfamilies," in Hetherington, E. M., and J. D. Arasteh (eds.), *Impact of Divorce, Single Parenting, and Stepparenting on Children* (Lawrence Erlbaum Associates, Publishers, Hillsdale, New Jersey, 1988).

Pasley, K., and M. Ihinger-Tallman, "Boundary Ambiguity in Remarriage: Does Ambiguity Differentiate Degree of Marital Adjustment and Interaction?" *Family Relations* **38**(1) (1989).

Pasley, K., and M. Ihinger-Tallman, "Family Boundary Ambiguity: Perception of Adult Remarried Family Members," in Pasley, K., and M. Ihinger-Tallman (eds.), *Remarriage and Stepparenting: Current Research and Theory* (Guilford Press, New York, 1987).

Pasley, K., and M. Ihinger-Tallman, "Stress in Second Families," *Family Perspective* **16**(4) 1982).

Perkins, R. F., and J. P. Kahan, "An Empiricial Comparison of Natural Father and Stepfather Family System," *Family Process* **18** (1979).

Peterson, J., and N. Zill, "Marital Disruption, Parent–Child Relationships, and Behavior Problems in Children," *Journal of Marriage and the Family* 48 (1986).
Pill, C. J., "Stepfamilies: Redefining the Family," *Family Relations* 39 (1990).
Pink, J., and K. Wampler, "Problem Areas in Stepfamilies: Cohesion, Adaptability, and the Stepfather–Adolescent Relationship," *Family Relations* 34 (1985).
Radomisli, M., "Stereotypes, Stepmothers, and Splitting," *The American Journal of Psychoanalysis* 41(2) (1981).
Ricci, I., *Mom's House, Dad's House: Making Shared Custody Work* (Collier Books, New York, 1980).
Russell, D. E. H., "The Prevalence and Seriousness of Incestuous Abuse: Stepfathers vs. biological Fathers," *Child Abuse and Neglect* 8 (1984).
Sager, C. J., E. Walker, H. S. Brown, H. Crohn, T. Engel, E. Rodstein, and L. Walker, *Treating the Remarried Family* Brunner/Mazel, New York, 1983).
Sanders, G. F., and D. W. Trygstad, "Stepgrandparents and Grandparents: The View from Young Adults. *Family Relations* 38(1) (1989).
Santrock, J. W., R. A. Warshak, and G. L. Elliott, "Social Development and Parent–Child Interaction in Father-Custody and Stepmother Families," in Lamb, M. E. (ed.), *Non-traditional Families: Parenting and Child Development* (Lawrence Erlbaum Associates, Publishers, Hillsdale, New Jersey, 1982).
Santrock, J. W., and K. A. Sitterle, "Parent–Child Relationships in Stepmother Families," in Pasley, K., and M. Ihinger-Tallman (eds.), *Remarriage and Stepparenting: Current Research and Theory* (Guilford Press, New York, 1987).
Schulman, G. L., "Myths that Intrude on the Adaptation of the Stepfamily," *Social Casework* 49 (1972).
Schwebel, A. I., M. A. Fine, and M. A. Renner, "A Study of Perception of the Stepparent Role," *Journal of Family Issues* 12(1) (1991).
Stern, P. N., "Stepfather Families: Integration around Child Discipline," *Issues in Mental Health Nursing* 1 (1976).
Stern, P. N., "Affiliating in Stepfather Families: Teachable Strategies Leading to Stepfather–Child Friendship," *Western Journal of Nursing Research* 4 (1982).
Victor, R. S., "Grandparent and Stepgrandparent Rights," *Trial* (April 1989).
Visher, E. B., and J. S. Visher, "Children in Stepfamilies," *Psychiatric Annals* 12(9), (1982).
Visher, E. B., and J. S. Visher, "Common Problems of Stepparents and Their Spouses," *American Journal of Orthopsychiatry* 48 (1978).
Visher, E. B., and J. S. Visher, "Major Areas of Difficulty for Stepparent Couples," *International Journal of Family Counseling* 6 (1978).
Visher, E. B., and J. S.Visher, *Old Loyalties, New Ties* (Brunner/Mazel, New York, 1988).
Visher, E. B., and J. S. Visher, "Parenting Coalitions after Remarriage: Dynamics and Therapeutic Guidelines," *Family Relations* 38(1) (1989).
Visher, E. B., and J. S. Visher, *Stepfamilies: A Guide to Working with Stepparents and Stepchildren* (Brunner/Mazel, New York, 1979).
Visher, E. B., and J. S. Visher, "Stepfamilies in the 1980's." in Hansen, J. C., and L. Messinger (eds.), *Therapy with Remarriage Families* (Aspen Publications, Rockville, Maryland, 1982).

Visher, E. B., and J. S. Visher, *Stepfamily Workship Manual* (1980).

Wald, E. *The Remarried Family. Challenge & Promise* (Family Service Association of America, New York, 1981).

Walker, K., and L. Messinger, "Remarriage after Divorce: Dissolution and Reconstruction of Family Boundaries," *Family Process* **18** (1979).

Walker, K., J. Roger, and L. Messinger, "Remarriage after Divorce: A Review," *Social Casework* **18**(2) (1977).

Wallerstein, J. S., "Children of Divorce: Preliminary Report of a Ten Year Follow-up of Older Children and Adolescents," *Journal of the Academy of Child Psychology* **24** (1985).

Wallerstein, J. S., "Children of Divorce: The Psychological Tasks of the Child," *American Journal of Orthopsychiatry* **53**(2) (1983).

Wallerstein, J. S., and S. Blakeslee, *Second Chances* (Ticknor & Fields, New York, 1989).

Wallerstein, J. S., S. B. Corbin, and J. M. Lewis, "Children of Divorce: A 10-Year Study," in Hetherington, E. M., and J. D. Arasteh (eds.), *Impact of Divorce, Single Parenting, and Stepparenting on Children* (Lawrence Erlbaum Associates, Publishers, Hillsdale, New Jersey, 1988).

Wallerstein, J. S., and J. B. Kelly, *Surviving the Break Up: How Children and Parents Cope with Divorce* (Basic Books, New York, 1980).

Weitzman, L., *The Divorce Revolution: The Unexpected Social and Economic Consequences for Women and Children in America* (Free Press, New York, 1985).

White, L. K., and A. Booth, "The Quality and Stability of Remarriages: The Role of Stepchildren," *American Sociological Review* **50** (1985).

Whiteside, M. F., "Families of Remarriage: The Weaving of Many Life Cycle Threads," *Family Therapy Collections* **7** (1983).

Whiteside, M. F., "Family Rituals as a Key to Kinship Connections in Remarried Families," *Family Relations* **38**(1) (1989).

Whiteside, M. F., "Remarried Systems," in Combrinck-Graham, L. (ed.), *Children in Family Contexts: Perspectives in Treatment* (Guilford Press, New York, 1989).

Whiteside, M. F., "The Role of Explicit Rule-making in the Early Stages of Remarriage," in Gurman, A. (ed.), *Questions and Answers in the Practice of Family Therapy*, vol. II, (Brunner/Mazel, New York, 1980).

Zill, N., "Behavior, Achievement, and Health Problems among Children in Stepfamilies," in Hetherington, E. M., and J. D. Arasteh (eds.), *Impact of Divorce, Single Parenting, and Stepparenting on Children* (Lawrence Erlbaum Associates, Publishers, Hillsdale, New Jersey, 1988).

Index